EVERY [BARCODE] 'S
B
LOVE & MARRIAGE
and FAMILY LIFE

First Edition

Icon Books
Cambridge,   U.K.

CONTENTS

Every Woman's Book of
LOVE AND
MARRIAGE
AND FAMILY LIFE

This edition published in the UK in 2003 by
Icon Books Ltd, Grange Road, Duxford, Cambridge CB2 4QF
e-mail: info@iconbooks.co.uk   www.iconbooks.co.uk

Originally published in the 1930s by The Amalgamated Press Ltd, London
(original publication date unknown). Every effort has been made to trace the
copyright holder of the material reproduced in this book. If notified, the publisher
will be pleased to acknowledge the use of any copyright material.

Sold in the UK, Europe, South Africa and Asia by Faber and Faber Ltd, 3 Queen
Square, London WC1N 3AU or their agents. Distributed in the UK, Europe,
South Africa and Asia by TBS Ltd, Frating Distribution Centre, Colchester Road,
Frating Green, Colchester CO7 7DW. Published in Australia in 2003 by Allen &
Unwin Pty Ltd, PO Box 8500, 83 Alexander Street, Crows Nest, NSW 2065.
Distributed in Canada by Penguin Books Canada, 10 Alcorn Avenue, Suite 300,
Toronto, Ontario M4V 3B2. Published in the USA in 2003 by Totem Books.
Inquiries to Icon Books, UK, as above. Distributed to the trade in the USA by
National Book Network Inc., 4720 Boston Way, Lanham, Maryland 20706.

ISBN 1 84046 484 4

Printed and bound in the UK by Mackays of Chatham plc

CHAPTER I

Preparing for Marriage

SO you and The Dearest Man In The World are engaged ? What joyous hopes cluster round your future ! How bright the path which winds away into the coming years.

Yes, now that you are actually planning your marriage, courtship days are filled with wonderful pictures of the golden future, aren't they ? You can begin stitching away at your bridal " pretties," and lovingly stocking the " bottom drawer " with everything you are going to provide for use in your very own home.

Marriage, with all its wonder and mystery, will set the final seal upon your mutual love, for, of course, it is the very crown of love.

Perhaps you have only just come to realise that, in giving yourselves in marriage, you are presenting each other with the completest gift possible, a gift which can never be taken back. It is a very solemn thought, and a very beautiful one to those who truly love each other.

But what is this deep and powerful emotion which is urging you on ? What is this love which demands the surrender of your whole self to the tender keeping of another ?

It is a bliss and ecstasy that cannot be described but only felt in every fibre of body and soul ; it is sex attraction, friendship and companionship, and it is also Nature's method of ensuring that the race shall be carried on.

Whether love has come suddenly, like a burst of sunshine in a dark room, or gradually like the breaking of the dawn creeping slowly to glorious noon, the happiest lovers feel sure it was " fate " that brought them together and meant them to stay together—and they are saved much heart-searching and worry. They are indeed among the world's fortunate ones, for their marriage is "made in Heaven."

Nevertheless, even after your engagement, it is as well to remember that your decision is a vital one, and marriage is for a lifetime —and be very sure you are not making a mistake, for, though it takes courage to break an engagement, it is nothing short of foolishness to continue if you are doubtful about the marriage at all.

Making Sure of Love

THOSE who are actually not quite sure of themselves and their love, should give themselves the following simple test :

Arrange not to see each other for a stated period, and see how you get along. If your feelings are deeply genuine, they will survive the separation and be stronger than ever at the end of it. If there is a mutual attraction only depending upon kisses and caresses—which can be so deceptive, and can so easily impersonate Love because they are so wrapped up with the real thing—separation, if long enough, will break the spell and destroy the glamour, restoring your clear-sightedness.

But even those of you who are sure would do wisely to ask yourselves very honestly the following "test" questions.

Is your feeling deeper than the mere passion which is a part of sex attraction ? Remember that Sex is so deeply-rooted an instinct that the touch of a hand and the nearness of an ardent young man is alone quite enough to kindle a physical response in the average girl.

Try, if you can, to separate that emotion from other equally important considerations. Is he—or she —the sort of person you can value as a *friend* ? That is to say, have you anything in common ? Do you appreciate the same sort of things, laugh at the same jokes, share the same sort of ideals, and like the same set of friends ? Do you think the same on the biggest topics of life and love and religion ?

Religion particularly is one of the important things that a couple must agree upon before marriage, for, while love and tolerance are fine, a certain oneness of mind is necessary, too, since marriage is a mingling of soul as well as body. Then there is, in the various forms of religion, certain definite teaching regarding marriage which should be fully understood and agreed upon by both people who intend to marry.

Another point of immense importance is the attitude of both regarding children.

Anyone who has had any experience of the confidence of women knows how serious a bar to happiness disagreement on this point may be.

"I love children and always pictured the joy of having a little one of my own, and now I find my husband is not willing," says a poor, bewildered new wife.

Now this is most definitely something she ought to have found out before marriage. It is difficult indeed to understand how she could fail to discover that her husband-to-be disliked the idea of having children, for in many an impersonal conversation there would be enough, one would suppose, to indicate such a trait even though the subject had never been directly discussed.

So a tremendous part of the happiness of married life, especially early married life, depends upon a clear understanding and agreement about this important point.

Now is there anything about your dear one that ever shocks or hurts or even outrages you—that you shrink from ? And, if so, is your love big enough to go on loving in spite of those things ?

Or do you, on the other hand, admire, appreciate, and approve of each other with all your heart and soul ?

Then ask yourselves this last searching question : Do you love each other enough to make ANY sacrifice—to share poverty, ill-health, and misfortune gladly together ? Would you rather have each other with any misfortune than live carefree apart ?

Only the other day a magistrate said about a young woman that she had shown that unmistakable sign of true love—willingness to sacrifice. Real love is always thinking more of the loved one than of oneself, isn't it ?

Sex Attraction

JUST one word about the girl who says: "I like him awfully but I hate being kissed." The element of sound, healthy sex-attraction should definitely enter in between two people who expect to find happiness in marriage—so, if there is no physical attraction on one side, think twice about continuing the courtship. If she loves a man, a girl ought to like being kissed ; she ought to want to kiss and be kissed. But of course, she may have some unnatural prejudice due to a wrong upbringing or a frightening experience in childhood which has affected her outlook, and, if so, love from a patient and understanding man may save her—it is indeed the only thing that can heal her and bring her back to normal.

Sometimes, most strangely, a definite dislike on one side often turns, in time, to love and attraction—and, love being so great a treasure, no girl should be in too much of a hurry to turn down a would-be lover.

Now let us consider some definite flaws in a man's character which are so obvious that a girl cannot miss them.

" I am unhappy because my fiancé is sometimes the worse for drink," many a girl has said. " He has promised to give it up when we are married. Do you think I dare risk my happiness with him ? I love him, but I hate this weakness."

Now, if this young man really cared enough for the girl to overcome this habit, he would do it during their period of courtship when his love, if anything, is at its height. If he does not do it then, the probability is that he never will.

Love is such a force that, under its mighty influence, men have done things which would seem almost impossible. Let the man prove to the woman *before he marries her* that he *can* master his weakness, whatever it may be ; but do not let her deceive herself into thinking that she will be able to *reform him after marriage*.

It may have been done in isolated cases but, speaking generally, what a man is before marriage that he will be after marriage—*only more so*.

If you are quite happy about all that has been said, and are satisfied that you truly love each other, and you mean to be married, then sooner or later you will share your lives together.

Perhaps, as yet, you have not thought very far beyond the wedding which will bring your dreams true as far as perpetual " togetherness " is concerned ; but, if you are average young folk,

If you think, "I like him awfully but I hate being kissed", think twice about continuing the courtship.

"I am unhappy because my fiancé is sometimes the worse for drink. He has promised to give it up when we are married, but do I dare risk my happiness with him?"

somewhere beyond that is the vague idea of building a nest and rearing a little family—and this book is written to help you in every way possible.

Engagement " Snags "

LET us first consider your engagement. The giving and the acceptance of the engagement ring means that you are provisionally promised one to the other. You are pledged to that degree of loyalty which may reasonably be expected from two people who, in due course, are going to belong wholly to each other.

So if you are a girl who, up till now, has had hosts of admirers, and outings with lots of men, thinking nothing of a playful kiss from your dance partner, you are now in honour bound to make a difference —as, of course, you will want to. For now you are promised to your fiancé, and your lips are his. Up to a point your free time is his, and all that part of life which is wrapped up with love is his.

You, too, young man, will have to make a difference. You are pledged to her, and, instead of the pleasant and harmless little flirtations you may have indulged in before, your affection, ardour, and kisses—indeed your whole love personality—rightfully and gladly belong to *her*.

But—and this is important— both of you must beware of becoming jealously possessive. Hold the reins lightly, and do not draw the silken cords of love into a fatal stranglehold.

Each of you should remember that the other has other claims— concerning mother, father, brothers, sisters, and even friends—and be reasonable and generous, won't you?

And remember, too, that getting engaged is only a *promise* of that full sharing of all life which one happy day you hope to enjoy. It is not in itself that sharing. It does not give unwise freedom. You have not yet entered the inner palace of love—you are, so far, only in the courtyard surrounding the palace—and you must not anticipate the joys of the inmost palace itself.

Because, you see, being engaged is not an irrevocable step. It is just possible that, in the closer intimacy of friendship involved in being engaged, one or both of you will find that you cannot, after all, face a lifetime of " togetherness." The engagement is a testing time, a trial time, a " preliminary canter " to see whether you two can run in double harness successfully. It is not yet too late to draw back.

Engaged couples cannot be too careful to preserve the bloom of their relationship and the sweetness of their love, knowing that, when their time of full possession comes, the entering into their palace of love will be all the more triumphant.

This particular difficulty is not ignored by the wise and open-eyed young couples of to-day, and, although it may be better not to mention it (because discussion is apt to concentrate attention upon it), there should be understanding about it.

Generally speaking it is easier for the girl than for the man to regulate the emotions because nature has made her less inflammable than he. So remember this always and, with gentleness and understanding, limit the kisses and the caresses, and realise the value of having some mutual hobby or interest which will act as an outlet for this energy of love which cannot yet have its natural fruition.

Without a single word on the subject being said, you can make the man you love realise that you understand his difficulty, and that you want to help him to be strong for the sake of your mutual love and all the beautiful things it is going to mean to you in the future.

You can avoid everything that is going to make things hard to keep your relationship within those bounds which hundreds of years of experience have proved to be wise and desirable and right and proper.

There will be times when things are hard for her too, young man, and then you must be the strong one. Indeed, in this delicate matter a mutual helpfulness, a mutual agreement and a mutual pride in the chivalrous protection of mutual respect, will increase the loving esteem in which you hold each other.

Looking Ahead

THERE is another matter of very great importance which is far better settled before marriage than after.

This is the satisfactory adjustment of financial arrangements.

So large a proportion of married-life quarrels come from misunderstandings and difficulties about money matters that every couple should have a clear understanding as to how they are going to manage this vital part of their domestic arrangements.

Together you should budget for your main expenses with the income as a starting point (see Chapter IV). Rent, rates, heating, lighting, housekeeping, clothes, insurance, possible doctor's bills, holidays, and other pleasures—all these should be taken into account and, with the figures before you in black and white, a mutual agreement should be arrived at as to the weekly sum available for each, and whether the whole shall be handed over to the wife to manage or whether she shall receive a certain amount weekly for her specific responsibilities (i.e. food, etc.) and the husband shall pay the rent, rates, insurances, etc.

Sometimes it is the girl who has the business head ; sometimes it is the man. Arrangements should be made accordingly. But always it is for the man to remember that, if she is giving up a well-paid situation to take on the job of being his wife, it is only fair to see that she receives the necessary funds according to his means.

It is for the wife to remember that spending *his* money is a sacred trust and one that requires as much skill and care as she is capable of. To spend the money wisely and well is a task that requires almost as much steady thought as the earning of it.

If, as is sometimes the case nowadays, there is an agreement that you shall carry on for the time being with your job, in order to make marriage possible at all, there should be a *definite* arrangement as to what expenses you will each be responsible for, and how much each of you is going to keep for personal use.

Unless these details are settled before marriage, they have a way of cropping up and causing untold difficulty later on.

When the husband is to be the sole wage-earner, a very fair arrangement is, after all necessary outgoings have been met, to divide what remains for pocket money.

Few husbands realise how humiliating it is to the young wife to be obliged to ask her husband for every penny she needs for herself, particularly if she had a job before marriage, and was used to

The engagement is a testing time, a preliminary canter to see whether you can run in double harness successfully.

It is usually easier for the girl than for the man to regulate the emotions. So you must ration the kisses and caresses and realise the value of a mutual hobby which will act as an outlet for this energy of love.

Beware of becoming possessive. Hold the reins lightly, and do not draw the silken cords of love into a fatal stranglehold.

spending what she needed. So, if you can, give her an allowance, however small, apart from her housekeeping money.

Education for Marriage

ENGAGED girls should be able to enrol for a " marriage course " and learn a number of necessary things about wifehood instead of being obliged, as so many are, to try out experiments on a poor long-suffering husband !

More happiness than we can estimate hangs upon a girl knowing how to cook, how to handle money to the best advantage, how to shop, how to run a house, and how to make and mend. So you will need to know about food values and well-balanced meals. The first need of a man, after all, is to be fed properly, and this is your responsibility, bride-to-be. So you need skill and wisdom and education.

Experience will educate you, of course, but you ought to have some ideas before marriage. If you are wise, you will take a few homely lessons from mother, not scorning to take a few tips about the shopping, the best markets, the cheapest cuts, and the economical hints—or to take a cookery course.

And then, as the marriage draws near, do take the trouble to educate yourself in that once most neglected branch of education—Sex. Fortunately you live in a day when most people are agreed on the importance of the wife understanding this side of marriage. No longer need you marry in an ignorance which was once miscalled innocence. No longer need you enter upon wifehood with only the vaguest ideas about physical relationships, or with an unhappy misgiving about that intimacy which is the basis of

marriage and the foundation stone of happy partnership.

There are, of course, other aspects of marriage equally important as the sex relationship, but the satisfactoriness of all these others really depends upon this.

It was once supposed that love and instinct were all that was necessary to teach a married couple what they should know, just as it was supposed that motherhood itself taught a woman how to manage her baby ! The modern mother, with her infant welfare centre and babycraft books, may well wonder how her grandmother managed. We know now that instinct, though a wonderful teacher, does not provide the actual knowledge.

Many a middle-aged woman to-day is a nervous wreck because she understood so little about Sex that this important part of her marriage went on the rocks, taking the rest of her happiness with it.

Many a home has been broken up because misery crept in *here* through pure and simple ignorance on one side or the other.

The education of both the man and the woman is equally important, and it is hoped that this little book will ensure that you do not embark upon the adventurous voyage without chart and compass. Chapter II deals fully and frankly with the question of sex relations.

The Marriage Eve

AS the great day approaches, you may be conscious of a curious lack of enthusiasm, bride-to-be. You may be worried because you cannot seem to work up any sense of joyous anticipation, of expectation, and you may even go so far as to wonder whether you are not making a mistake after all.

This is a sort of natural reaction to all the excitement of planning the wedding, sending out invitations, sewing, buying, and arranging. Probably you are tired out. These last weeks before the wedding are a great physical and emotional strain, but you need not worry or doubt yourself or your lover. Long ago you decided that he was worthy of your love and trust and, deep in your heart, you are sure of him. The quiet communion of the honeymoon days will set right this vague sense of fear and flatness which may have caused you such depression. So don't worry.

Of the great day itself one need not say much. It is bound to be one of the outstanding days of your life, a day to look back upon as a sweet and wonderful memory.

But do not imagine that, because you have got married, you will necessarily live " happy ever after." So ends the fairytale beloved by each of us in our childhood, but it can only end like that for humans if the two people concerned are prepared to *learn* a lot and *love* a lot.

In other chapters we shall consider some of the things it is most important to learn.

At the moment the most important question that may arise is—shall we have a honeymoon or not ?

Of course, you will realise that a honeymoon is going to cost money —money that might be spent on something for the home. Would it not be better, you wonder, so to spend it, and forego that week of honeymoon holiday at the beginning of married life ? Why not have the honeymoon later on, when it may be better afforded ? you may think.

Now there are some cases where such economy is necessary, but, speaking generally, the honeymoon should not be sacrificed.

The Need for a Honeymoon

IT is, you see, a unique holiday. You will never have another quite like it. If you postpone it, you will lose its full flavour of mystery, romance, ecstasy and bliss. After all the preparation and fuss and excitement of the actual wedding-day, you *need* to get away alone together to find yourselves and each other and peace. You need time for this—time from which rush and hurry and flurry are eliminated.

In these golden days you will savour the utmost sweetness of the first complete expression of your mutual love, and for this wonderful experience quietness and leisure and being away from all other claims and demands whatsoever are almost absolutely necessary conditions.

" Going home " will be full of joy, of course, in any case, but, if it is preceded by a week, or even only a week-end, when you can be at complete leisure to devote yourselves to each other, your whole life will be enriched by the memory —and the " great adventure " of married life will have the grand send-off it deserves.

A *

CHAPTER II

Sex Relations

SUCH a book as this would not be complete without a chapter on those intimate relations between man and wife which can make or mar the perfect harmony of their life together.

Some may feel that this is not a subject which can be discussed in print, for we are still, unfortunately, suffering from the repression of the Victorian age which regarded all sex matters as unmentionable. Yet those who are best qualified to judge—ministers of religion, social workers, doctors, and all psychologists, agree that without proper sex education there can be no upholding of the high standard of married relationships on which we have always prided ourselves as a nation.

The Birmingham branch of the British Social Hygiene Council, in a recent report, said: "Most of the young women who have appealed to the Council for advice have been in good circumstances, but, lacking a sense of responsibility, have become involved in liaisons with men, and frequently married men. These men give them what is known as a 'good time' in return for a relationship that has had tragic results.

" These experiences are sufficient to emphasise again the need for greater knowledge of the moral, social and physical aspect of sex for young people of both sexes."

Some time ago the Archbishop of Canterbury said: "I would rather have all the risks which come from a free discussion of sex than the great risks we run by a conspiracy of silence. . . . We want to liberate the sex impulse from the impression that it is always to be surrounded by negative warnings and restraints, and to place it in its rightful place among the great creative and formative things."

To put it in its rightful place; that is to be our task in this chapter, for the benefit of three different groups of women : (1) the engaged girl ; (2) the bride ; (3) the wife who has entered upon married life with no proper knowledge of the physical side of that relationship and has found herself confronted with difficulties whose existence she had never imagined.

Let us think, then, of the origin of this physical union of husband and wife which is the essential foundation upon which all marriage rests. The Bible, with its noble frankness, does not attempt to disguise this basis of earthly union : " Male and female created He them," says Genesis, and later He bade them " Be fruitful and multiply." And marriage lifted the act of reproduction from the purely physical meaning it has among animals, and made it not merely a bodily union but one of mind and soul as well, sanctified by the mutual love of husband and wife.

Christianity, with its noble insistence upon personal chastity, and its teaching that marriage was blessed by God mainly for the share it gave man in exercising the divine power of creating life, has done much to enrich and beautify the ideal of earthly union. But even in pagan times there was a persistent belief in monogamy— that is, of one husband for one wife. The ancient Egyptians and Greeks and Romans and those races of the Far East of which the Chinese are the oldest example, though they tolerated the possession by a man of several women, accorded to only one woman the rank of wife, and granted to that wife maternal rights and privileges over any offspring that might be born to her husband from a union with other women. The wife, *as wife,* had a place and dignity all her own, and the husband who remained true to her was looked upon with respect.

These being the facts, we ask ourselves, How does it come about that even in countries where the youth of both sexes are allowed to mix freely with each other and select, according to their own hearts, their life partners, there should be so much sexual frustration, so much married unhappiness, so many cases of infidelity to marriage vows ?

Causes of Failure

TWO main causes may be said to account for these failures on the part of husband and wife. The first of these is ignorance and the second selfishness.

There are other causes, of course. People do exist, it is undeniable, whom some mysterious nervous instability render entirely unsuitable for marriage. These unfortunate cases are the subject at present of careful investigation by psychologists. Often their failure is traceable to some shock in early childhood : this may be entirely forgotten in adult life, yet it remains in the secret recesses of the inner consciousness, producing a sense of fear and incompetence in the face of sexual relationship which is a cause of infinite distress to both partners.

These, however, are medical cases, which may be left to the experts who are rapidly gaining knowledge of the cause and the suitable means for their cure. Our concern is with the ordinary run of sane, healthy-minded folk who, having every physical requisite for a life of married happiness, yet fail to achieve this to the full.

We have mentioned ignorance as the first cause for marriage failure. To act properly one must understand properly, and primitive peoples are perhaps wiser than we in the way they prepare their young people for marriage. When boys and girls reach the age of puberty they are taken apart by experienced and trusted persons of their own sex, who devote a considerable time to instructing them in the new and important field of human activity which they will shortly enter.

Modern education is returning to this practice by means of sex instruction given to adolescent pupils. This, in view of the reluctance on the part of many fathers and mothers to speak freely to their boys and girls on sex subjects, is an excellent thing.

Many people well qualified to judge consider, however, that such instruction is much better given in the home. They believe that it should be started at a very early age by telling the small boy or girl in a casual chatty way " where baby comes from." As a seed sown in the child's garden produces in proper season a flower, so the seed planted by God in the mother's body produces in due time another human being. More than one mother, imparting such knowledge to her little son, has been touched by the passionate hug with which the little fellow greeted the news that from the very first he had been in such close physical contact with her.

You will find helpful advice on this subject in Chapter IX.

The further knowledge, as to the exact process by which the germ of life reaches the mother, may well be left till the age of adolescence when, whether parents choose to face the fact or not, their young people begin to feel a strong—and,

frankly, a perfectly natural and healthy—interest in sexual mysteries. A sensible and reassuring talk between father and son, and mother and daughter, at that period may form the basis of a sound and healthy attitude towards sex matters which will stand the youngsters in good stead throughout their subsequent life.

Preparation

HOW, then, is this instruction to be given to adolescents ?

The matter offers many difficulties even when the necessity for imparting information is clear. Often the elders are too shackled by taboos and repressions to speak plainly ; sometimes they feel that their methods will be too crude and the explanations too clumsy to be helpful. All too frequently they themselves lack the necessary sex knowledge with which to enlighten a younger generation.

Because it is certain that no book dealing with the subject of marriage could be helpful without giving definite information regarding the physical side of married life, we cannot shirk this responsibility. It is hoped that the following explanations will help not only young married couples standing on the threshold of their life together, but also parents of almost-grown-up children.

In considering the subject of the physical relationship of marriage we must first of all decide what elements go to make it satisfactory. These must be divided into two classes ; those which spring from the mind, and those which are of bodily origin. The sex act is in one way a simple and natural union, but, viewed in another light, it is the most complicated experience

A man, as a rule, regards the sex act more naturally. As his satisfaction is more easily attained, he must teach himself to be patient.

Lack of response on one side or lack of consideration on the other can lead to frayed nerves, bitterness, and even a parting of the ways.

that falls to the adult human being. This is because the mental and the physical elements are so closely combined in it. When bridal couples fail on the physical side of married life it is either because they do not know what to expect or else because, realising in a measure what the experience should be, they lack the knowledge which will bring about the desired results.

To begin with, it is important that when sexual union is desired the minds of both husband and wife should be in a state of rest. They must, for the time being, have banished all their mental burdens ; they must be free from external worries and anxieties. Their thoughts must be care-free and unfettered just as much as their bodies must be free from pain or illness.

The wife who wishes to get the best out of married life must prepare her mind for the sex act by banishing any fears and any holding-back of her true nature. Only if her mind and spirit are in real sympathy with the physical experience will she know the complete satisfaction which can come from it. Therefore there must be mental preparation for the experience, a sweeping away of the modest restraints of her earlier years, a breaking down of mental barriers, a willing and joyous yielding of herself to the man of her choice.

The husband's preparation is of quite a different character. A man, as a rule, regards the sex act more naturally ; his sexual instinct, for reasons that will be explained later, is more quickly aroused. Just because in his case satisfaction is more easily attained, he must teach himself to be patient ; his task must be to set himself to imagine what difficulties are facing his wife and, by all possible means,

to make the way easy for her. Very often, at the beginning of marriage, he must act as teacher and initiator ; in the carrying out of such roles lies his special mental preparation for sexual union. At first it might seem that such a situation involved much self-denial and restraint, but it is not really so.

Organs of the Body

SO much for mental preparation for the sex life. The physical element must now be considered. It is here that the actual bodies of husband and wife are concerned ; it is here that an explanation of the functions and reactions of the sexual organs is so essential if there is to be a healthy physical union.

In the man the sex organs are partly within and partly outside the body. It is important to note that they form one continuous system, for this is not the case where the female organs are concerned. The male sex organs consist of two organs named testicles, which hang in a pouch of skin known as the scrotum, and a tube-like organ known as the penis. Both penis and scrotum are external to the body. The testicles may be regarded as a factory of the life-cells or sperms which are the man's offering towards the awakening of life in his children.

The internal structure of the testicles is very marvellous and also extremely complicated, and the actual method by which the sperms are formed has yet to be discovered ; all that is known at present is that, from the time of adolescence onwards, these life-cells are continuously being made and stored away in very fine tubes which fit like a cap over the surface of the testicle. These tubes open into larger tubes known as the spermatic ducts, one of which runs from each testicle in an upward and backward direction into the abdomen ; there they join together to form one short duct which passes forward again and through the length of the penis. At the culmination of the sex act millions of sperms are ejected in a flow of seminal fluid.

The sexual organs of the woman are quite different, since they are to serve a different purpose. They consist of two ovaries and a womb with two tubes leading from it ; the womb hangs down into a short passage known as the vagina, which opens externally ; none of the actual sexual organs of the female are external to the body.

In a way, the ovaries are the counterpart of the testicles in the male, but the likeness is really very slight. Whereas, in the male, the sperms only begin to form when the boy reaches his " teens " in the case of the girl-child, the " eggs " are present in the ovaries a considerable time before birth. Their number is never increased as time goes on ; the girl starts life with the full number allotted to her. When menstruation commences one of those " eggs "—or ova, to give them their correct name—is liberated from the ovary every month.

The next female sex organ to be considered is the womb itself. This is a hollow, muscular organ which at normal times is about three inches in length and two inches in width ; the walls are very thick and will allow of an enormous amount of expansion, for it is within the womb that the child will grow until the time comes for its birth. Two tubes lead from the upper surface of the womb (the organ is more or less pear-shaped, and is so placed that the " stalk "

hangs down into the vagina) and these tubes open blindly into the free cavity of the lower abdomen ; the ends are fringed and, in the fluid that is found in this cavity, they move about rather like seaweed in the ocean. There is no direct connection between womb and ovaries ; the ova are released into the abdominal cavity and gradually, through the waving motion of the fringed ends of the tubes, they are swept into the womb.

Conception

THERE one of two things may happen. Either the ovum may be met by a male sperm, in which case a union or fusion will take place between the male and female germ and conception takes place. The impregnated ovum will then fasten itself to the inner surface of the womb and the infant will proceed to grow and, normally, will continue growing for the nine months of pregnancy.

If conception does not take place, the ovum passes out through the mouth of the womb and into the vagina, together with a discharge of blood and mucus from the lining of the womb, at the next menstrual period.

Before leaving this subject of the sex organs, it may be mentioned that, in most virgins, a piece of tissue extends across the vagina just below the neck of the womb, partially but not entirely closing the passage ; an aperture remains through which menstruation takes place. This tissue is known as the hymen (maidenhead) and further reference will be made to it later.

Having described the actual sexual organs, it remains to explain what happens when a physical union takes place. In the first

We would suggest to the bridegroom that the idea of consummating the marriage on the wedding night should be given up. The wise bridegroom may not take the final step for several days.

place, the male penis during periods of sexual excitement becomes erect. In this condition it can be inserted into the vagina much as a finger into a glove. A series of movements instinctively follows, after which an ejaculation of seminal fluid takes place, releasing millions of sperms, only one of which is required for the fertilisation of the female ovum. The rest are lost and die off on exposure to the air.

That is the comparatively simple process which takes place during sexual intercourse. It is in its relationship to the mental and spiritual requirements of the civilised man and woman that this sex act becomes so complicated. How are they going to reconcile what is apparently more or less of an animal instinct with the view that in the sex relationship lies one of the most valuable and uplifting experiences of their mutual life? It is obvious that some fresh element must come in to convert a mere instinct into something that partakes of the nature of a sacrament.

Love

THAT element is the love that has sprung up between the man and the woman, the affection that is full of tenderness and sacrifice but which is also fired by a passion which demands the closest possible contact with the person of the loved one, which sweeps away all barriers until it finds complete satisfaction in what is actually an elemental instinct. To those who say that there should be other and " higher " planes on which this mutual love should be expressed, we can only say that this sex instinct has been implanted, to a varying degree, in all normal human beings and that by denying its existence or refusing

it a lawful outlet we should be starving a definite side of our nature.

Just think for a moment and you will realise that we receive almost all the impressions in life which enrich us through our senses ; colour pleases our eye, music our ears, smooth surfaces our sense of touch. Why do we hasten to clasp the hand of a friend or to kiss some loved one ? Simply because such actions convey pleasure, through nerve-endings to our brains. Why then deny the sex instinct, which has been specially implanted for the closest of all possible unions between a man and a woman who have entered into the partnership of marriage ?

Results of Ignorance

STILL, it is not sufficient for young people on the threshold of marriage to love each other and recognise that proper scope must be given to the fulfilment of their sexual instinct. Those are more or less abstract conditions, and it is practical advice that is needed to bring the two into harmony.

The aim of this chapter is to spare young married people the trials of an " experimental " stage in their physical relationships ; such a course in most cases leads to disappointments and experience has proved that thousands of married couples never get past the experimental stage. In other words they miss the rich experience that should be theirs just because they have not given sufficient thought to the subject in advance, because they have come together without proper sex knowledge.

It is of the utmost importance that there should be correct understanding of the physical side of married life from the outset. Without it not only will one side of the man's and the woman's nature be starved, but there is another still more serious effect. This thwarting of a natural instinct almost invariably leads to a certain lack of mental balance. It may be very slight—perhaps a gradual inability in fixing the attention, a poor memory, a slight hesitation in speech or manner or action, but it may lead to some breakdown of a much more serious nature. Again, so many of the disagreements between married couples are really due to dissatisfaction where the sex life is concerned. Lack of response on one side or lack of consideration on the other will all too quickly lead to frayed nerves, bitterness, and perhaps eventually a parting of the ways.

Sex Harmony

WHEREIN then does this question of sex education lie and why is it that there are so many failures ? The whole trouble is that people do not always recognise the fundamental differences between a man's and a woman's response to sex stimulation. Once that difference has been appreciated and carefully studied most of the pitfalls are removed.

We have already said that, provided the right circumstances are present, the sex instinct is easily roused in the man ; this is largely due to the conditions which arise when the stimulus occurs. Unless the brain is temporarily occupied with some other interest, the moment of relief comes swiftly. This condition does not arise in the case of the woman, however. Her desires are neither quickly roused nor speedily satisfied. This is a fundamental point which should be recognised at once by all inexperienced married people.

We have also said that, at the commencement of marriage, the husband has frequently to act as teacher and guide to the wife who lacks sex education. The man who is engaged on the task of awakening sexual desire in his wife should retard the moment of his own satisfaction until she, too, has reached the climax of her pleasurable sensations, the " orgasm " as it is called. It is extremely important that this should be done unless the wife is to miss all physical reaction to the union and to remain disturbed and dissatisfied.

How is this to be done ? First of all, we would suggest to the bridegroom that the common idea of consummating marriage on the wedding-night should be given up. Its drawbacks are manifold ; first of all the pair have probably a very fatiguing day behind them and they usually find themselves among strange surroundings by night. The wife is perhaps in a state of emotional turmoil already, knowing that her unmarried life with all its manifold interests lies behind her and that the future is quite unknown. That is no time for thrusting a still more bewildering experience upon her.

Indeed the wise bridegroom will move very cautiously, in order that he may avoid every false and clumsy step. He may even have to make up his mind that the final step shall not be taken for several days. Yet all the time he should be leaving no stone unturned to awaken the sex instinct in his wife. If he does this skilfully he will probably find that she will presently take the initiative in showing him that she is eager for the physical side of his love. The wife who has set herself to understand her husband will realise that he is using restraint in order to make the way easy for her, and will appreciate his tact. If she is wise she will give herself gladly as soon as she has become accustomed to the change in her immediate circumstances.

Difficulties

SOMETIMES the first occasions of intercourse are marked with definite pain for the wife, however carefully the husband may act. There are several reasons for this. There may still be a definite amount of nervousness on her part which leads to contraction of the muscles ; in that case the husband will have to make further efforts to win the wife's complete confidence and desire.

Very often the trouble is due to a particularly tough hymen. Normally this ruptures on the first few occasions of intercourse, but this is not always the case. Unfortunately, in Europe a great deal of unnecessary importance is attached to this matter of the unruptured hymen. In the East it is ruptured by the midwife's fingers as soon as a baby girl is born, but in the Western hemisphere the unbroken hymen is felt to be such a definite sign of chastity that the idea of an artificial rupture is rarely considered.

Occasionally the vagina is particularly narrow, even when the hymen has been ruptured. In that case it is wise for the wife to arrange for the very minor operation known as dilatation, or stretching, which will only keep her a very few days in hospital but will certainly add enormously to her comfort and satisfaction once it has been carried out.

It is undoubtedly the duty of every wife to take steps of this kind when it is obvious after a few occasions that all is not perfectly normal. The wife who goes on, month after month, postponing her visit to the doctor out of a sense of false shame or embarrassment, is not only acting selfishly as regards her husband, she is also defeating her own interests. She is trying to satisfy herself with a very poor second best where her married life is concerned.

Sometimes in these early relationships the sex act is found to be difficult owing to a dryness of the vaginal walls, but here again Nature has made ample provision. Special glands are placed at the entrance to the vagina which contain a lubricating fluid, but it must be remembered that these glands only function when the wife's desire has been sufficiently aroused.

Health and the Sex Life

THE question is often asked whether full enjoyment of the sex act is necessary to the health of husband and wife and, if so, whether unmarried women or celibate men do not suffer from lack of such relationships. There is no doubt whatever that to married people, whose desires are constantly being aroused by close proximity to each other, full enjoyment of the sexual act is an absolute necessity if they are to enjoy good health.

By continuously creating a demand with no means of satisfying it properly, the system is bound to suffer in time. Couples who suffer from this great disadvantage often seem to age prematurely, and there seems to be a general sapping of their vitality. This condition

After the completion of the act, there comes the calmest of sleeps and you awake strengthened by the fullness of the experience.

The sex instincts of many wives are never awakened, yet they still have big families. But some doctors say that the children in these families have not quite the same vitality.

does not normally arise, however, with unmarried women and celibates, simply because no demand is made on their sexual instincts.

We have mentioned the harm done when married people do not get satisfaction from the sex act, but it would also be well to point out the positive side of this matter and to dwell on the tremendous improvement in the health of both man and wife after a few months of married life in which their sexual relationships have been satisfying to both. Such people have grasped the importance of sex in their lives; they have shown consideration for each other, they have learned how to satisfy each other's desires. After the completion of the act there has come the calmest and most refreshing of all sleeps, from which they have awakened to face another day, strengthened by the fullness of the experience that has been theirs, knowing themselves more deeply in love than ever.

Mention has not, so far, been made of the matter of parenthood, but this is because our object has been to consider the physical relationship as it concerned the two principal actors in their sex life. There is no doubt that no married life is really complete without the arrival of children, and it is a recognised fact that the wife who is most deeply in love wishes to bear the children begotten of her husband's love in her body just as the husband is equally anxious to give her children.

Not for a moment would we suggest that it is difficult for the wife whose desires have never been roused to conceive and bear children. There are thousands of wives whose sex instincts have never been awakened and yet who have nevertheless become the mothers of large families. But many doctors and midwives state that children born in those circumstances have not quite the same vitality and that they do not progress so smoothly as those whose parents obtained the deepest satisfaction from their physical life. Be that as it may, the wife who has never known pleasure in marital relations is not necessarily debarred from motherhood; often she is a very successful mother, finding the joy in her children which has either been denied to her, or which she has sometimes denied herself.

Adjustments in Married Life

BUT the perfect performance of the sex act is not the only matter of importance in an ideal sex life. As the years go by new conditions are constantly arising which call for a special adjustment and special study. So often one is asked for a little definite advice on the question of how frequently the sex act should take place. Unfortunately this is not a matter which can be decided for others; it is entirely a matter for the discretion of the individuals concerned.

Both husband and wife should keep a careful watch to see that no over-exhaustion is following their physical relationship. Provided they both enjoy quiet sleep after these occasions they can feel that they are following the right path. This is a matter which should be frankly discussed between them. The act should never take place when either partner is over-tired; when husband and wife have to work hard during the day they are often very weary at bedtime and in those circumstances it has often been found a wise plan to delay the sex act until both have been refreshed by sleep. Very often it has been found advisable to give up these relationships for two or three weeks if either husband or wife is at all run-down. The great point to remember is that the act should on all occasions be spontaneous.

Occasionally a married couple who have enjoyed complete satisfaction from the sex act for a considerable time begin to find that it is losing interest for them. In such cases a short period of abstention will often put matters right. At the same time it must never be forgotten that each separate occasion of sexual intercourse should be regarded as something quite complete in itself, and that it should be faced with fresh zest and interest.

At first the husband will have to remind himself that his wife is to be won afresh on each occasion, and just the same forethought and care must be exercised in approaching the sex act. Gradually, however, as time goes on, the positions may come to be reversed. The wife will set herself to attract her husband all over again, using all her tact and ingenuity to appear before him in some fresh and attractive light. Neither husband nor wife dare grow slack, lest indifference take the place of the rapture of early married life. This is a duty which opens up endless possibilities for the clever wife who has studied her husband. It is an art in itself, and how well worth while is this careful re-kindling of the fire that is going to bring life-giving warmth right through married life.

Probably both men and women have times at which their desires are specially aroused. It is certainly so in the case of the wife, and she is well advised to make a note of those times, which are likely to recur in fairly regular cycles. Many wives find that they are sexually roused for a few days before a period, but this is not true of all women. The wife might well make a note of her particular dates and take full advantage of them for her own and her husband's satisfaction.

Some wives are worried because they find that the sex act has inadvertently taken place either just before the end of a period or immediately after its onset. Others again find that the time of keenest sexual desire actually occurs during the course of menstruation. This need cause no anxiety, however. Admittedly most wives feel that they need extra rest at those times, and the idea of the sex act is then distasteful to them, but no harm is done if sexual intercourse takes place then. Certainly in the case of that small percentage of wives who feel that this is their time of greatest desire, the occasion should not be avoided.

During Pregnancy

AGAIN, some wives are anxious to know whether it is advisable to continue sexual relationships during pregnancy. Here, again, much depends upon individual tastes. Many mothers-to-be have no longer any definite sex desire during the waiting months; others, however, feel a definite sexual excitement from time to time during pregnancy. Here, again, the thoughtful husband will respect his wife's wishes.

Towards the end of pregnancy, intercourse will probably be too fatiguing and uncomfortable for the mother and she will be prepared to give it up until she has recovered from her confinement. In any case it is best to avoid it from the seventh month until six weeks after the birth. It is also wise to refrain throughout the waiting months at those times when a period would normally have occurred. These are the times when a miscarriage is most easily brought on and a wife should therefore keep as quiet as possible.

The young mother may, however, have no desire for the sex act for many months after the birth of her child, especially if she is nursing her baby. In such circumstances both husband and wife must exercise careful discretion. The wise wife will know how to show her husband affection without actual indulgence in the sex act, and she will study his feelings lest he should for a moment feel that his child has ousted him from her affection. So many happy marriages have been upset before now by neglect of this important precaution. This is just one of those occasions on which the wife must try to place herself in her husband's position, just as he tried to consider her inner feelings in the weeks that followed their marriage.

In Later Life

SOMETIMES people inquire how late in life the sex organs can function pleasurably and for the good health of man and wife. Here, again, the reply must be that all depends upon the individuals concerned and on the use they have made of the sex act in their younger years.

There is no function of the body that will suffer more quickly and be used up more rapidly than that of the sex organs if they are not treated rightly. If the sex nature of husband and wife has been well cared for and properly used during their earlier years, if it has not been restrained and also not overused, then the sex organs will continue to function to the satisfaction of both husband and wife through the passage of long years.

This is an important physiological fact and serves as additional proof of the fact that sex, where human beings are concerned, serves a purpose other than the reproduction of the species.

Advice to Brides

IT may be helpful to brides to have a few words of advice on the hygiene of the physical side of their married lives so as to save them anything in the way of embarrassment on what should be particularly happy occasions.

Some wives feel it necessary to douche in the morning after intercourse as a hygienic measure ; indeed some do so quite regularly. This should not be necessary, however, provided the parts are carefully washed in the usual way. There is a theory that some of the seminal fluid is absorbed into the vaginal walls, and that this is beneficial to the wife.

Brides who find that certain muscles are apt to contract at the early stage of the sex act, thus making its completion a difficult matter, would be well advised to take a warm bath before retiring for the night. This helps to relax the muscles generally, which will help them very definitely.

The arrangement of the wedding-day is usually left to the bride. This allows her to make a careful calculation to see that it will not fall during a period. This may save her a good deal of embarrassment during her honeymoon and, because in her sexual life she must never lose sight of the importance of perfect personal daintiness and freshness, she should be specially careful about these matters. If all girls realised just how important these details are they would be doing an enormous amount to smooth out the difficulties of adjustment that can so easily arise in those early days.

It is hoped that all those who are about to embark on marriage, or who have recently been married, will not only read this chapter through once, but that they will give it careful study, for it has been written in the hope that it will meet their special needs and that it will serve them as a guide in matters which are all too difficult to explain by word of mouth.

The Reward of Unselfishness

TRUE marriage, as everyone knows, is a matter of mutual unselfishness and this is particularly true in sex matters.

The unselfish husband will realise the need for patience, in order that he may enable his wife to share his joy.

The wife must realise that to play her part adequately in the sex side of marriage, she has to think as much of her partner's interests as of her own. Sexual life, like every other human activity, needs the use of the mind as well as the body. For the wife to play a part that is merely submissive and inactive means throwing an unfair share upon the partner. For the young bride entering married life, it is important to remember that she thereby constitutes herself the guardian of her husband's purity. A man who takes a wife, meaning to fulfil honourably his vow of fidelity, steels himself to resist the advances of other women who may try to attract him. He is surely entitled to look for a constant effort to attract from the woman whom he has chosen to share his life.

Joy, mutual and invigorating, should be the invariable atmosphere in which love comes to its fulfilment. From such blissful moments all anxieties, all reproaches, all of the tiresome discussions of ways and means which fill the everyday hours of most of us, should be excluded.

This joy, however, cannot always be mutual. As has been said, woman, by virtue of her physical make-up, does not experience passion so easily as man. She cannot therefore always come to these marriage encounters in quite the same eager spirit as her husband. It is here that unselfishness is called into action, and such unselfishness makes it necessary sometimes for the wife to play a part and enjoy her husband's pleasure even if she cannot share it fully herself. Any wife who does this consistently will get a full and certain reward.

Men, even the cleverest of them, are creatures of habit. A husband who has always gained full and complete satisfaction from his wife, who has never been repelled or made to feel himself a creature of brute impulses, will be safe from other women, not because he may not find them beautiful or charming, but because ingrained custom has taught him to consider any sex relationship as only enjoyable as well as permissible with his wife.

The Sacred Bond

AND when, as age comes on and the sexual impulse slackens and eventually fades into a pleasant memory, there will remain rooted deep in the inner consciousness of both husband and wife a dependence one upon the other and a mutual confidence which will be like that of a child who, after having run habitually to its parents for the fulfilling of its legitimate needs, continues in after-life to love father and mother with a deep loyalty that is born of the loving satisfaction given to those earlier claims.

Too much attention cannot be given to these aspects of the marriage bond. For married love, perfect and complete, is something unique in the experience of the human race. No other satisfaction even remotely approaches it. Material and yet spiritual, it has its roots in mother earth and yet reaches out towards that other world of which, without knowing much about it, all of us are conscious. Marriage is the one thing that belongs to every race and to every class of man. Properly exercised, its pleasures can heal the worst of human sorrows.

For the young bride entering married life, it is important to remember that she thereby constitutes herself the guardian of her husband's purity.

CHAPTER III

Settling Down

OFF for the honeymoon! Who would ever think there is anything that anyone could possible teach you about your honeymoon? You've been planning it for weeks, probably—you are going to your favourite spot, maybe, or you are going to some new fairyland neither of you has been to before. And anyhow, you say, it doesn't matter where you are going—you will be together, and that is enough to ensure that you have a perfect honeymoon.

It may be. The honeymoon is the beginning of your grand adventure. It will give you memories to look back on all your life. It must be as perfect as possible. And yet just the fact that you both want it to be perfect will not make it so. Like most of the other worth-while things in life, it must be thought about first.

Before the wedding, you looked into your financial position and planned out your budget as you were advised in Chapter I; you saw to it that your new home would be ready for your return, and everything was put in order so that there would be no worries, no bothers, but just plain sailing. You found out just how much you would have to live on, and now you are fully prepared to go home after the honeymoon and start housekeeping. You feel you know what is before you, and you are ready to greet it.

But with a honeymoon there is sometimes rather a different feeling. You have lived in houses all your life: you know something at least about the difficulties and joys of running a home. But to the bride and bridegroom marriage itself is a completely new experience, and it is just as essential that they understand that and feel ready to greet the honeymoon—in fact, of the two, learning to express one's love is more important than learning to manage one's home.

The great thing to remember is to yield to the impulses that love inspires in you. Just as love taught you the thrill of kissing and of holding hands in your engagement days, so married love will unfold its beauties before you. Now that you are married, there is no need for those restraints you exercised so conscientiously before—yet to the shy bride that prospect is a little frightening. It is not easy to cast off the habits one has carefully acquired. You may find you are filled with a wonderful happiness at the prospect of giving yourself to your new husband, mixed with a vague sense of uneasiness because of the new experience.

Do not worry. When you are alone together, that first night of your honeymoon, as your love goes out to meet his in a kiss, you will be led on and on until, almost without realising it, you will find that your marriage has been consummated—you have given yourself to him, he has given himself to you, spontaneously, gladly and naturally.

Wooing a Wife

THOUGH, in the joy of being together, it is usual for intercourse to take place on your first night together, it is by no means always the case, and as has been said in Chapter II it is not the best time for all couples, particularly if they have had a tiring day.

But, just as it is the wife's duty to understand the laws of housekeeping so that she can run the home smoothly, so is it the man's duty to understand her in order that their love life may run smoothly —and a whole chapter has been devoted to the subject, see page 10, which you would do well to study together before going on your honeymoon, in order that your first coming together may be a happy and satisfactory experience for both of you—born of a mutual longing for nearness that will not be denied.

You see, it is the husband's privilege to lead his loved one on gently step by step until she shares his own desires—for, though it is generally thought that the man's needs are more urgent, because they are more quickly aroused, the wife, too, is capable of equally powerful longing, but her feelings take longer to arouse. She likes to be made love to—to be " courted " and " wooed " and won ; even though, young bridegroom, she is now no longer only your sweetheart, her feelings are just as shy, as it were—and perhaps your " conquest " is even more beautiful just because of that.

But, if she seems tired on your first night together, remember the nervous strain she has been through, for a wedding is no light undertaking, you know, no matter how much in love you may be ! Be gentle with her, and understanding. Let her curl up in your arms and go to sleep if she feels like it. You have all your lives before you, and it will be better for both of you if your first experience of the greatest bond of all is shared when you are both keyed up and ready for it.

Glorious leisure for love-making is the greatest boon a honeymoon has to offer. It gives you plenty of time alone together to study each other, time to love unreservedly and to enjoy the beatyu of being together at last, for always. It is a time to look back on for the whole of your lives. Make it indeed the happiest beginning imaginable —and you will have your reward.

And so the honeymoon passes, and we come to that delightful business of settling down in the new home. It is a grand adventure, isn't it? You are thrilled to be the privileged one to get up and cook your man's breakfast; you delight in sharing it with him, and in waving him off to work—and you are happy to wander round dusting your new possessions, planning out tasty meals to prepare for him each evening, washing up and making the bed, and getting to know your neighbours.

It is thrilling to know that, as newlyweds, you are causing a mild sensation in your road—that you are the object of much interest to your friends and relations, just now.

And so the honeymoon glamour goes on. Outwardly, it may fade with the passage of time, but in your hearts it will last just as long as you let it—so don't let it wane.

A Home of Your Own

SOON people will stop pointing you out as " The Newlyweds "; they will take you as a matter of course, as one of themselves—and very proud you will feel, too, no doubt, for you will have achieved a real place for yourselves in the world. You are no longer just a woman now, little bride; you are a wife with responsibilities and a man to care for—a man whose well-being depends on you. And your man is a husband with a home to support. You have each reached a great landmark in your lives.

Be proud of your achievement, and be very determined to keep your marriage as something to be proud of, remembering that a little forethought now, in the early days, will save you a lot of trouble later on.

Just now life seems to be full of thrills, and loving comes so naturally that you may think it is stupid to imagine that there will ever come a time when it will need attention. Nevertheless, the rarest flowers need the most care, and a little thought will prove to you that nothing really worth having remains valuable if it is left entirely to itself —so guard your love, watch it and tend it as your most treasured possession. Others may take it for granted that, now the honeymoon is over, you will settle down to a happy marriage, but never fall into the habit of taking it for granted yourselves. A happy marriage has to be worked for with every part of your being; it does not just follow on naturally.

There is one great thing to remember, and that is that, when you were on your honeymoon, every hour was yours to spend together as you wished; but now that you are safely settled in your home there is work to be done to support it, and things are apt to be a little different.

Yes, you are probably saying, there is work to occupy the husband all day, and housekeeping to keep the wife busy—but there are still the precious evenings we can spend together, so things are not so very different. Yet they are. You are each likely to expect the other to be as fresh and charming, when you do have time to be together, as you were when there was nothing else but loving to occupy your attention—and is that going to be easy to achieve always?

Glamour was born when you first fell in love; it was nourished in your engagement days by the young man showering his fiancée with attentions, and it blossomed right out under the romance of your honeymoon days when both of you could express your love in ideal circumstances. Now, if that glamour is to continue to thrive, you, young wife, in particular must do something about it.

Do not be hurt if the man who swept you into his arms so lovingly one evening on his return home, only sinks into his arm-chair the next evening, and looks as if he has every intention of staying there. He does not love you any less because he is tired. Give him the benefit of the loving understanding you will expect from him when *you* are tired. Fetch his slippers, and hurry on the supper ; listen sympathetically to his tale of woe afterwards, or let him sit quietly reading while you bring out some mending. Your most valuable offering, at such a time, is a sense of peaceful relaxation. He has been working for you—and this is one way in which you can say " thank you."

Home is the place where one naturally expects to be oneself and to be loved because of it. As your fiancé, he would hardly have allowed himself to fall asleep when visiting you, but that did not prevent him from feeling tired, after a hard day's work, and half wishing that he could do so. Now that you are so much more than just sweethearts, it is right that he should feel perfectly at ease in your company. It would not be a compliment to your fitness as a wife if he felt he must always entertain you—for good wives have plenty of common sense mixed with their love.

But even a tired husband can buy a little bunch of flowers on his way home, or a few of her favourite sweets ; he can manage a smile when the wife runs to meet him, and a remark on her appearance, for, of course, she will have made herself look pretty to greet him.

Love can be expressed in such a number of ways, and, with sympathy on one side and appreciation on the other, hand-in-hand you can surmount this tiredness which is perhaps the first enemy of after-honeymoon glamour.

" Marriage Measles "

MOST young things in the course of growing up suffer with little illnesses which, though not serious, nevertheless cause quite a little trouble—and newlyweds are no exception, for " marriage measles " often set in, and, unless they have careful treatment, they are apt to leave a few scars ! So " inoculate " yourselves at once with a strong sense of humour which will save the situation.

As you may have guessed, " marriage measles " is just the process of getting used to each other's funny little ways, and of settling down together. It is likely that they might never occur if only people would stop putting their loved ones on pedestals—but they always have done so, and they probably always will ; and, after all, it is rather inspiring to know that one's husband or wife thinks there is no one else in the world to compare with one. It gives one something to aim at, and ideals to live up to.

The home is your mutual possession, but, because it falls to her lot to care for it, the wife is apt to look upon that expensive carpet as " her " carpet, or the spotless bathroom as " hers." If you leave lather on the bathroom mirror, or ash on the carpet, young husband, she will probably have something to say about it—and your first attack of measles is upon you !

The quickest way is to say you're sorry and prove it by helping to

Do not be hurt if the man who swept you into his arms so lovingly one evening, only sinks into his armchair the next evening and looks as if he has every intention of staying there.

Fetch his slippers, and hurry on the supper; listen to his tale of woe afterwards or let him sit quietly reading while you bring out some mending.

repair the damage. Of course, it is your home, too, and supposedly you have a perfect right to drop ash on the carpet if you wish, but it is hardly worth while reminding her of that, since you only did it by mistake, and since obviously you must be just as keen as she is to have a home you can be proud of.

On the other hand, little bride, you can make his life a misery by insisting that the home should remain a spotless house with no sign that it has ever been lived in. A home should be comfortable, bursting with life and love and laughter. If you cannot bear to see the cushions out of place, do not follow him round with injunctions to put them back and leave everything just so. Remember that it *is* his home as well as yours, and either resolve to give in gracefully about the cushions, or else put them tidy yourself with some joking remark about your being so houseproud.

Laugh it Off

JOKING solves most problems, you will find in these early stages. If he fell in love with your curls, it will be disillusioning for him to see you having to do them up in curlers each night—but it's no good your crying about that. You have two courses open to you, unless you have a permanent wave. One, you can laughingly say : " Well, now you're learning all my beauty secrets," and cheerfully put your head of curlers in a pretty little sleeping cap—or you can do them up after he has gone to work, and make yourself a smart cap to wear while you are doing your housework.

Then, too, you will certainly find that he has some annoying little habits ! Impossible as it seems for the one-man-in-all-the-world to have bad manners, perhaps your husband will be one of those who always feel grouchy before breakfast ; he may insist on giving you a prickly kiss before he shaves, or he may be addicted to reading the paper at meals. Whatever little faults—or even large ones—you may discover, determine to joke him out of them. It can be done, and it is so much more pleasant than " pitching into " him !

At the same time, because he gets out of bed on the wrong side one morning, there is no need to assume that he is always going to do so. In fact, many a " habit " has been cured instantaneously by the husband or wife laughing it off the first time it occurred, and assuming that it was something most unusual.

Let " Look On The Funny Side " be your motto for a bit, and see how much it helps. It is disappointing when the bride prepares a special meal for her man, and then he is unexpectedly late home from work ; it is annoying when that special cake she made flops in the middle and has to be given to the dog. Yes, and irritation is so easy to give way to—but bring your sense of humour to your aid, and half the trouble will have vanished.

But laugh *with* each other and not *at* each other, for that will do anything but soothe ! A kiss and a hug should bring the first smile, and a joking remark will do the rest. We all live and learn, and later on, when you look back on those first days of your marriage, you will find the heartaches and disappointments will be no less poignant for being framed in love and laughter—but they will be infinitely more worth while recalling.

The First Quarrel

THE most bitter attack of "marriage measles" comes perhaps with the first harsh word. Whatever its cause—tiredness, thoughtlessness or mere sudden irritation—it hurts terribly, and, though it may soon be forgotten in the joy of kissing and asking for forgiveness, unfortunately it gives newlymarrieds a taste of the thrills of "making it up," which leads to the mistaken belief that an occasional quarrel sharpens the wits, and that the joy of "making it up" afterwards is well worth the hurt one suffers at the time.

The truth of the matter is that every single quarrel leaves its mark, and it is certainly *not* advisable to give way to them. One soon loses the joy of "making it up" if quarrels become frequent—and there is no way of limiting the number once you start !—then, from being a surprising occurrence, they become a usual thing, and continual bickering sets in, which naturally does not make for marriage harmony.

How can one avoid them ? you ask. Well, the way to avoid a second quarrel is never to have a first. It takes two to make a quarrel, but it only takes the presence of mind of one to avoid it. A laugh, a kiss, or a joking remark will turn a cross word—or, if things have gone beyond endurance— a pleasant: " Well, don't let's get annoyed with each other ; we'll continue the discussion when I come back," will give the other person time to think calmly—and you, too, incidentally—while you leave the room on some excuse or other. No one can quarrel by himself, and a stern refusal to join in should put an end to the attempt.

At the same time, there are occasions when either husband or wife will lose his or her sense of proportion, and something may occur which is too serious to be laughed off ; it may be a subject on which you cannot agree—then would it not be better to keep your opinions to yourself ? Remember that everyone has a right to his or her ideas, and none of us has a right to force our own particular ones on anyone, even our life-partner. But, if you must come to some decision, talk the matter over calmly and avoid unpleasantness at all costs. There is a great deal of fun to be had out of discussions and debates, but, as soon as the slightest sign of annoyance creeps in, then be on your guard.

If you reach a deadlock, you can always ask the opinion of a reliable friend who will give you an impersonal view—but, if you do this, it would be fairer just to state the facts, for and against the case, and not say which of you holds which opinion. Then, when you have finally agreed on a decision, let the matter rest. It can do no good to start talking about it all over again.

" Making it Up "

YOU will certainly not be popular with your friends if you disagree in public ! Think back, from your own experience. There really is nothing that makes us quite so uncomfortable as being spectators at a quarrel, is there ? Sometimes it has far-reaching effects, too—for, in an effort to end the discussion, or to stand by their own particular friend, your pals will take sides, and so the argument grows. Long after you have " kissed and made it up," they still remember all about it, and probably they will never feel the same towards your life partner again.

We all have our own funny little ways, and it is certainly not worth while quarrelling about them. If you cannot cure them pleasantly, then resolve to take them as part and parcel of your dear one. You fell in love with each other just as you were—not as you hoped he or she might be—and no amount of quarrelling can alter a person's character for the better, though it can easily turn a once-happy couple into a nagging woman and a hen-pecked, rebellious husband.

One last word on the subject will remind you that a wise rule is never, never to go to sleep with a quarrel hanging over you. Get it settled before you go to bed—or at least reach an agreement which makes for happiness and leaves you no chance of sulking and refusing kisses that can do so much to heal that wounded feeling, once the real cure—of getting the matter right—has been started.

The thought of sharing the same room and all those precious little intimacies of marriage when your hearts are miles apart is nothing short of horrible. It is only right that when two people come together in the great bond of the marriage union, their hearts and minds should be in tune as well. Yet to refuse this privilege and cling to the quarrel is equally damaging to your love. No matter v ho is in the wrong, when one makes a move to end the distressing situation, do go forward to meet him or her halfway. Maybe she ought to " climb down," or he should apologise first—but be generous, and, knowing this, make it easy for the one who is wrong to get back into favour again. None of us can be right all the time !

And then, when everything is settled, let the quarrel die a natural death—do not bring it up again the next time you have a disagreement. There are so many nice things to remember that quarrels are far better forgotten at once.

When Life Feels Flat

AND so life flows smoothly on. With the honeymoon, all your dreams of happiness seemed to come true suddenly, leaving you perhaps a little breathless with the wonder of it all. Then came the added thrills of settling down—and you both reached a very pinnacle of happiness.

Is it any wonder then, if, one day, you suddenly wake up and wonder why things seem to have gone a little flat ? Like small children at Christmas-time, you have opened all the surprise packets within reach, and happiness has overflowed. It is natural that a reaction should set in. It will not last for long—indeed, only for as long as you yourselves let it—so it is up to you to make short work of it, realising that it is, after all, a perfectly natural reaction, and that a little good, honest, hard work—such as turning out a room, on the wife's part—will soon send it packing.

If possible, arrange to go on a little jaunt together, visit friends, or the Pictures, to take you out of yourselves. Up to now you have had little else to think of other than " Am I happy ? " " Am I making my husband (or wife) as happy as I thought I could ? " " Is our marriage a success ? "

That is good, but nothing will thrive if you keep on looking at it from all angles, and never leave it alone at all. Give yourselves other things to think about and enjoy

One undesirable result of a wife going to work is the effect on her husband. He can't adopt the attitude of the male hunter if his wife does the wage earning too. It gives him an inferiority complex.

occasionally, and your marriage will be all the fuller for it.

This brings us to the interesting subject of "friends." Naturally enough, you, young bride, will have your own friends, and you, her husband, also have yours. Some of them you will both like, which is fortunate, for you can exchange visits, and make up happy parties at no great expense, providing you with that outside interest which is so necessary in married life.

It is not good, of course, to remain wrapped up in each other to the exclusion of everyone and everything else. Maybe you do not understand why that should be, in these early days when all you want is to be alone together—but later on you will see. Mixing with other people gives you new ideas, and fresh things to talk about; it keeps up your interest in life, and promotes a certain amount of competitive feeling which prevents your marriage growing slack. It makes you move with the times; helps you to count your blessings, when you meet those less well off than yourself—and to strive for better things when you come in contact with those who have achieved success with their marriage.

It keeps you young in spirit, and cheerful, and it saves you many a lonely hour when for some reason you cannot be together. It broadens your outlook, and gives you the opportunity of standing by when a friend is in need—and of having staunch pals to stand by you yourself when clouds are on your horizon. Married people who keep too much to themselves soon grow to think only of themselves—and are generally most uninteresting people !

So much for the friends you both like. But there are nearly always one or two special pals who mean a lot to you, but whom hubby openly admits he can't stand—and the problem arises : Should you give up the friends your life-partner does not like ? It cuts both ways, you see, for there may be a chum of his that *you* cannot take to.

Your Friends, and His

THE best way—and the most tactful—is to arrange with each other that your meetings with these friends shall take place when your life partner is not there to be bothered with them. A married woman can always invite her friends to drop in while her husband is at work, and, excusing herself with the fact that she has his evening meal to prepare, can persuade them to leave before his return. And for the husband there are, say, odd games of billiards on the way home from work, or Saturday football matches in which the wife is not particularly interested, to which he can invite his friends. Or you can arrange an occasional " bachelor evening " when he is at liberty to meet, away from your home, those friends of his whom you do not find congenial.

Naturally, if you have little parties, all your friends can be invited together, for, if they *are* your friends, neither of you would wish them to feel that they were not welcomed by your life-partner —and, in this way, no feelings are hurt.

But first it is well to listen to your husband's (or your wife's) objections to these friends. Maybe they are reasonable, and you would do well to drop the acquaintance by degrees. Perhaps Mrs. Jones is a dreadful gossip, or Tom Green may be too fond of his little drink— perhaps, without your realising it, they have a bad influence on you, and you are a much nicer person when they are not there. Listen to the objections, and remember that it is the voice of love speaking, and act accordingly.

But do not be in a hurry to discard your old friends. Gradually, you will make new, mutual friends —on holiday perhaps, or the people living near you—and only the very special old friends will continue to visit you much. For the others, an occasional letter may take the place of their visits—and so the situation will ease itself. Letters brighten one up enormously, you know, and you will find yourself just waiting for the postman, bringing you news from your old home-town, your former school-friends and work-mates. Old friends are usually the staunchest, and there is no reason why, just because you have married, you should cut yourself off from communication with your old life, is there ?

Letting Each Other Down

WHETHER you like it or not, the friends on both sides are bound to watch you to see what kind of a success your marriage is going to be ; and it is useless putting on your party manners when they come to call, for friends have an uncanny way of reading between the lines !

Remember, young husband, that, when her friends come to see you, she wants to be proud of you. She doesn't want you appearing at the door in your old carpet slippers, full of grumbles because things went wrong at work, or you could not find your blue-striped shirt anywhere when you wanted to put it on. Keep the " family secrets " to yourself till after the visitors have gone !

And you, little bride, when he invites his friends home, be prepared for them to think to themselves : " I wonder what sort of wife old John has married ? " and show them that he is a very lucky man. Make yourself look your prettiest—even if it is only for his old aunt—and don't let anything ruffle you while they are there. Your husband may be clumsy, and you may long to scold him, but remember that it is an ordeal, in a sense, for him, too. He is so desperately anxious that you shall appear as wonderful to them as you do to him.

Since practice makes perfect, the only way to be sure of not letting your life-partner down when people are there is never to do it at all. Remember, hubby, that she expects you to stand by her as staunchly as she is ready to stand by you. Even the best of friends and relations are apt to criticise at times. Listen to what they say with a smile, but make it quite plain that you are very satisfied with the way your wife manages—even if, after the guests have gone, you do think one of the suggestions worth passing on to her.

And, young bride, the same applies to you. Your friends may try to find out what he is earning, but that is really your own business, isn't it ? Keep private things to yourself. If you want your friends to think your husband is marvellous, and what good taste you had to marry him, you must let them know everything there is to be proud of about him, but staunchly hide his little faults from everyone, even his own relations.

Yet it is not only the things which are said which let the dear one down. It is the things we do, too. For instance, your girl-friends will

not think much of your consideration, young bride, if, should you be
invited out for a while just as hubby
is due home, you agree to go,
without so much as letting him
know, in a little note, that you are
sorry not to be there to greet him,
and that you have only popped
round to So-and-So's house and
will soon be back. That anything-
will-do-for-him attitude may seem
smart and rather a contrast to the
one they are obviously expecting
from you as a bride—and it may
create an impression just at first,
but it will be just the sort of
impression you should wish to
avoid, and one which you would
hate hubby to give about you !

How Would He Like It ?

" DO as you would be done by "
is a splendid motto, and, no
matter what your friends may say
to the contrary, they will really
envy you your happines and mutual
consideration if you both make a
point of following it. Where everything is concerned your first thought
should be for each other : " How
will this affect the wife ? " " Will
hubby mind if I do that ? " Put
yourself in the other's place, for a
moment ; picture how you would feel
if he—or she—did the same thing,
and then see if you still want to
do it.

If you make a promise, do your
utmost to keep it ; inspire trust
in each other, and, though you may
have many failures, one way and
another, let each be sure of the
other's confidence and determination to win through. Remember
that you are two people, but your
lives are one, and, unless you live
in sympathy with each other, those
lives will never make a splendid
marriage.

You, young bride, must put
your man's comfort before anything
else. You must learn to cook well,
if you cannot do so already, for he
has a right to expect that of you,
though, if he loves you, he may
never mention that right ; you
must mend his clothes, and not
leave buttons off, and holes in his
socks, just because something else
turned up to take your attention.

Before marriage, when you
worked for your living, you would
not have dreamed of neglecting
any part of your job, would you ?
It is much the same now. *He* is
your job, and he depends on you
to look after him and make him
happy in every way possible—
mentally, spiritually, bodily, and
in all the little everyday ways
which one is apt to think of apart
from the bigger and seemingly more
important things. Each one of
those " little things " is a stitch
in the fabric of love's cloak, which
is made up of the three larger
" materials "—the heart, the soul,
and the body. And, if you fail him
in the least of them, you are
letting him down.

Read the marriage vows through
together sometimes, and see if you
are carrying out your part of the
bargain which you made so readily
on your wedding-day. " To have
and to hold," " To love and to
cherish," " In sickness and in
health "—all these are not just
idle words ; they are meant to
help you to know what is expected
of you.

And do not think, young husband,
that if you bring home the weekly
wage envelope, you have done
your part. She wants more than a
wage-earner to keep her ; she wants
the lover-like sweetheart who used
to court her, who took her to dances
sometimes, and to the Pictures, who
was extra tender when she was not

PLATE 1

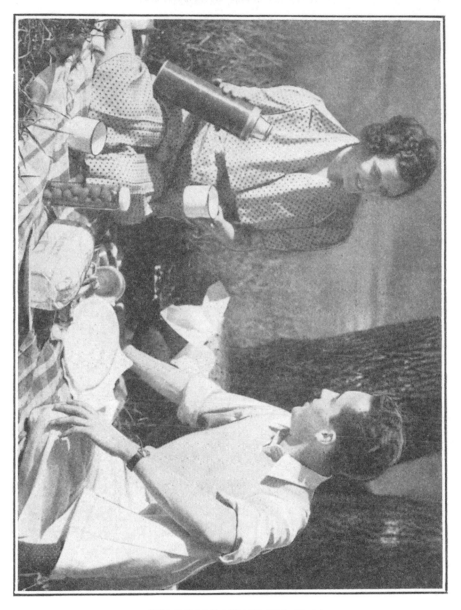

HAPPY DAYS

COURTSHIP time is a time of glamour, when you are both on your very best behaviour and eager to agree with each other. But wise couples frankly exchange views on money matters, children and other subjects that count so vitally in the making of a happy marriage. Advice on courtship days will be found in Chapter I.

PLATE 2

PARTNERS

TO make marriage a success, husband and wife must truly be partners. They must pull together in keeping love alive, in bringing up the children, and in managing their money. There must be no secrets between them, about money matters or any others. Then they will manage well—and though money does not make happiness, mismanagement of it may bring misery. The Money Side of Married Life is dealt with in Chapter IV

PLATE 3

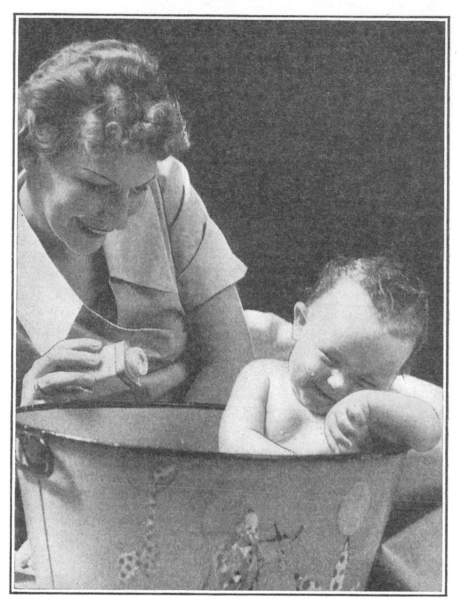

MOTHERHOOD

THE coming of a baby crowns a happy marriage. However content are the two who have become one, they do not know the full joys of married life until they have become three, and baby smiles are bringing fresh sunshine into their home. Advice on adapting your domestic routine to the changes that a baby makes in it, and on giving the little precious a good start in life, is given in Chapter VI.

PLATE 4

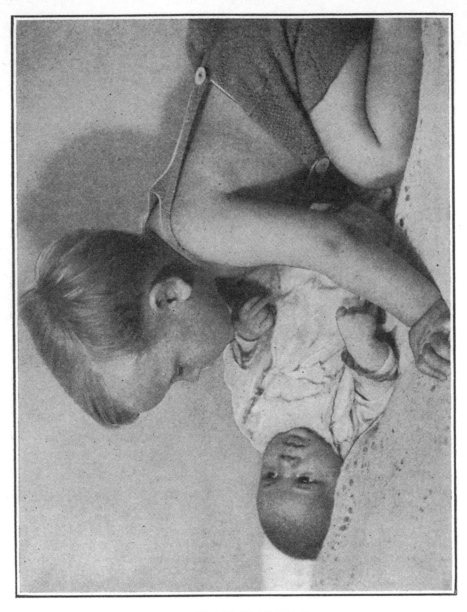

*NO NOSE
OUT OF
JOINT*

WHEN a
second baby
comes there is
always the risk that
the firstborn may
feel neglected, but
if the problem is
dealt with in the
right way he can be
taught to love his
baby brother or
sister and never
feel jealous.   See
Chapter IX.

very well, and who did all he could to help her. You will be letting her down if you fail to fulfil one single need in her life—and she in yours ; when you come across a bad point, look immediately for two good ones, and see what fun it can be being loyal and true in every department of your life.

" In-Laws "

BE specially careful not to let each other down before " in-laws," for they are the people on whom we are anxious to create a good impression, and who like to talk to us about our dear ones, and advise us in their own way.

As we noticed before, it is wise to listen to their advice, remembering (1) that they will be flattered if you do, instead of feeling offended because you do not, and (2) that, since they must have had a good deal of experience, they probably do know what they are talking about, and there may be something useful in the knowledge they are imparting.

Utterly refuse to have any unpleasantness with any of them—which will be quite easy if you maintain a smiling manner and the utmost confidence in your life-partner. If you can, invite most of them separately, so that they can come on a special visit to sample the wife's cooking, and inspect your little home, and really feel that you want to get to know them, and to be one large happy family.

Here it seems a suitable moment to mention wedding presents. So many people are under the impression that, once a present has been given, you must keep it, and use it —or at least bring it out, and look as if you are using it !—when the donor visits you. But that always seems to be such a dreadful waste.

You do not like it, but the intention of the donor was to give you pleasure, and, unless it does, it is a complete waste of time and money, isn't it ?

Of course, if you are going to do anything about it, great tact must be exercised, but it is sometimes possible to notice, as each present is unwrapped, which shop it came from, and make a little note of it together with the name. Then, when you are writing to say " thank you very much," if it seems a likely possibility to you, why not say something like this : " We loved the blue vase you sent us and should so much like to put it on the sitting-room mantelpiece, but, unfortunately, it does not go well with our colour-scheme, which is yellow. Shall we put it away, ready for the time when we redecorate (many moons ahead, I'm afraid !) or shall we change it at the shop for another colour ? " Nine times out of ten you will be told to change it for something more to your taste, and then, when the donor visits you, you will be able to show her with real pride just how and where you are actually using her gift.

Family Skeletons

THERE are secrets and sorrow in most families, and, because some well-meaning aunt of your husband's tells you that one member of their family was a terrible drunkard, there is no reason to suppose that your dear man will inherit the failing ! Look back into your own family. Do you remember the cousin twice removed who left her husband and went on the stage ? Well, there is no likelihood of your doing the same thing, is there ? In fact the idea is laughable ! Well, treat all those little confidences in the same way, and do not attach any importance to them. Even if there is hereditable illness somewhere in the family, comfort yourself with the thought that you have both been medically examined—if you were wise—before marriage, and pronounced perfectly fit for the adventure.

Now, you must expect a little criticism! Remember that to your in-laws, as a rule, you could not possibly be good enough to marry their precious John, or their wonderful Lucy. Treat that with an understanding smile, and be glad they are so proud of her, young husband—or that they think so highly of your husband, little bride. In time you can easily prove to them that you are, in fact, the only possible person who could have made their darling happy— and that is a little secret which you are going to let them into by degrees, and by experience, and which you are going to take a pride in doing.

Living with " In-Laws "

AT all cost avoid making trouble with the " in-laws." You did not marry them and you will only have to visit them, or have them visit you, occasionally—but if you hurt your husband—or your wife —by some rude reference to them, or by repeating seriously some little insult which you could easily treat as a joke, you are laying up an unknown amount of difficulties for the future. Peace of mind is such a wonderful gift that it is worth fighting hard to preserve it.

As a rule, it is best to live in one room alone together where you can have complete privacy, than to attempt to share a home with your " in-laws " no matter how well you get on together.

You see, it is the man's privilege to support his wife and to provide for her himself. It is his nature, and he cannot be really happy unless he has achieved this. Little quarrels arise, born of a sense of inferiority in his heart, of which he may not even be conscious—he wishes he could do more for his wife, and, failing, feels resentful. A resentful man is never very cheerful to live with, and the wife becomes restless, and perhaps a little sorry for herself. Nothing can make up to her for the fact that she does not possess a real home of her own. One shared with " in-laws " is at the best only temporary, and one cannot blame her for lacking enthusiasm in respect of it.

Then friction is almost sure to arise between her and the mother, or mother-in-law, who cannot help reminding herself occasionally that she is really the mistress of this home, and who naturally wishes to run it in her own way.

Sharing a home when both wives are at home all day is a venture to be avoided unless it simply cannot be helped. No matter how small your home is, have it to yourselves, at any rate at first. It gives you something to aim at, to build round and to be proud of. It is yours. You are responsible for it. You can invite your friends there, and you can do what you will without any fear of worrying your " in-laws." You can entertain them at your place—no matter how humbly —and they can exchange visits with you. At least, young husband, you can show " her " people that you are able to support her yourself, and that, by degrees, you are determined to do even better.

That is if, as is to be sincerely hoped, you are going to be able to live on the young husband's wages, and there will be no need for the bride to keep on her old job, or get another, after marriage.

If she has to work, then perhaps if the " in-laws " are kind enough to offer you a home with them, it might be a good idea for you to consider it. You could offer to go as " paying guests," handing over a reasonable amount for your board and lodging, and for any other expenses that crop up. This will relieve the bride of the added responsibility of housekeeping while she is also holding down a job, and will leave you both free to enjoy each other's company in the evenings, and over the week-ends.

Wives Who Go Out to Work

BUT nature does not provide for the young bride having to work, and she usually gets upset in one way or another if she has to. You see, the laws of marriage are based on the age-old idea that man should do the " hunting," the providing and the wooing—that he should, indeed, be a real he-man, and that woman should give herself to him, acknowledging him as master, and fulfilling the other half of marriage which consists of bearing the children and caring for the home.

This she cannot do to the best advantage if she, too, is being a " he-man " in some degree. For if she spends at some place of business the time when she would normally be doing her housework, then, when she returns, she must do the little jobs that are waiting for her—and the husband, coming home and wanting loving arms to greet him, and a hot supper on the table, finds instead a little wife who is nobly trying to come up to expec-

tations, but who is really just as tired out as he is, and needs just as much sympathy and under-standing.

Though, of course, modern women realise that they are able to do much more than their ancestors—and they do it admirably, whatever they undertake—one cannot get away from the fact that funda-mentally women were intended to be in the home, and that is their real place, completing the other half of the life they agreed to share when they married.

If you can possibly manage on your husband's wage, do so, young bride. It is praiseworthy of you to consider going out to work, and starting all over again the business of wage-earning which you had every right to expect to leave behind you when you married—but, before you decide to do it, ask yourself if the money you gain will really make up to you both for the comfort you will each miss. If you can be relieved of the responsibility of running a home, then you might manage it satisfactorily for a while—but it is not the wife's real voca-tion, and she cannot make her husband completely happy while she is doing this. For one thing, when both partners are working, an air of " You-go-your-way ; I'll-go-mine " is bound to arise—there is no time, perhaps, for you to wave hubby off to work, and you may not be in in time to greet him on his return. If someone else is doing the catering for you, you do not get much chance to plan out his favourite meals, and, if you yourself are seeing to them, then, more often than not, you have to rush in and buy something on your way home, which is rather comfortless.

Work has to take the first place in your considerations—you must not arrive late, but occasions may

The laws of marriage are based on the age-old idea that the man should do the hunting. The woman must give herself up to him, acknowledge him as master and fulfil the other half of marriage – bearing the children and caring for the home.

Little bride, you must learn to be your husband's nurse when he is ill, his companion when he's well, his cook, his housekeeper, his valet, his comforter when he's down and his sweetheart when he's in good spirits.

arise when you have to stay late, and, no matter how much you may worry over hubby's feelings, you cannot do very much ; in fact he has to take a back seat—and so, by degrees, an air of casualness dims the romance of your marriage, and you settle down to the fact that you cannot possibly hope to welcome a baby while you are working, and the magic tint fades from your dreams.

There seems to be no reason why, if you find you have time on your hands, and not much money in the bank, you should not take up some part-time work which will not interfere too much with your other arrangements—but, other than that, take a pride in seeing how well you can manage on even a small wage, study special little economies, and learn to make your own clothes. It will be quite a good " game "— and such a very worth-while one.

Changing Characters

ONE of the most undesirable effects of both partners going out to work is the effect it has on their characters.

For instance, the husband can scarcely adopt the right attitude of the male if his wife does the wage earning, too ! It gives him an inferiority complex, whether he realises it or not—and she becomes dissatisfied, and may well wonder, sometimes, why she married at all, because all she seems to have gained is added responsibility. It is easy to say " But that wouldn't happen with us ; we understand each other." Probably the people it does happen to understand each other all right—but all the same they find that they cannot account for sudden changes, for little dissatisfactions and quarrels, for this,

that, and the other—and it all boils down to the fact that their natural reactions have been upset by the fact that they are both trying to do the man's part.

Which brings us to the point of discussing characters. What sort of wife have you become ? What sort of husband ? Perhaps you think it is not worth while considering such a thing. You each married the other because you liked each other as you were, and presumably your characters will remain the same for always. But that is not so.

Strange as it may seem, love is the chief offender in this case. A doting young husband spoils his wife for the sheer pleasure of giving her her own way—perhaps he cannot afford to give her very much else, and that is his way of making up for his lack of worldly possessions. Glady she accepts his attentions, lets him give her her own way, and glories in the happiness of her new-found pleasure. That is all right for a little while. But one day, perhaps, he begins to realise that there are times when her own way is by no means the best way—he may be weak enough to go on giving it to her, and things end in disaster —or he may be strong enough to refuse to let her ruin both their lives, and then she immediately jumps to the conclusion that he no longer loves her. Poor little wife, you cannot blame her—and you cannot blame him, either. Nor could you blame them if the circumstances were reversed, and it was the wife who always gave her husband his own way. Love began the mistaken kindness, and human nature expected it to continue.

Henpecked husbands and down-trodden wives did not start their marriage in such an ignominious state. They started by loving too much.

And so we see that love should consist of giving and taking in almost equal proportions. It is not only not wise, it is not even kind to your life-partner always to be self-effacing and only anxious to please. Even such precious offerings can become monotonous, you know, and the receiver of them may long to do a little such giving on his own account—so don't be " selfish " ; don't try to do all the pleasing, but give your life-partner a chance to prove his—or her—love, too.

It is a well-known thing that we all have something of the male about us, and something of the female, and according to how well that " something " is developed, so we see the various temperaments. For instance, you can meet a domineering woman, more like the usual idea of a man than a typical shy, modest little wife—or you can meet a retiring young man, much more like a sensitive girl than the usual idea of a hearty young fellow.

Because your husband is not very go-ahead, young bride, and you are, be careful of always taking the lead and letting him follow. He may be very glad to. But it is bad for him. You will not be helping him to become more manly, and you are making him into a henpecked husband ! Talk things over together, by all means, and help him by letting him know your point of view, but force him to make the actual decisions sometimes and to think for himself. Look to him for help, too, instead of always expecting him to look to you. Encourage him to overcome this shyness, or whatever it may be. The man should always take the lead, outwardly at least—even if behind him is the wife skilfully guiding him, so that, perhaps, even he himself does not realise it.

Don't be a " Doormat "

ON the other hand, if you feel that he is far wiser than you are, do not just do as he says because he says so, waiting for him to speak or command you, glad to obey him, because you love him so. Men do not appreciate " doormat " wives—and justly so : if you think you are so far below your man's intelligence, and you seem to have no ideas of your own, no opinions save his, and are only too glad to fetch and carry for him, like a slave in olden days, how can you expect him to look up to you ? How can he respect you ? Can you blame him if he learns to look down on you, taught by your own behaviour and self-admitted inferiority ?

By all means fetch and carry because you love him—but let him perform the same service for you sometimes ; show him that you expect it, not as a return duty, but, as the occasion arises, as an act of love. Maybe his opinions are sounder than yours—are more often right ; but at all events have some opinion to offer, give him the joy of explaining how he arrived at his ; learn from his greater powers of reasoning, and teach yourself to think things out so that your opinions may be of value, too.

Marriage is a partnership, and it is not right that one partner should have all the responsibility—whether it is in work, when the husband should do the wage-earning and the wife care for the home, or whether it is in planning your lives, when you should both do a little hard thinking occasionally. Try to share everything and leave nothing entirely to one person—neither the loving, nor the giving. Watch your characters and adjust them as the years go by, for they really do need the utmost care.

Do not always be the one to give in or the one to command, for you should each pull your own weight ; but you will need to be tactful when you see the need for adjustment arising. You know your life-partner best. Some respond to being joked out of a habit, and some will take just a hint if it is handed to them smilingly—others hate you to think they are in the wrong at all, so you must tactfully change your own behaviour. If love is sincere it must take as well as give, you see.

" Quick-change " Wives

IN fact, married life requires a number of variety acts from each partner ! And, to be efficient, you must be a quick-change artist. Little bride, you must learn to be your husband's nurse when he's ill, his companion when he's well, his housekeeper all the time, his cook, and his " valet," mending his clothes and caring for them ; his comforter when he's " down," and his sweetheart when he's in good spirits, his counsellor, his helpmate, his entertainer—in fact there is hardly anything you are not called upon to be to him during the course of your life together.

And you, hubby, what can you offer the woman who means so much to you ? Nothing less than all the things she needs in life, of course. So, between you, you will have your work cut out in perfecting each little " part " you must play on life's stage. Study first aid together, so that you can read a thermometer if necessary, and do well all the hundred-and-one little things that need to be done in a sick-room ; learn how to be the very best companions possible— and aim at filling each " rôle " as well as you can.

Remember that, now you are married, you are each the only sweetheart the other has left. For you, the man, she may have given up a rich admirer who showered her with gifts, or a devoted one who followed her round with compliments that made her thrill with happiness—or he may have given up for you, young bride, the most famous beauty in his town, who knitted him lovely warm pull-overs with her own fair fingers. Whether you each had a dozen admirers, or whether you fell in love with each other first, you are still the only sweethearts left now, and you must make the most of that privilege.

Do not spend your time wondering if you are as pretty as his other girl-friends used to be, little bride —make the most of yourself, and see to it that you are as pretty as you possibly can be, and as attractive as you were when he fell in love with you.

Keep a diary, and read it together when you are having a quiet evening sometimes—so that you can play the game of " Do You Remember ? " and recapture the thrill of those days gone by— keeping young together, and in tune with each other, enjoying life to the uttermost—putting into it the very best you have to offer, and taking out of it the resulting happiness and peace.

Surprise each other with little kisses and caresses. Yes, you are married now, but romance flows just as strongly in your veins. Make it worth each other's while to go for a moonlight stroll, and keep the glamour alive. If you leave nothing to be desired in your marriage—every part of it filled with joy and happiness, what have you to fear even though an " old flame " suddenly turns up ?

True, old flames spell romance, but it is past romance ; if an old flame cannot fill any place in your dear one's life, for the simple reason that it is already filled to overflowing, then there is no danger.

" Old Flames "

REMEMBER that the old flame lost the love of your dear one, and you won it ; show plainly that you know you have nothing to fear, joke about the little feelings of jealousy which will probably trouble your heart, and see to it that, when the old flame finally departs, you have a jolly evening on your own together—perhaps visiting a dance or a show of some sort, so that there is no time for morbid thoughts of the might-have-been.

Here the question arises : Should you confess your previous love affairs to your dear one ? Perhaps you were a little unwise in your extreme youth, and it would ease your conscience to explain and know that you were forgiven. But, before you do this, you must ask yourself if the comfort you would be giving yourself would really be worth the great pain you must naturally inflict on the dear one—for, though you may readily be forgiven, perhaps the incident will never be forgotten, and something may die in your dear one's heart that can never be brought to life again.

The real time for confession is before you agree to marry each other. Then, if your past, whatever it may be, affects your dear one too much, he or she has at least the chance of going away from you, and trying to forget you—or else you know that you are fully forgiven and it will never come between you.

Once you are married, silence is best—unless the truth is likely to come out from any other quarter, and ruin your happiness when you least expect it. It is not the silence of fear, but of love that would rather suffer alone, unforgiven, than trouble the heart that now knows only happiness because of you. Confession is not the only way of atoning for the past ; perhaps an even better way is to make the most of the present, learning from your great mistake, and letting the experience make a better person of you.

Ideals are so very precious ; nothing can make up for the loss of them. Let your life-partner think you are the most wonderful person there is—and determine to be so, as far as you are able !

CHAPTER IV

The Money Side

MONEY does not make happiness, but mismanagement of money can cause a great deal of misery in what might otherwise be a very happy home. It is not merely a husband's duty to earn as much money as he honestly can for his wife and family : it is his duty to spend it to the best advantage, and it is the wife's duty to help him—not only by judicious handling of the housekeeping allowance and by not being extravagant personally, but by understanding and discussing with him the entire expenditure of their income.

Look upon this as a business matter in which you two are partners, with no secrets from each other, working together to make the best of your income, whatever it may be, and to achieve that vitally important thing—to live within your means. If you manage to make ends meet you will be free from worry and care, and the nerve-strain that worry brings. You will have to go without many things you would like to have, but the peace of feeling secure, of knowing that you can pay your way, is well worth it.

Now the basis of living within one's means is the making of a hard-and-fast budget and sticking to it. On one side is placed all the family income and on the other side the various outgoings. Then the account must be balanced, leaving a margin for such emergencies as are bound to crop up in the best organised of homes. It is practically impossible to lay down any rules as to how much money, or even what proportion of the income, should be spent on housekeeping, how much for rent or house-purchase, and so on. Not only do incomes vary, but conditions are different in nearly every home.

The Household Budget

THE thing to do is to put down first the expenses to which you are definitely committed, and which cannot be avoided or reduced —rent or house-purchase instalments, income-tax, rates, insurances, light, fuel and payments for anything you may be purchasing by instalments. These amounts *must* be paid regularly, and never let yourselves be tempted to " borrow " from them for any other purpose—except in an absolute crisis.

Next allot a definite amount for housekeeping. People have widely differing ideas as to what this should be, and some families can live on less than others. But whatever it is, young husband, regard it as a thing that must not be cut down except from sheer necessity, and you, young wife, keep within it at all costs. (Incidentally, hubby, *give* it to her when it is due : she will hate having to ask you for it.)

Then comes the husband's necessary personal expenses—fares, clothes, midday meals and a reasonable allowance for tobacco, papers and other incidentals.

In most homes, the wife takes her small personal expenses out of the housekeeping and asks her husband for money when she needs something definite such as a new frock. This usually works very well, but it is much more satisfactory if the husband gives his wife, in addition to the housekeeping money, a definite personal allowance, however small as was suggested in Chapter I. This saves

B *

the wife from having to ask him for money whenever she wants to buy herself a hat or pair of gloves, and saves him from a sudden demand for the price of a new frock when he didn't expect it and cannot conveniently meet it. With a very small income this method is not perhaps practicable, but it is a good one to follow whenever possible. But talk the matter well over together, because you, young husband, in the glamour of the early days, will probably promise her more than you afterwards find you can afford, and to have to cut down her allowance later will be uncomfortable for both of you.

After that come amusements and sundries—and you will be astonished at the way the sundries mount up. Repairs to shoes, replacements of household articles, and so on, run away with far more than you estimate. Then if you are buying your home you must allow something for household repairs and decorations. You must have a margin for doctors' bills and medicines, you must put something by for your annual holiday. And then there is the baby you hope will come to make your happiness complete ; his needs will cost you something, and the very beginning is not too soon to start saving up for him.

And in some way or other you must save for the future, either by setting aside a definite regular amount, by one of the methods explained later on, or by putting aside what is left over each week. But so often there is little or nothing left over that some definite form of saving, which you stick to as firmly as you pay your rates and taxes, is the only satisfactory way. In any case, however you frame your budget, don't allot every penny of your income ; allow a margin for unforeseen extras. You'll need it.

How to Save Money

THE secret of keeping to your budget is to avoid money being frittered away—a thing that happens very easily. The only way to prevent this is by keeping accounts. It is not necessary to account for every penny spent through the year, but husband and wife should be able to say pretty well where the personal allowance, and the housekeeping money, go. And at certain periods of the year, for two or three weeks at a time you should keep close accounts, showing practically every penny spent. In this way you will know exactly where the money goes, because well-kept accounts are just like signposts. You may find you are spending too much on some particular commodity, or allowing yourself to buy things you do not need.

Good housekeeping consists of systematic marketing, i.e., knowing the best days of the week on which to shop, the best shops to patronise, where there are most likely to be bargains and so forth. Where you have weekly books, pay them every week on the same regular days. Except where inconvenient, pay spot cash, buying no more of a thing than you need, because this is always the most economical way. Some commodities, however—such as soap and candles, for instance— are best bought in bulk because you save money by so doing. Soda, on the other hand, is an example of the things it is not wise to buy in quantities, because it does not improve with keeping.

Labour-saving appliances, providing you buy wisely, are almost always good investments. Having a proper brush for each domestic task is an economy, and so are such things as stainless steel knives, an efficient cinder-sifter, a vacuum cleaner, an electric iron and so forth.

Every husband or wife should carefully compare the gas and electricity accounts as they come in with those of the corresponding quarter in previous years and seek out the reason if there is an increase. The housewife should keep her receipts with care, and she should have reliable scales and occasionally check off the weights of goods as they are delivered. In other words, she wants to make an absolute career of being a good housekeeper, always bearing in mind that her husband has to work for the home income and that it is a matter of duty to secure the best possible return for the money she spends.

All this kind of thing is being thrifty in the best possible sense. It is the pennies we save methodically that mount up over a period of years far more than the pounds we set aside.

Thrift

THERE are, of course, other forms of thrift. It is genuine thrift to buy your house with the aid of a mortgage, because this is really saving up a substantial capital sum for one's middle life. Insurance is also thrift in its best sense, because it is compulsory saving ; you are bound to set by the money needed for the premiums. Going back to our budget, however, there is still scope for thrift both to the wife and to the husband, she from her housekeeping and personal allowance and he from his expense allowance. If you have a little left over at the end of the week, don't spend it : put it aside for emergencies.

It may sound rather like a child's money-box, but the Home Safe is a wonderful method of saving small amounts. It should, of course, be used to " feed " an account with the Post Office Savings Bank ; an investment account in a building society ; or an account at one of the big joint stock banks. Money in a Home Safe earns no interest until it can be credited to the actual account, so that as soon as there is a good deal of small change in the safe it should be taken to the post office, building society's office or bank to be opened. Usually the interest paid on accounts of this kind is 2½ per cent, that is to say, sixpence in the pound per year.

So far as the Post Office Savings Bank is concerned, it is a pity that its many advantages are not better known than they are. A depositor can, for example, arrange for fixed, regular payments such as rent, building society instalments, insurance premiums, subscriptions and so forth to be paid automatically and without cost from a Post Office account—provided, of course, that the money is there. And there are special arrangements for the savings of children, even in pennies, by means of Savings Slips. When required, you can draw up to £3 on demand from the P.O.S.B., and other withdrawals are very easily arranged, by telegraph if necessary.

It is quite a good idea for both wife and husband to have their own Home Safes, and also their own separate accounts in the P.O. Savings Bank, and it is really wonderful how small sums do accumulate in the course of a few years of systematic saving.

Another good way of saving is by means of National Savings Certificates, which are a sound investment. Provided the certificates run their full time, they yield interest at the rate of £2 18s. 4d. per cent per annum on the money invested, and Income Tax is not payable on this. A single certificate costs 15s. and its rate of growth in value is as follows :

1 year	15s. 3d.
3 years	16s. 0d.
5 years	17s. 3d.
10 years	20s. 0d.

For £3 15s. you can buy a single document representing five certificates ; for £7 10s. one representing ten Certificates ; for £18 15s. one representing twenty-five certificates and so on.

If you wish, you may accumulate the 15s. necessary for the purchase of one certificate by means of Savings Stamps costing 6d. each at a Post Office, but the most thrifty plan of all is to belong to a local Savings Association, the address of which can be obtained by writing to the Secretary, National Savings Committee, Sanctuary Buildings, Westminster, London, S.W.1. Certificates may also be purchased in the names of children.

Insurance

INSURANCE, of course, is one of the necessary expenses of a secure home. If you are buying your house with the aid of a mortgage you will be compelled to insure the structure against fire, but it is prudent to go much further than this and also insure the contents of the house against the same risk. To insure the bare structure costs 1s. 6d. a year for every £100 of the value of the house, but for 2s. per £100 per annum you can insure both the house and its contents.

This, however, is insufficient, for there are other contingencies beside fire. There are, for instance, housebreaking (breaking in and stealing during daylight), burglary (breaking in and stealing during the night hours) ; larceny (theft by people who have a right to be in the house); ordinary theft, without breaking in, and so forth. Then there are such risks as losses by storm, frost and flood ; the impact of aeroplanes or road vehicles into the house ; the claims by the public if a tile should fall from the roof and do damage ; and liability towards charwomen and other domestic servants.

All these risks, including those of fire, can be covered under one " Comprehensive " policy, which has been specially planned for owner-occupiers. The cost is usually 5s. per annum on each £100 of value, but, of course, the property has to be insured up to its full value. Jewellery and similar valuables are included in one of these Comprehensive policies so long as they are not out of proportion to the other items.

Life Insurance

COMING now to life insurance, it is the duty of every husband to insure his life in such a way that a lump sum of money would be forthcoming for his wife if he were taken. This is one of the chief objects of life insurance, but it is also a sound investment and a splendid form of thrift, for your savings invested in this way can never depreciate in value.

One of the most simple forms of life insurance is that affected by the " industrial " branch of an insurance company. In this branch the premiums are usually in mul- tiples of a penny per week and are collected at the door by an agent who calls. If a baby were insured by his parents at 2d. per week, and he kept up the 2d. premium through his life, he would, at the age of sixty-four, be entitled to £50, plus a bonus probably amounting to £54 8s., or £104 8s. in all— a remarkable return for only 2d. a week, and an example of the value of saving small sums regularly.

Next to the industrial branch of a company we come to the " ordinary " branch, which issues several different kinds of life policy, such as whole life and endowment, policies with profits and those without profits.

Generally speaking, a Whole Life policy is one where the premiums have to be kept up all through life, but in some cases there is a system of paying the premiums for a limited time—say for twenty-five or thirty years—though still the sum insured is not payable until the death of the person concerned. An Endowment policy is one where the sum assured is paid out when the person reaches a certain age or at death if that should take place sooner. " With profits " means that the policy-holder receives a share in the profits of the insurance company, his share being added to the sum assured in the form of bonuses. In each of these cases the premiums are higher than those for an ordinary and " without profits " policy.

A young husband naturally wishes for the smallest outlay to insure the largest possible sum for his wife and the cheapest form of life insurance is Whole Life, without profits. Under this scheme a husband aged twenty-seven next birthday could insure that his wife would receive £1000 cash at

his death by paying £15 13s. a year.
(The amount of the premium varies
according to the age of the insurer.)
These premiums would have to
be kept up all through life, but
they represent the highest cover
for the smallest premium. In
some instances, when the policies
have been in force a few years, it
is possible to convert them into
Endowment policies, but the rules
of the different companies vary.

A similar policy to the above but
"with profits" would cost £21 6s. 8d.
a year. The bonuses would amount
to not less than thirty shillings
a year for each £100 insured, so
that of the two this is probably
the better investment. A Whole
Life policy with profits for £100,
the applicant being aged twenty-
seven next birthday, would cost
£2 3s. 3d. in yearly premium.

Coming now to the question of
Endowment policies, a husband
aged twenty-seven next birthday
could insure for £1000 with profits,
payable in twenty-five years, or at
death if that should take place
sooner, for £38 15s. 1od. a year ; or
for £100 when he reached the age of
sixty-five for £2 12s. a year. It
should be remembered also in all
these matters of insurance that
there is an allowance to be taken
off one's Income Tax for the
premiums paid.

If preferred, husband and wife
could take up a Joint Policy on
their lives, the amount assured
becoming payable on the death of
whichever of the two partners is
taken first. In this case, if the
young couple are aged twenty-seven
next birthday the annual premium
necessary to insure £100 would be
£3 7s. 5d., the policy being " with
profits." On the whole, though,
it is far better for insurance in a
domestic sense to be always on the
life of the breadwinner.

Some young parents are anxious
to insure the lives of their children,
but it is not legal to insure a child's
life for more than a merely nominal
sum. As a matter of fact, a penny-a-
week industrial policy will provide
all that the law permits in this
respect, the actual amounts being :

A child dying under the
    age of 3 . . . £6
A child dying between 3 and 6 £10
A child dying between 6
    and 10 . . . £15

One could, of course, take out
one of the 2d. " Old Age Endowment " industrial policies mentioned before, but if the child
should die very young the payments
made by the insurance company
could not exceed these legal limits.

" Raising the Wind "

A POINT which some young
couples are rather apt to over-
look is that a Life Insurance policy
becomes real property, especially
an Endowment policy that has
been running a few years. After
about the third year, such a
policy acquires what is known as a
" Surrender Value," which is the
sum the Company would pay out
if it were surrendered to them with
all its rights and privileges. Generally speaking, it would, of course,
be very bad business indeed to
surrender a policy, except in circumstances of the gravest emergency,
for every policy with a surrender
value has also a loan value, which
means that one may raise money
upon its security without giving
up or reducing the sum assured
and any bonuses involved.

Thus if you happened, perhaps,
through something quite beyond
your control, to be desperately in
need of immediate cash, you could

raise a loan from the insurance company at no more cost than a fee of a few shillings for registration and stamp duty. You would, of course, have to pay interest on the loan, and if the policy holder should die, the amount of the loan and unpaid interest would be deducted from the sum assured and bonuses. On the other hand, if you have an account with one of the joint stock banks your manager would probably be quite willing to arrange for you to have an overdraft on the security of the Life policy, only asking to see the receipts for the premiums as they became due.

An Endowment Insurance policy is sound from every aspect. It forms a sound investment and a splendid form of thrift ; it provides for one's dependents in case of death ; and it is something very substantial to have " up one's sleeve " if ever the affairs of the home got into one of those " tight corners " which sometimes arise in spite of all one's efforts.

" Paid-up " Policies

BUT, you may ask, what about repaying the loan to the insurance company ? The answer is that you are at liberty to repay the loan when convenient, or you need not repay it at all until the policy matures so long as you regularly pay the interest, and, of course, the premiums to keep the policy " alive ". On the other hand, if you do not keep up the premiums and the interest the company will regard the policy as being surrendered, take what is due to them out of the surrender value, and remit you the change, whatever it might be.

Sometimes, when misfortune temporarily overtakes a married couple, there is much heart-searching about giving up an Insurance policy which has perhaps meant a good deal of effort in the way of saving. To meet such cases there are what are called " Paid-up " or " Fully-paid " policies. This means that all the original conditions of the policy, particularly the date when it matures, are carried out, but that no more premiums are payable and the actual sum assured proportionately smaller.

As a case in point, let us suppose that Mr. A. is a young husband who took up an Endowment policy for £500, payable when he was fifty-five, or say for twenty years. At the end of ten years he finds things very difficult and cannot keep up the premiums any longer. This being so, he can convert the policy into one for £250, the sum to be paid at the time when the £500 would normally have become due. Mr. A. pays no more premiums, but if he should die his dependents would be entitled to draw the £250 at once. As for bonuses, those for the first ten years would be added to the sum assured, but there would, of course, be no further bonuses after the date of the conversion.

There is one more form of insurance of the utmost interest, and that is the National Health Insurance. If a person has been compulsorily insured and then earns a salary which takes him beyond this form of insurance in a compulsory sense, is it worth while to become a Voluntary Contributor and keep up the stamped cards ? The answer is that in most cases it is definitely a great advantage to become a Voluntary Contributor, though a good deal depends upon the record cards and the actual position of the insured person. In cases such as this, one should take one's record card to the office of the particular Approved Society and seek advice there.

Annuities are, of course, quite different from insurance. In this case you put down a lump sum and receive an income in return, which stops at your death. Because we are, as a nation, tending to live much longer than was once the case, the rates are higher than they were. A man of fifty-five years of age would receive an annuity of about £8 for every £100 he put down, whilst a woman of the same age would receive about £7, or slightly less. Thus to provide for life an income of only £1 a week one would, at fifty-five, have to put down about £700, the annuity being payable half-yearly so long as you lived ; of course the capital is not returned. People who have no dependents at all, and wish to get the highest return on their capital, might well take up an annuity because of the complete security, but it would scarcely be a wise thing for a husband to do unless he took up a joint annuity on behalf of his wife and himself, to be continued until they both passed on.

Making a Will

THE making of a will is another business duty of every husband, and it ought to be done immediately after marriage—not before, because marriage revokes, that is to say cancels, a will. The will should be drawn up by a solicitor, who will arrange for the necessary witnesses. The fees depend upon the number of pages in the will, but in most instances all the wishes can be set out in few words and at a small cost. You can, of course, buy a blank will form from a stationer for sixpence, but it is wiser and safer to consult a solicitor. You don't want to run a risk of your widow having difficulty in obtaining what money you leave.

The Instalment System

IN the course of home business affairs wife and husband must often have occasion to discuss buying things on the instalment system. There is nothing unthrifty about this plan so long as you know for certain that you can meet the payments as they fall due. Of course, you pay more for an article in this way than if you paid cash, but this does not mean that it is extravagant to take advantage of the instalment plan, for very often you would never own some particular article at all if it were not for this plan.

" Hire purchase " is not quite the same thing as payment by instalments and married couples should understand the legal considerations of a hire-purchase agreement. Under such an agreement you are merely the hirer of the particular article or articles, and you must on no account sell or pledge them. The money you pay is legally for hire and not for purchase at all, and until the final payment has been made and the agreement terminated the things are not your property. Thus, when you are half-way through the agreed period you have not paid for half the furniture ; in fact, by law, you have not paid for any, but have merely been keeping up the hire charges. This is a point which ought to be clearly understood because it applies not only to furniture but also to a motor-car, wireless set, gas stove or anything else which one buys under the system of hire purchase.

House-Purchase

IN house purchase things are quite different. When you buy a house through a building society or some similar body, you do not rent it until you have finished paying for it; you do actually buy it outright, with borrowed money. In other words, you get into debt for what appears to be an enormous sum and then by thrifty methods gradually extinguish the debt and become possessed of very substantial capital. It is one of the singularly few cases where getting into debt is of real advantage.

Having found a house that suits you, the next step is to find out how much may be borrowed towards its cost. This is usually done by making a formal application to a building society, and this makes you liable for a valuation fee, whether business results or not. As a rule £1 1s. is charged for surveying a property of a value not exceeding £500 and within reasonable reach of the building society's office; between £500 and £1000 the fee is £2 2s., with £1 1s. additional for each further £1000 or part thereof.

Assuming that all goes well, there will come in the course of a week or ten days a notice of the full amount the building society is prepared to advance on the property and an intimation of the deposit required—usually about 15 per cent of the purchase price, though it is possible in several ways to have this reduced to 10 per cent. Thus, if you are borrowing £1000 you have to find £150 as deposit; or, on the lower scale, £100. You have

also to become a member of the society, which usually means entrance fees of about 3s. per £100 advanced.

From start to finish a mortgage transaction should be completed in about three weeks, unless there are any complications of title and such matters, and you will find then that you have to make monthly repayments to the building society, these instalments including both interest and return of principal. The actual charges depend upon the term and of course the shorter you can make this term the more interest you save yourself in the long run.

Here are the repayment rates of a large London building society, this scale being the actual amount of the monthly instalment for every £100 you borrow :

20 years, 12 monthly repayments
    per year of 12s. 10d.
18 years, 12 monthly repayments
    per year of 13s. 9d.
15 years, 12 monthly repayments
    per year of 15s. 7d.
10 years, 12 monthly repayments
    per year of 21s. 1d.

You may be doubtful upon which term of years to fix when taking up a building society's mortgage. Many prospective owner-occupiers are young married couples with their way to make in the world and not too much money. To them a long-term mortgage is best, because though they pay more interest in the long run, the monthly repayments are so much smaller.

As time goes on, however, you may be better off, and in such circumstances it is wise to approach the society and ask for the term to be reduced so that larger instalments can be paid. The effect of this is not only to discharge the mortgage much more quickly but also to save interest, and this interest is the greater part of the cost of house purchase by instalments.

So long as you keep up these monthly repayments you have absolute security and there is no calling in the mortgage or anything of that sort. You must, however, insure the structure against fire and, of course, keep it in a reasonable state of repair—though you would do that in your own interests.

I have mentioned the initial survey or valuation fees, but there are also certain legal expenses to be met by the purchaser. As a rule it costs £1 1s. to investigate the title and make a report, and the mortgage deed for an advance over £300 but not exceeding £500 would cost £2 12s. 6d., whilst one between £500 and £1000 would be £3 3s.—beyond that 5s. per £100 in addition. The Inland Revenue stamps on the mortgage deed average about 2s. 6d. per £100. There are further small fees when the mortgage is finally discharged.

House-Purchase by Insurance

IN some places the local council makes advances for house purchase, and inquiry should be made at the town hall or council offices regarding what arrangements there are. As a rule a loan from a local council is a little cheaper than that from a building society, but there is not likely to be much difference in the initial expenses.

A third method is to do the business through an insurance company. Here the idea is to take up an Endowment Life Insurance policy at least for the sum borrowed, so that one has to keep up the premiums on this policy. Usually an insurance company lends slightly less than a building society—in other words, the purchaser must find a rather larger deposit—but if anything should happen to the bread-winner there is always the cash from the insurance with which to redeem the mortgage, and this in itself is a great comfort to a wife. With an insurance company one has, of course, to pay interest on the money borrowed, but you need not repay the capital as with a council or building society's mortgage. You can do so if you choose, but there is not the same necessity, because it is always represented by the actual insurance policy. Of the three methods the council is the cheapest and then comes the building society. The insurance company is perhaps slightly the more expensive, but then one has all the advantages of life insurance.

To carry out the idea of married partnership to the extent of buying the house in the joint names of husband and wife is a good idea. In itself it provides an even greater incentive to work together to pay off the mortgage in the quickest possible time. The legal method known as "joint tenancy" is the best way of arranging this matter, because it means that when one of the pair dies the property passes automatically to the other with no conveyance, stamp duties or anything of that nature. It does not mean that death duties would be avoided, but if three years had elapsed since the date of conveyance, the death duties payable would only be on half the value of the house.

If you as a married couple feel you cannot shoulder the responsibility of buying a house, you will become tenants of a house, flat, maisonette or some such dwelling. Here the chief point is to have whatever arrangement you make put clearly into writing in the form of an agreement, and in most cases it would be money thoroughly well spent to engage a solicitor to act for you in overlooking the document.

In any event, the agreement should give a description of the property; the amount of the rent; when rent is payable; the period of the agreement; who pays rates and taxes; what happens if the tenant does not pay his rent; what power the tenant has to sub-let; whether the tenant has the option of renewing and on what terms; and who carries out the repairs and decorations. Very often, even when you contemplate buying a house, it would be prudent to become a rent-paying tenant for one year round so that you may ascertain if the district suits you; in this event, you should obtain a written option to purchase the property at a fixed price.

CHAPTER V

Parenthood in Prospect

SOONER or later in your early married life, the day will almost certainly come when you will whisper a tender little secret in hubby's ear; the wonderful news that a baby is coming to make your happiness complete.

After your delight has decreased a little you will begin to plan—joyously but carefully—for the days ahead, because you will realise that this is going to make a difference in your married life. Adjustments must be made, routine altered, many things will be looked at differently now that, by the curious arithmetic of marriage, you two who became one have now become three! Both you and hubby need to consider carefully what you must do, and avoid doing, during the next few months.

The first thing to be said about pregnancy is that it is *not* an illness.

Even in these enlightened days there are still misguided though well-meaning people who would persuade the expectant mother that she ought to regard herself as an invalid. To follow their advice is to make the nine months of waiting a nine-months' purgatory instead of the period of increased health and vitality they should be.

It cannot be too strongly emphasised that pregnancy is as natural as eating and sleeping and the other normal functions of the body.

If that is the case, you may say, why is it necessary to devote a chapter of this book to it ? Why cannot it be left to take its course without any special attention ?

Unfortunately, the conditions of our modern life make that impossible. There is so much that is unnatural in our diet and other habits of living that when a woman comes to the age-old task of bearing a baby, she has to start a kind of " back to Nature " campaign.

If she will follow the path I am going to outline in this chapter, I can promise that the journey will be a smooth one, with none of the setbacks and dangers that the " killjoys " would prophesy.

Symptoms of Pregnancy

THE first sign of pregnancy is the cessation of the periods. It is not by any means a sure sign, of course. An attack of influenza, anæmia, chronic ill-health or even a serious shock to the nervous system will delay the periods, and sometimes stop them. When it occurs in conjunction with some at least of the other symptoms which I am about to mention, however, the failure of a healthy wife's period to appear at the usual date gives her good reason to suspect that she is going to have a baby.

The next symptom is often—though not always—morning sickness. The sickness may be experienced even before the periods cease, but as a rule it begins about six weeks after conception. Normally, it is a sensation of nausea when you first wake, or more often, when you first get out of bed. There is slight vomiting, which should pass off during the morning.

The third symptom, which may also be felt before the periods cease, is a sensation of fullness, soreness, and tingling of the breasts. Generally it shows itself six to eight weeks after pregnancy has begun.

During the second four weeks of pregnancy, there may be irritability of the bladder, a frequent desire to pass water. After eight weeks have passed there are more definite signs.

The breasts begin to enlarge and feel tender when touched. The brownish ring you have been accustomed to see round the nipple, which is called the areola, becomes darker in colour, though in the case of very fair women this is not so noticeable. Sometimes a fainter ring makes its appearance outside the areola.

About the tenth to eleventh weeks you will find it is possible to squeeze a little watery fluid from the nipples.

By the fourth four weeks you yourself will notice some enlargement of the abdomen for the first time, although no change in your figure will be visible to other people.

Then, at about four and a half months,—half-time—there comes a quickening—the moment when the mother-to-be first feels the movements of her child within her. The first time it may be so faint as to be unrecognisable, but day by day it gets stronger until it cannot be mistaken.

During the second half of the waiting-time, not only does baby make his presence felt by moving about more and more vigorously, but other unmistakable signs of your condition make their appearance.

The lower part of the abdomen becomes more prominent, and you may notice marks on the abdominal wall. These need not alarm you, however. They are simply due to over-stretching of the skin.

During the later months, too, a doctor can detect the beating of the child's heart.

In the case of a first baby it is only after the sixth month that the expectant mother's condition becomes really noticeable, for between the sixth and eighth months the womb is gradually rising above the level of the navel. At the end of the eighth month it reaches its highest level, and the pressure on the lower part of the chest produces that shortness of breath which makes this stage of pregnancy rather trying to some mothers.

Then comes the " drop." A few weeks before term, with a first baby, the level of the upper part of the womb begins to fall again, as baby settles down into the right position for the coming birth. At the same time the breathing is much easier and there is greater freedom of movement. This occurrence is appropriately named " lightening."

Calculating the Date of Birth

THE duration of pregnancy is ten lunar months, that is to say, ten months of four weeks, not calendar months of thirty or thirty-one days. It is impossible to calculate *exactly* the date of birth because it is difficult to determine when conception took place, but a good approximate date may be arrived at by counting seven days and nine calendar months from the first day of the last normal period. There *are* cases where one or even two periods appear after conception has taken place, but these are generally scantier than usual and may only last for one or two days.

Let us suppose that your last normal period commenced on January 20th. You add on seven days which brings you to January 27th, and from here you count forward nine calendar months. This brings you to October 27th for the probable date of birth.

A newly married wife who has seen no period since her marriage should count seven days and nine months from her wedding day.

As soon as you feel reasonably certain that you are pregnant— that is, if you have missed two periods and have noticed any of the other symptoms already mentioned—you should lose no time in choosing your medical attendant and placing yourself under his or her care for the rest of the nine months.

You have quite a wide choice. Either you can go to your doctor now and ask him to attend you at your confinement, or you can make similar arrangements with a qualified nurse or midwife, or you can attend one of the splendid ante-natal clinics, which are among the greatest blessings that modern medical science has placed at the service of every woman to-day. There is one such clinic in connection with practically every large hospital, and there you can be sure of the best possible attention.

This supervision may seem to you unnecessary. You may think it will be time enough to see about a doctor when your time is drawing near, but, especially with a first baby, it is essential that he should keep his eye on you from the earliest days. Only in this way can any slight abnormality be detected and corrected before it has gone too far.

At each visit the doctor or nurse will test the urine to see that the kidneys are all right, the rate of the child's growth can be measured, and towards the very end its " lie " can be ascertained. The way a baby lies in the mother's womb is most important. If it is in the right position for being born, an easy, normal labour is probable. If there is anything wrong with the position, then very often the doctor can put it right before labour begins. At any rate, " forewarned is forearmed," and your guide knows exactly how the case is going on.

The Ideal Diet during Pregnancy

NOW comes the question of the kind of life you should lead while your baby is on the way. One important detail is diet. The mother gives so much to her baby that it is a time of extra strain on her body, and unless she understands the right diet, her own health is bound to suffer, and unless the baby receives the right kind of nourishment she cannot expect him to be sturdy.

The diet should consist, as far as possible, of uncooked, fresh, live foods.

Do not eat too much ; it is not necessary. A big appetite is largely a matter of habit. Over-eating is the chief cause of heartburn and other such discomforts in the second half of pregnancy.

To try to " eat for two " is positively dangerous, as it may put more strain on the kidneys than they can bear.

Babies rarely suffer through lack of food, as they have the power to draw on their mother's reserves. If you are losing flesh, you ought to consult a doctor about it. If you are putting on flesh, you are eating more than you need and will be wise to cut down the more solid items in your diet, especially meat.

All changes should be made very gradually, however, for the digestive organs need time to adjust themselves to deal with different food.

Do not eat much meat ; once a day is quite enough, and then not too large a helping. This is specially important in the last six weeks.

Fresh fish (especially herrings), cheese, nuts, peas, beans, and lentils, wholemeal bread and—in strict moderation—eggs provide just as much nourishment but in a cleaner form and can take the place of meat.

Eat plenty of fresh fruit as part of your daily food and not as an extra —oranges, apples, bananas, pears, plums, dates, figs, grapes, raisins, strawberries, and any other fruits which are available.

Never cook fruit that you can eat raw, for your baby has need of vitamins, which are spoilt by cooking. All fresh vegetables and salads of all kinds, including cucumber and tomato, are specially valuable. It is a very good thing to add a little raw grated carrot.

If you are eating plenty of fresh, uncooked food, you will not need any extra milk. If you do take it, drink it *with* meals and not between them. Remember that milk is a food and not merely a beverage like tea or lemonade.

Make it a strict rule not to eat between meals. If you really feel the need of something, take a fruit drink or eat some fruit.

It is best to eat the main meal in the middle of the day, to avoid indigestion and heartburn in the evening.

It is best to avoid all alcoholic drinks, for alcohol passes into baby's blood, and hinders his development.

Water, barley water, fruit juice, fruit juice and water, weak tea and mineral waters are good. Never take tea which is strong and over-drawn, as it seriously interferes with proper digestion.

You should take about four pints of fluid altogether in the day, but avoid drinking with meals.

Your Daily Life

THE pregnant woman needs reasonable exercise and plenty of fresh air and sunshine. It is not necessary for her to spend most of her time with her feet up on a sofa. A brisk daily walk—not a " Shop crawl "—is essential, and there is no need to fear the effects of ordinary housework so long as the lifting of heavy weights is not undertaken. Long standing at the wash-tub or kitchen table is not advisable, since it tends to produce varicose veins, so prepare your vegetables sitting down with your feet up on another chair or stool.

An occasional party or visit to the cinema will not hurt you, but late nights must be the exception and not the rule. You need eight or nine hours' sleep in a well-ventilated room to give your body a chance to restore the energies used up in building another little life.

Clothing plays an important part in the life of the expectant mother. If she is conscious of looking well, she will *feel* all the better, but apart from the question of appearance, unsuitable dress can produce acute discomfort. There must be no tightness anywhere. All garments should hang from the shoulder and garters and knicker elastic must be avoided.

At any rate during the later months the support of a special maternity belt will be needed for the abdomen.

An uplift brassière should be worn to give support to the enlarging breasts.

Preparation for Breast Feeding

EVERY mother-to-be worth her salt wants to feed her baby and in order to be sure of doing this successfully when the time comes, she must start her preparation some months beforehand. The half-way signal—quickening—is a warning that it is time to begin.

Every day bathe the breasts with hot and cold water alternately, making the change from one to the other as quickly as possible. This tones up the breasts and stimulates the glands to secrete milk.

The nipples must stand out well so that baby's little lips may grasp them. You must therefore try to draw them forward, massaging them gently between the finger and thumb which have been soaped or oiled with olive oil.

Some Ailments of Pregnancy

BY adopting the course of life, and especially the diet already advised, you ought to avoid most of the common ailments and discomforts of the waiting-time.

For instance, constipation, morning sickness, and indigestion should be unknown to the expectant mother who diets wisely.

However, constipation remains a very common and, it must be realised, a very dangerous enemy at this time, and it must not be tolerated for a single day. Until the good effects of her diet begin to show themselves the sufferer from constipation must have recourse to such safe medicines as liquid cascara and senna tea and to the lubricant, medicinal paraffin. Strong purgatives and salts are to be avoided.

The sensation of nausea known as morning sickness usually vanishes after a cup of weak tea taken before rising. Some women find relief in smelling the rind of a lemon. If morning sickness persists for longer than six weeks, or if it continues all day, the doctor's advice must be sought.

Indigestion and heartburn also yield to a properly adjusted diet which does not include too many starchy foods. Drinking with meals is strictly forbidden, and the principal meal should be taken at midday. Soda-mint tablets are a harmless remedy, but no cure.

Miscarriages, which mean the premature loss of the tiny unborn baby, most commonly occur during the third month of pregnancy, but apart from this the risk is greatest at the time when the period would normally have been due.

If you should notice a loss of blood, which may be accompanied by pains rather like period pains, the first thing to do is to go to bed and lie there quietly; the second is to send for a doctor. He will very probably be able to save the little one, though he may not, but no mother should attempt to get over a miscarriage without medical attention. Untold harm may be done by neglect of this precaution.

Marital Relations

MANY expectant mothers are perplexed on the subject of whether sexual intercourse should continue during the waiting-time or not. Doctors are divided in their opinion as to the wisdom of abstaining during the first six months, but agree very definitely on two points. There should be no intercourse for a pregnant woman during those days in the first four months when her periods would be present had she not conceived. Sexual relationships at these times could easily bring about a miscarriage. Secondly, there should be no intercourse after the sixth month of pregnancy until such time as the mother has completely recovered from her confinement.

CHAPTER VI

Young Parents

AND now your dearest dream has come true, and the two of you have become three ; a real little family—mother, father, and baby. No longer are you just married sweethearts, but parents with a glorious responsibility. Life is an adventure for three now—an adventure in which not only are you two explorers, but you must' be guides, too. But the way is marked for you in this work, and if you follow it, all three of you will have a happy journey, avoiding most of the snags and pitfalls that beset the path of parenthood.

The secret of a happy, smoothly run home, is of course a well-trained baby. From the day that nurse leaves you or you return from hospital, young mother, you should make a routine for baby's day and *stick to it.* Here is a very good one which should fit in with most households :

6 a.m. Baby wakes, ready for his first meal. Hold him out, feed, hold out again, put on fresh napkins and return to cot.

9.30 a.m. Lift baby, hold out, bath, dress, and feed. Put in pram out of doors.

2 p.m. Lift, hold out, feed, hold out, change nappies. In pram again.

5 p.m. Lift, hold out, do not put clean nappies on, but let baby kick and play on your knee.

5.30–6 p.m. Undress baby, " top and tail " him, feed, hold out, put on clean nappies and put to bed in unlighted, well-ventilated room.

10 p.m. Rouse baby for last feed. After this hold out and change nappies. He should then sleep till next morning.

If baby *should* wake in the night, on no account give him a feed or ask daddy to walk the floor with him. Give him a drink of cool, boiled water and turn him over on his other side. He will soon learn that this is not worth waking for !

Of course, you will breast-feed baby if you can. There is nothing *quite* equal to human milk for a human baby, and natural feeding has these further advantages for the mother herself : it costs nothing ; it saves work ; in a wonderful way it helps the womb to contract so that you regain your figure.

Artificial Feeding

IF your doctor advises you not to nurse baby, then the next best thing for him is humanised milk, which you yourself can make up to resemble mother's milk as closely as possible.

The ingredients are the best milk you can afford (Grade A, tuberculin-tested if possible), water (which must always be boiled), lime water, sugar of milk, and Crooke's cod-liver oil emulsion (all of which are obtainable from the chemist). The milk should be brought quickly to the boil as soon as it is delivered and then rapidly cooled by standing in a basin under running water. Here is the recipe to make 5 ounces :

HUMANISED MILK

2 *oz. of milk.*
$\frac{1}{4}$ *oz. of lime water.*
$2\frac{3}{4}$ *oz. of water.*
2 *teaspoonfuls of sugar of milk.*
1 *teaspoonful of emulsion.*

Add the sugar of milk to the milk and stir until dissolved, then the lime water and lastly the cold boiled water. Measure the exact amount of emulsion required for the day into a cup. Stand the mixed food in a jug covered with butter muslin in a basin under running water until quite cold.

At feeding time measure the amount of food and add the correct quantity of emulsion. The food should be given at blood heat. (Test this by holding the bottle against your bare forearm near the elbow.)

When making up the food in larger quantities be sure to mix the ingredients in exactly the same proportions.

A healthy baby requires the following quantities of food at each feed : 3rd day, 1 oz. : 4th day, $1\frac{1}{2}$ oz. ; 5th day, 2 oz. ; 7th day, $2\frac{1}{2}$ oz. ; 8th day, 3 oz. ; 10th day, $3\frac{1}{2}$ oz. ; 3rd week, 4 oz. ; 4th week, $4\frac{1}{2}$ oz. ; 2nd month, 5 oz. ; 3rd month, $5\frac{1}{2}$ oz. ; 4th month, 6 oz. ; 5th month, $6\frac{1}{2}$ oz. ; 6th month, 7 oz. ; 7th month, $7\frac{1}{2}$ oz. ; 8th month, 8 oz. ; 9th month, 8 oz.

If it is necessary to bottle-feed baby from birth, however, you must give only half a teaspoonful of emulsion in the 24 hours to start with, increasing by half a teaspoonful every day until the correct amount is reached.

For the first two months of baby's life whole humanised milk must not be given. The quantity made up for the day's five meals should be diluted with water as follows :

	Humanised milk.		Boiled water.
3rd day	$1\frac{3}{4}$ oz.	to	$3\frac{1}{4}$ oz.
4th day	$3\frac{1}{2}$ oz.	,,	4 oz.
5th day	5 oz.	,,	5 oz.
7th day	$6\frac{1}{2}$ oz.	,,	6 oz.
8th day	8 oz.	,,	7 oz.
10th day	12 oz.	,,	$5\frac{1}{2}$ oz.
3rd week	15 oz.	,,	5 oz.
4th week	18 oz.	,,	$4\frac{1}{2}$ oz.
2nd month	21 oz.	,,	4 oz.

After this you give baby undiluted humanised milk as given above. The quantities given in the table should be mixed and kept in a scrupulously clean jug, and measured out in feeds as required.

Weaning

IT is usual to continue breast-feeding for eight or nine months and then comes the weaning period, which is spread over four weeks. If this gradual process is followed neither you nor baby will be upset in the least.

1st Week

Breast feeds at 6 a.m., 10 a.m., 6 p.m., and 10 p.m. Bottle feed at 2 p.m.

Milk brought to boil	2½ oz.
Lime water . .	2 teaspoonfuls
Cane sugar . .	1 teaspoonful
Cold boiled water .	4½ oz.
Cod-liver oil emulsion . .	1 level teaspoonful

Sufficient for 1 feed

2nd Week

Breast feeds at 6 a.m., 2 p.m., and 10 p.m. Bottles at 10 a.m. and 6 p.m.

Milk (boiled). .	7½ oz.
Lime water . .	1 oz.
Sugar . . .	1 tablespoonful
Cold boiled water .	6½ oz.
Emulsion . .	3 teaspoonfuls

Sufficient for 2 feeds

3rd Week

Breast feeds at 6 a.m. and 10 p.m. Bottles at 10 a.m., 2 p.m., and 6 p.m.

Milk (boiled). .	12 oz.
Lime water . .	1½ oz.
Sugar . . .	1½ tablespoonfuls
Cold boiled water .	10½ oz.
Emulsion . .	1 tablespoonful and 1 teaspoonful

Sufficient for 3 feeds

4th Week

Breast feed at 6 a.m. Bottles at 10 a.m., 2 p.m., 6 p.m., and 10 p.m.

Milk (boiled). .	16 oz.
Lime water . .	2 oz.
Sugar . . .	2 tablespoonfuls
Cold boiled water .	14 oz.
Emulsion . .	1½ tablespoonfuls

Sufficient for 4 feeds

5th Week
All Bottle Feeds

Milk (boiled). .	1 pint
Lime water . .	2 oz.
Sugar . . .	2½ tablespoonfuls
Cold boiled water .	18 oz.
Emulsion . .	2 tablespoonfuls

Mix the food as directed on page 58, using cane sugar in place of sugar of milk.

Introducing the First Solids

WHEN baby is nine months old a teaspoonful of barley jelly may be added to the 10 a.m. bottle feed, working up to 2 tablespoonfuls by the end of the month. During the second half of the month a taste of rice pudding should be given before the 2 p.m. feed every other day. On alternate days give water flavoured with a little vegetable extract. Before the 10 a.m., 2 p.m., and 6 p.m. feeds give baby a hard-baked finger of wholemeal brown bread.

At ten months 2 tablespoonfuls of barley jelly can be added to the 10 a.m. feed. At 1.30 p.m. baby can have 3 ounces of water in which green vegetables have been cooked, with a pinch of iodised salt added. At 2 p.m. give him 2 tablespoonfuls of rice pudding into which a tiny quantity of vegetable extract (about the size of a green pea) has been stirred. Follow this with 5 oz. of bottle food. Give fingers of brown bread as before.

At eleven months he should have 3 tablespoonfuls of barley jelly with the 10 a.m. bottle feed, green vegetable water as above at 1.30 and 3 tablespoonfuls of rice pudding with vegetable extract or baked custard (but not more than once a week).

The 10 p.m. bottle feed can now be given up, but a little water should

Baby may smile in his sleep at a very early age, but that is because of wind. He may give you a real smile from four weeks old, but don't try to make him smile. It is bad for his nerves.

Sucking at a dummy spoils the shape of a baby's mouth and his gums and it also introduces harmful germs into his system.

be given in its place. A small piece of brown toast with butter can be introduced at the 10 a.m. feed.

From the time weaning commences baby needs a drink of orange juice daily at 9 a.m. or 5 p.m. To make this, add an ounce of orange juice, freshly squeezed from the fruit, to an ounce of cold, boiled water. Sweeten as little as possible.

Vaccination

WHEN baby is a few weeks old you will have to consider the question of vaccination. The earlier this is done, within reason, the better. The Public Vaccinator will carry it out free of charge, or if you prefer it, your own doctor will do it. There is very little doubt nowadays that this is a very valuable means of stamping out the terrible disease smallpox, and you are bound by law to have it done within six months of birth, unless you have a real objection to it, in which case you must swear a Statutory Declaration before a Commissioner of Oaths or a J.P. within four months of the child's birth.

Baby's Progress

EVERY proud mother eagerly watches her little one's progress and it will be as well to outline the "milestones" you should look out for.

The average baby weighs about 7 lb. at birth and is 20 inches high. From the first to the sixth month you may expect baby to gain 6 to 7 oz. a week. After that a gain of 4 oz. weekly is sufficient. Babies vary very much, however. As long as the weekly gain is regular and baby seems healthy in appearances, has normal motions, and seems contented, there is no need to worry.

The second standard of progress, which all your friends and relations will take an interest in, is teething. This, of course, does not start till baby is between six and eight months old, when the two lower central teeth come through. These are followed by the four upper central teeth (between 6 and 12 months). Next come the two lateral lower central teeth and the four front double teeth (12 to 18 months). The four canine teeth appear between the 18th and 24th months and the whole set is completed when the four back double teeth or molars come through, some time between the 24th and 30th months.

Some of the most wonderful moments of motherhood are those in which baby first begins to " take notice." Raptly you watch him learning the use of his senses ; watch that miracle of everyday life, the dawning and development of his intelligence.

You will look eagerly for the first real smile. He may smile in his sleep at a very early age, but that is his reaction to wind or swallowed air. He *may* give you a real smile at from four to six weeks old, but don't be disappointed if he doesn't acknowledge you in this way much before he is three months. One thing you must not do is try to *make* him smile. This is definitely bad for his nerves.

In the same way, when he discovers the precious faculty of laughter, do not stimulate it by tickling him, but let him enjoy his own secret jokes to the full. Spontaneous, natural laughter is good for him.

Baby's next most important adventure is in the direction of " finding his feet." He will show

You must play fair for father, little mother. You must do your very best for baby, but remember that hubby is used to having your attention and he will feel terribly hurt if you unwittingly push him out of the picture.

When hubby comes home, let him find the new arrival tucked up in his cot, either sleeping soundly or waiting for daddy's goodnight kiss.

signs of wanting to sit up, roll about, and perhaps even to crawl at about six months. Let him make his own experiments and, whether he is forward or backward, never force his pace. Nature knows when his muscles are strong enough to support him and will teach him how to use them. Some babies walk at a year old, some a month or two later. If your little one is very late in walking, do not *make* him stand, but take him to the doctor or clinic and find out if there is any error in his diet.

The first words usually follow the first steps and here you can help baby by talking to him. He learns by imitation and association. Possibly at a year old, but more likely at eighteen months, he will say " Dad-dad " or " Mum-mum " and make some attempt at naming familiar objects such as cake or pussy. He will, of course, find some words easier to say than others, and will probably show a preference for addressing his daddy —which does not necessarily mean that he loves his mummy less !

How Father Can Help

BUT bringing up baby on the correct lines is not the whole secret of successful parenthood in the early days. There are other ways in which the young father and mother must work together to keep in the home the atmosphere of love and happiness that should surround every child. If baby has this, all the wealth in the world could not give him more.

" I'm a family man now," thinks the very new father importantly, and he makes a lot of plans for working extra hard so that there is enough money for all their needs. But do remember, young husband,

that being a good father only *starts* there. There are numbers of other things you can do if you really intend to take your fair share in the wee one's upbringing, right from the beginning.

Do you remember how, when you knew the baby was on the way, you made sure your wife did everything she ought to do—visited the doctor regularly, and the dentist—how you helped her prepare the cot, perhaps even making it yourself ? You were so anxious that everything should be as perfect as possible for your beloved when she went on that journey to meet the child of your mutual love, weren't you ?

Well, don't imagine that, because they have both come safely through the experience, there is nothing more that you can do to help, other than earning money.

For one thing, the wife will be glad of your assistance in the matter of heavy household jobs, such as lifting weights about, and fetching in the coals. She is not very strong yet, remember, and she needs you to look after her every bit as much as the youngster needs her to look after him.

Naturally things will not be quite the same now that there is an addition to the family, and it is up to you to help all you can, and keep cheerful when things seem to be going wrong. If baby is fretful, don't get grumpy and urge her to give him a dummy. It may keep him quiet for a little while—but ask your doctor if he thinks it is a good idea, and he will tell you that sucking at a dummy not only spoils the shape of a baby's mouth and also his gums, and makes him liable to adenoids, but—since it is impossible to keep a dummy really clean—it is a method of introducing myriads of harmful germs into baby's system.

The most trying time, of course, is if, at first, the baby wakes up in the night, and it is then that the would-be perfect father shows himself in his true colours. Remember that it is every bit as important that the wife should have an undisturbed night as that you should—for, while you are out at work all day, she, at home with the baby, is working very hard, too. Rest and lack of worry are essential to a new mother, so help her all you can, even if it is only with ready sympathy.

It is easy to see that if father is doing his bit, the new mother will be encouraged to remain his sweetheart as well as the baby's mother, for she will feel happy in the knowledge that they are working together still.

Fair Play for Father

AND that is perhaps the first consideration for you, little mother. In your determination to do your very best for the baby, do remember that hubby is used to having the first claim on your attention, and he is going to feel unbearably hurt if you unwittingly push him out of the picture.

Baby's presence will have made alterations in your domestic routine, but try to avoid its interfering with hubby's comfort. When the little fellow has his six o'clock feed in the morning change him and put him back in his cot for another little nap, or a happy kicking period, while you get on with hubby's breakfast. If baby is well, he will be quite happy in his cot and hubby will be able to have your undivided attention before he goes off to work, and there will be nothing to prevent your waving him off as usual and sending him out with that warm well-loved feeling that makes life seem so worth while.

When he comes home, let him find that you have had time to make yourself look pretty and are ready to greet him as you always did before the baby came.

Let him find the new arrival tucked up in his cot, either sleeping soundly, or drowsily waiting for daddy's " good-night " kiss. You can tell hubby of all the wonderful things baby has done, during the evening, and during the week-end he can see these wonders for himself and take an active part in bringing up baby.

As a general rule, you share everything you can about the baby, but there is just one item which you would do well to keep to yourself, little mother—and that is His Little Lordship's washing. Of course there is bound to be a lot every day, while the little chap wears nappies, but a clothes-horse full of damp clothes drying round the fire is no welcome for daddy when he comes in at night, is it ?

Of course, when space is limited, and it is too wet to dry the clothes outside, there often seems to be no alternative. But try and dry off all you will need during the daytime, so that daddy will not have the feeling that baby's coming has completely upset his comfort. He may not *say* anything about it, but he cannot help feeling it, and it is up to you to see how little your happy evenings together need be upset by the addition to the family.

And don't become one of those mothers who spend their evenings with one ear cocked for sounds from the little room upstairs ; who hardly hear what their husbands are saying because they are listening in case baby whimpers ; who start up every now and again to run

Don't let motherhood side-track you into not caring about your appearance. Baby wants to be proud of you as a mummy, doesn't he? And hubby is still as keen that his pals should see that he has married the most attractive little woman imaginable!

Don't always let your conversation be about baby. Your friends will be interested but they will be glad to see that you still want to hear about the latest fashions and the newest recipes.

upstairs because they " think they heard baby ;" who speak in whispers and go about on tiptoe for fear of waking him.

If he's well, the little precious will sleep solidly until ten o'clock approaches. If you have trained him in that way from the beginning, you can talk and laugh and even have the wireless on without disturbing him in the least.

Do remember that, while you have been absorbed in the coming of your baby during the waiting time and, later, have been taken up with all the wonderful new duties before you, your husband has only been able to stand by in case you needed him, and help in little ways that could not possibly absorb all his attention. His life has been going on in much the same way—off to work each day, and home again—with the exception that whereas before he could sometimes take you out on a little jaunt, or to visit friends, whenever you happened to feel like it, for the last few months he has had to give up those treats—or else go without you, which is not at all the same thing—and, no matter how much he may love the little baby that has come to your home, one big thought in his mind is bound to be : " When can we go out and enjoy ourselves again ? "

It is very understandable, isn't it ? And the wise wife, as soon as she feels strong enough to enjoy a little jaunt with him, occasionally gets grandma or a kindly neighbour to look after the new baby for a few hours, and gives herself up to her husband's company.

Or, once you have got the child safely to bed, there is really nothing to prevent your having a few friends to your home, is there ? They needn't make *much* noise, and, as

has been said, a reasonable amount will not awaken baby.

Remember that, though your world has changed so completely now, the " outside " world is still going on, and there are still a lot of interesting things in it ! Hubby still wants to know how his favourite team is getting on, and it does him good to discuss its chances with the friends who drop in—while you talk to the wives.

And do not always let your conversation be about the baby. Your friends will be interested, of course, but not as completely as you are, and they will be glad to find that you are still the girl you used to be, who wanted to hear about the latest fashions and the newest recipes.

Don't " Let Yourself Go."

DON'T let motherhood side-track you into not caring any more about your appearance. It is a poor excuse that baby takes so much time, these days, that you have none left to spruce yourself up in. Baby wants to be proud of you as a mummy, doesn't he ? And hubby is still every bit as keen as he used to be that his pals should realise he has married the most attractive little woman imaginable !

You will not be a perfect mother if you lose your old personality. " No," you are probably interrupting, " but money is not so plentiful now as it used to be. Would you rather I spent it all on clothes and neglected my baby in consequence ? " Of course not, but why should that be necessary ? In these days one can ring the changes so delightfully, and at such a small cost, that even an old dress can look neat and attractive— stockings can be darned, and shoes polished up.

Christening

WHILE we are on the subject of clothes—what about the little one's christening robe ? If there is not a special robe in the family that has been used for generations and generations, it is rather a delightful idea to make a robe out of your wedding dress. Failing that, any dainty long white frock will do, with a shawl and—if you wish, just for this one occasion —a veil, which should be thrown well back when the child is handed to the clergyman, so that there will be nothing to get in the way.

The ceremony, of course, is different in the various places of worship, and it is not always necessary to have godparents. But in the Church of England a little boy has two godfathers and one godmother, and a small girl has two godmothers and one godfather, who make the vows for the child, and promise to see that he or she is Confirmed when he or she is old enough to keep the vows.

If you are not quite sure what happens you should read through the service in your Prayer Book, beforehand ; and ask the clergyman himself to explain just what is expected of you; so there is really nothing to worry about, is there ?

Afterwards, if you like, it would be nice to have a Christening party, for the guests who go to the ceremony. This need not be an extravagant affair—all you need is a white cake, with perhaps a cradle on top, a few sandwiches and biscuits, and whatever you fancy to drink.

Care should be taken with the choice of godparents if you are having any. They need not be rich in money so long as they are rich in the love they have to offer, and so long as they are people you

yourselves love and respect—for you are giving them a share in your precious baby, and the right to have a say in its upbringing.

Care should also be taken with the names you give your wee one. For he or she will not thank you if the initials of the names you choose spell some unfortunate word that will mean severe teasing wherever he or she goes !

And so the little one begins to grow up. Naturally you do not want to forget all the tender little memories which mean so much to you at the moment, but it would need an exceptional brain to remember everything clearly right from the little one's babyhood until it has grown even to school age. So why not start a Baby's Diary just as soon as you can ? You can buy these all ready mapped out for you—or a clever father could no doubt make a delightful one in his spare time. In it you record everything that is of special interest about your child—the photos you have taken ; the funny little things he, or she, says ; the date when he took his first step, and the first time he really smiled. There are a hundred-and-one things worthy of recording, as of course you will agree—and what fun you will have bringing out the diary and looking back on these wonderfully happy days.

Childless Wives

WHAT of those wives who do not become mothers, who do not know the joy of feeling their own little one's arms round their necks, and hearing his baby voice whisper " Mummy " ?

It is dreadfully hard to weave dreams of little babies, only to find that they may never come true ;

PLATE 5

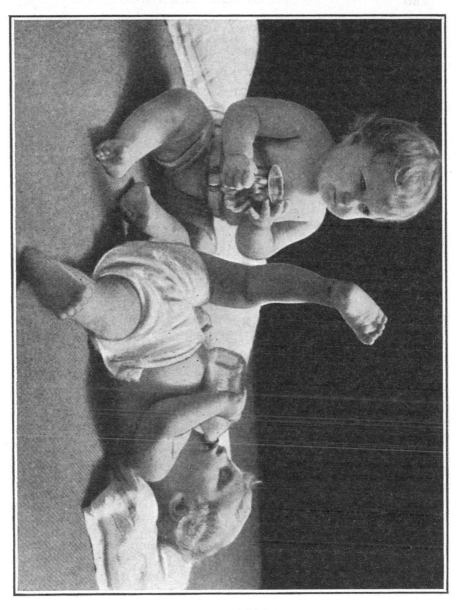

LITTLE CHUMS

EVEN when they are quite tiny, children should be accustomed to the society of other little ones, and there is no prettier sight than happy, healthy toddlers playing together. Advice on the bringing up of tinies, and treating the ailments they may develop, will be found in Chapters VII and VIII.

PLATE 6

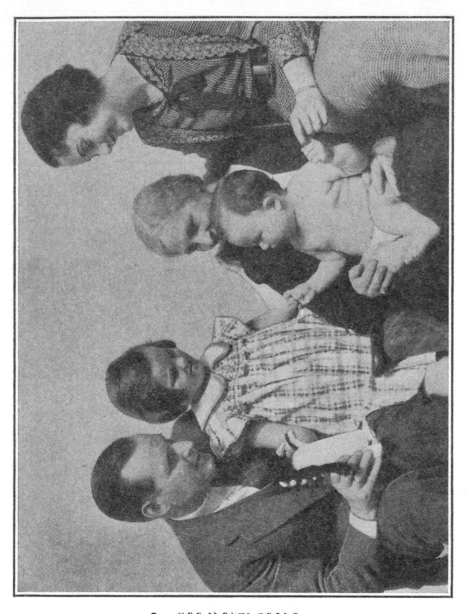

THE SPACED
FAMILY

IT is better, not
only for the
mother but for the
children themselves,
if the second baby
comes when the
firstborn is three or
four. She is then old
enough to "mother"
him. But the gap in
age should not be
too wide, or the two
cannot play happily
together. See
Chapter IX.

PLATE 7

"I DON'T LIKE IT, MUMMY"

FEW mothers escape the child who at some time in his or her life is faddy about food, refusing to eat this and dawdling over that. This is seldom due to a genuine distaste or lack of appetite, but more often springs from a desire to attract attention to herself. Advice on how to handle this awkward problem will be found in Chapter VII.

PLATE 8

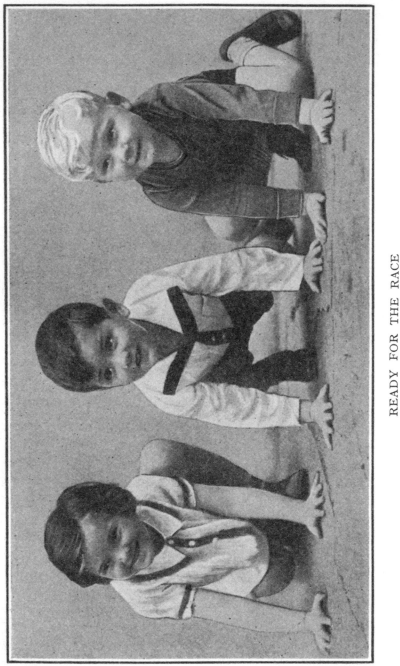

READY FOR THE RACE

GAMES in which children compete against each other are good, even for tinies. They encourage them to exert their capabilities, and teach them to be good losers and generous sportsmanlike winners. But keep your eye on the child who never wins; he will not only be unhappy but he may acquire an inferiority complex that will hamper him all his life. Find some game in which he *can* excel, and so give him a chance to beat the others sometimes. See Chapter VIII.

but in these days no wife should allow herself to accept such a disappointment as a matter of course. Medical science has advanced, and we know, now, that sometimes it is only a little thing that stands between such wives and their desires.

If the years are passing, and still there is no promise of a little one, you and your husband should go and see your doctor about it. There is no need to feel shy. To your doctor you are only another patient in whom he is deeply interested ; he is used to similar cases, and he will be glad to help you.

Yes, the first thing for a childless wife to decide is whether she really never will be able to have a little one of her own. If it is really so, the next thing is to ask herself what she is going to do to fill the gap in her life. In a great many cases a satisfactory answer will be found in the word " adoption."

Adoption Societies

SURELY, since you have a home and love waiting for a little one, if only heaven would please to grant your wish, by far the best thing is to adopt a wee one who is longing for a mother and father just as much as you are longing for a child ?

Give some homeless little one the chance to prove what a difference a child could make in your lives— and what an enormous benefit love and parental care can make in his —or her—life. Turn the sorrow in your lives into the joy in a little orphan's, instead of letting bitterness creep into your happiness.

But how, you may ask, shall I find a baby whom I can love and be glad to make my own ?

Well, now, in London there are several societies that provide for childless wives. One is the National Adoption Society, 4 Baker Street, W.1., which makes no hard and fast rule concerning the income of the would-be adopters, though naturally inquiries are made as to their ability to keep the child properly, and, as far as possible, children are placed in the kind of homes they would have had if their parents could have kept them.

This society makes it a condition that every child taken must be legally adopted. This makes the baby as much the child of the adopting parents as if it had been their natural baby, and is an advantage to the child and the " parents " alike. No one need worry about the legal proceedings, for there is very little publicity over them, and, while the cost varies, it is never much, and sometimes considerably less than two pounds.

The adopting parents are not given the name of the natural parents, but they are told the baby's history and the circumstances of his or her birth.

From this, as from most other adoption societies, a child may be taken on a month's probation, and if, for any reason, the adopting parents do not take to the child, or feel that, after all, the responsibility is more than they imagined it would be, they may return the little one without any further obligation. So it is worth while trying the experiment, isn't it ?

When the child is fetched, it is dressed ready for the journey, but no stock of clothing is given with it, and in no circumstances is any payment made.

The Adoption Society, The Church House, Bloomsbury Court, London, W.C.1, has much the same rules, but it also has a special fund for children when, for some reason or other—usually the death of one or both of the adoptive

C

parents—the adoption has failed. The child is then taken back, educated, and given a good start in life. So, you see, the fear of unknown calamities in the future need not haunt you unduly.

Information about adoption in Scotland can be obtained from the National Children Adoption Association, if you write to Miss White, Child Welfare Dept., Johnson Terrace, Edinburgh. And those living in Wales can write to The Governor, John Gibbs Home, Penarth, Glamorganshire—a branch of the National Children's Home and Orphanage—of which there is also an affiliated branch in Northern Ireland. It is the Craigmore Home For Boys, Lurgan, near Belfast.

It is best to take the child as young as possible, as this makes a more enduring link between the adoptive mother and child.

Then it is also best to tell the little one of its adoption as soon as you can—otherwise the news may come as rather a bad shock—for a small child takes whatever you tell it as a matter of course, and will not mind whether you are its real parents or not, so long as you don't have to part !

In most societies girl babies seem to be scarce, and, if you want a little daughter, you may have to wait some time for her. But to have a little treasure in your home, either a girl or a boy, is worth waiting for if necessary, isn'tit ?

If, however, you do not feel able to take over the complete responsibility of adopting a child, have you thought of opening your home to several as little foster-children ? Many adoption societies board their kiddies out, and, if you write to the nearest one to your home, and ask for information, you will find a new field of adventure opening up before you. Here, of course, you receive a small sum to help pay for their keep. But the main difference is that the children can never really be yours—they may have to leave you just when you are growing most fond of them. One idea worth trying might be to start with foster-children, to see how you get on, and then, if that is a success, to adopt a little one of your very own.

CHAPTER VII

Healthy Little People

FROM the first to the fifth year, from the time when baby is emancipated from his cradle and begins to " find his feet," till the day he enters upon his school career, is perhaps the most momentous period in his life. Upon the habits of health formed then will depend his future health and development.

During these years the child's mind and body are growing very rapidly, and as his activity grows so the need for mother's vigilance becomes greater.

She knows that the little one can no longer be put in cot or pram and left to sleep peacefully most of the day. Little hands and feet are busy exploring every corner of the child's world, and this instinct for exploring, for growing up and achieving independence should be encouraged, not checked. The sooner baby can be trusted to

attend to the everyday necessities of his life, to dress and feed himself, go to the toilet, the lighter will his mother's burden be.

The clockwork regularity which made his infancy pass so smoothly should govern his toddler days. His routine will, of course, have to be adapted according to his growing needs, but it is possible to give you at least some idea how to plan out your child's day. The actual hours will depend largely on the times father leaves home in the morning and returns in the evening. For instance, it will probably be convenient to postpone baby's tub till after daddy has gone or get it over before he comes in wanting his tea. The main thing is to fix a routine and *stick to it*. Then there will be no " tummy " upsets or disturbed nights for the kiddie. The following time-tables should be useful as a guide :

TODDLER'S TIME-TABLE

(Age 1–2 years.)

6–7 a.m.	Toilet. Wash hands and face. Clean teeth First meal. Toilet for bowel movement. Sleep or play in cot.
8–9 a.m.	Toilet. Bath and dress. (Or bath can be given at night if more convenient.) Out of doors as soon as possible in pram or playpen.
10–11 a.m.	Toilet. Wash hands. Second meal. Out of doors when possible or in airy bedroom for morning nap.
1.30–2.30 p.m.	Toilet. Wash hands. Third meal. Out of doors again as long as weather permits. Visit to toilet and wash hands half-way through afternoon.
5–6 p.m.	Toilet. Last meal. Brush teeth. Bath (if not given in morning). Undress for night. Toilet. Wash hands. Bed.

OLDER CHILD'S TIME-TABLE

(Age 2–4 years.)

7 a.m.	Toilet. Wash hands and face. Fruit and drink of water. Brush teeth. Bath if convenient (or may be given at night). Play quietly in cot till mother is free to dress him.
8–9 a.m.	Breakfast. Toilet for bowel movement. Wash hands. Out of doors as soon as possible.
Mid-morning.	Toilet. Wash hands. Milk or fruit if needed. Morning nap (or if more convenient, sleep may be taken in afternoon).
12–1 p.m.	Toilet. Wash hands and face. Dinner. Toilet. Wash hands.
1–2 p.m.	Out of doors to play or out for walk with mother, or afternoon nap if more convenient than morning.
3–4 p.m.	Toilet. Wash hands. Drink of milk or fruit juice if needed. Out of doors as long as possible.
4.45 p.m.	Toilet. Bath (if not given in morning).
5.15 p.m.	Supper. Toilet. Wash. Brush teeth.
6 p.m.	Bed.

It will be seen from these tables that the toddler's health routine falls under five headings—sleep, fresh air and exercise, food, habits of elimination, and hygiene or the care of the body. In each of these it is the child himself who must be trained to form good habits, learning to recognise what is expected of him as he learns to use his growing powers of brain and body. So let us consider each of these subjects briefly and find out how these good habits may best be formed.

Sleep

A SMALL child needs from eleven to thirteen hours' sleep every night, and he should be put to bed always at the same time—six o'clock up to the age of four or five and afterwards not later than seven. He also needs a nap of one or two hours in the middle of the day.

He must, of course, have a bed —if possible a room—to himself and it is essential that the window should be open. Don't start the practice of putting a nightlight in your child's room unless he himself shows signs of being afraid of the dark. With some children this fear seems to be instinctive and should be treated sympathetically, as explained in Chapter VIII, but there is no sense in *suggesting* a fear of the dark to a child who is free from this inherited instinct.

Don't let him expect you to stay with him until he goes to sleep. If bedtime is treated in a matter-of-fact way from the first, it will present no difficulties later on.

There is one point I would like to emphasise. Make bedtime a *happy* time. A child neither sleeps well nor gets the full benefit of sleep if he goes to bed disturbed by correction or reproaches.

The mid-day nap is needed to compensate for the tremendous amount of energy used up in the day's play. The nap may take place in the morning or afternoon— whichever fits in best with the day's routine and the necessity for getting all the sunshine possible.

Up to the age of four or five the child should be undressed for his nap, and in any case he should be put in his own bed and left alone with the door shut and the window open. Even if he does not sleep, be firm about keeping him lying down. Do not let him sleep longer than two hours.

Fresh Air and Exercise

A LL children need all the open air and sunshine they can get. Sunlight actually contains certain vitamins which help their bodies to grow straight and strong. During the summer months it is an excellent plan to give a daily sunbath, starting very gradually with an exposure of one and a half minutes each, back and front, and increasing the time by two minutes every second day till the sunbath is lasting for twenty minutes. After that you can make ten-minute increases.

Remember, too, that artificial sunlight treatment is now obtainable for children in most big cities, and if your child is weakly or inclined to catch cold easily in winter, it would be worth while inquiring at the local hospital or clinic about ultra-violet treatment.

Let your child play out of doors as much as possible, even in winter. Active youngsters do not feel the cold intensely as long as they are adequately clothed (*see* page 74) and protected from the full force of the wind. For instance, on a cold, bright day they can quite well play in the sunny part of the garden or yard if it is sheltered by a wall.

In very hot weather, they should not be allowed to play in the sun during the middle part of the day, and their necks should always be protected by a wide-brimmed hat. This is most important if the risk of sunstroke is to be avoided.

Children, like puppies and kittens, and indeed, all young things, instinctively exercise *all* their muscles, by crawling, banging things, digging, pushing, throwing, and by all the restless, inquisitive activities of their supple little bodies. Arms and trunk need exercise as well as legs and feet, and that is another reason why crawling should not be altogether discouraged in favour of walking. Remember that shouting, singing and even crying have their value in strengthening the chest muscles. A noisy, bouncing youngster is a healthy one who needs plenty of outlet for his store of energy. As soon as he becomes cross or restless you may know that he is tired, even though he won't say so, and he should be given a rest. Another time the tendency to over-tire himself can be lessened by giving him some quieter form of occupation for part of the day.

Tinies Need Change

IT is mother's task to steer childish energies into the right channels, acting more by suggestion than by command, introducing a toy or game which can be played sitting down, reading a story or inviting the little one to watch something that is going on instead of actively doing anything himself. A little child cannot be expected to keep up any one occupation for long, and mother must adapt herself as quickly as he to each new interest.

Remember, too, that his tender little muscles are not fitted for performing any one task for long at a stretch. When you take him for a walk, beware of making him hold your hand continuously and also of walking too fast for him. It is pathetic to see a gallant little chubby figure being hustled along a busy street by a preoccupied grown-up, his arm dragged up to reach her hand and his feet taking a run every now and then to keep up with her stride !

Food

A HEALTHY child should always be ready for his meals. If he is not, there is something amiss and you must find out what it is. Don't give snacks in between meals, which ruin both appetite and digestion, and don't rely upon coaxing.

A child soon learns that by creating a fuss over his meals he becomes the centre of attraction, but if the food he refuses is quietly taken away from him and nothing more offered until the next meal-time, he will soon settle down and eat his food in a sensible manner.

Above all, see that he has his meals at regular hours.

A child of under two years is not really old enough to come to table, and, if possible, his mother should let him feed by himself. He will, of course, get very messy, but take no notice of this—he will soon learn to be cleaner !

Then, when he is old and experienced enough to sit at table, treat him just as one of the family. Serve him in his turn with his own food only, and don't give him pieces from your plate. Make him behave properly from the start ! If he gobbles up his food, in order to get down quickly and continue a game, just make him sit still till the rest of the family have finished. This will soon stop his eating quickly, will teach him good manners and he won't get indigestion.

It is important that the child's diet should be properly balanced, containing the right amount of body-building foods (proteins), sugars and starches for energy, fats and mineral salts. The following diet sheets will enable you to make sure that you are giving these necessary elements in the right proportions.

DIET BETWEEN TWO AND THREE YEARS OLD

Four meals a day should be sufficient for the normal toddler. They should be given at strictly regular hours with no snacks whatsoever between meals. At any hour of the day or night children should be allowed to drink water.

ON WAKING

An orange or an apple or any other fruit in season. A drink of water.

BREAKFAST

Porridge or cereal breakfast food. (This is in no sense a meal and only very little should be given.)

A coddled egg two or three times a week, or lettuce or tomato sandwiches, or steamed white fish.

Fingers of crisp toast with butter. Eight ounces of milk, including that used with the first course.

DINNER

One level tablespoonful of any of the following : fish (boiled or steamed), or minced chicken or finely minced under-done steak or Irish stew (without onions).

One heaped tablespoonful of steamed, baked, or mashed potato. Mashed sprouts, cabbage, spinach, greens, cauliflower, carrot, or lettuce.

Milk pudding with stewed apples, prunes, junket, or custard.

TEA-SUPPER

Rusks or baked fingers of bread or crisp toast or thin bread-and-butter with a little honey, seedless jam, jelly, junket, custard, or stewed fruit.

A small piece of sponge cake. Eight ounces of milk to drink.

A slice of raw, ripe apple or two sections of an orange should be given to the child at the end of every meal in order to ensure that no particles of soft food are left between the teeth.

Half a teaspoonful of cod-liver oil or cod-liver oil and malt should be given twice a day either before or after meals.

All solids should be eaten first and the liquids reserved to the end of the meal. If the child shows an aversion to any special article of diet such as vegetables, it is best to give these first, and then to continue with the more favoured food. By this means he will be trained to eat whatever is put before him and trouble over meals will be minimised.

Many mothers are over-anxious because so often at this age children begin to lose their baby roundness. If the child is normally hungry, eats plain food willingly and is alert and active, all is well. The mother should never attempt to " stuff " him, for by so doing she will only irritate his digestive organs and retard his progress.

Continue to give him plenty of exercise for his jaws.

DIET BETWEEN THREE AND FIVE YEARS

The pre-school child needs nearly a pint of good milk daily. The food given to him should continue to be free from paps and have plenty of hard, tough characteristics so that he may be induced to chew it slowly and thoroughly. If a child has been properly trained to use his teeth he may now be given such substances as oatcakes, nuts and raw celery.

Slices of bread-and-butter, cakes, and sweets should never be given between meals. A stick of barley sugar or a few boiled sweets may safely be given after meals, but the teeth should be well brushed afterwards.

A teaspoonful of cod-liver oil should be given daily all the year round except in the hottest weather.

BREAKFAST

Fresh fruit.

Porridge in winter. Cereal with stewed fruit in summer. (The child's appetite should not be satisfied with this course.)

An egg or fish or tomato and lettuce sandwiches, or potatoes mashed and browned.

Crisp toast and butter. Eight ounces of milk or milky tea.

DINNER

Vegetable broth or a milk soup.

One tablespoonful of any of the following : Cutlet, mince or stew, under-done beef or steak finely cut up, brains, fish, chicken, or sweetbreads.

One heaped tablespoonful of boiled, baked, or mashed potato.

One heaped tablespoonful of any vegetable with the exception of parsnips or ordinary onions.

One heaped tablespoonful of milk pudding with stewed fruit or steamed pudding (not suet) or custard.

Fresh fruit may be given at this course in place of pudding.

TEA-SUPPER

Crisply toasted wholemeal or brown bread, thin bread-and-butter, rusks and butter or cream cheese sandwiches.

Mashed ripe banana or salad or stewed fruit ; seedless jam or honey or golden syrup ; jelly, junket, or custard.

A small piece of sponge cake ; milk or milky tea.

A quarter of an apple or two sections of an orange should still be given to the child at the end of each meal.

UNSUITABLE FOODS

The following articles of diet are unsuitable for a child.

MEATS.—Sausages, pork in all forms, twice-cooked meat, tinned meats, salt fish, goose, game, kidneys, and all fried foods.

VEGETABLES.—Cucumber, onions (except the large Spanish variety), radishes, and parsnips.

BREAD AND CAKE.—All new bread, buttered scones, rich and heavily-iced fruit cakes, pastries of all kinds.

DRINKS.—Strong tea, coffee, wine, beer, soda-water, cider.

FRUITS.—All unripe fruits and all stale fruits which have been exposed for sale in dusty streets. Unsound fruit is one of the principal causes of summer diarrhœa and colic in children. Tinned fruits in syrup have very little dietetic value.

Toilet Training

SO much extra work and anxiety is entailed for mother as well as harmful effects on the child by imperfect training in habits of elimination that it is worth while taking pains over this matter.

A small child should have one or two regular bowel actions a day, and accidents should be rare after he is one year old. He should be practically dry in the daytime after eighteen months, and bedwetting should be rare after two years. By this time he is old enough to ask to go to the toilet, but if he *does* have an accident, do not scold him. The way to clean habits lies through encouragement and praise for good behaviour, not reproach for lapses.

There are several ways in which you can help your child to form these essential good habits. One is to treat the whole business in a matter-of-fact way. Let the visit to the toilet after meals (a bowel movement should always take place after breakfast) be part of the normal routine of the day, and teach the little one to wash his hands afterwards.

A tiny child should not, however, be expected to use a toilet constructed for adults without its being adjusted for him. Most of these are much too high, and there should be a box to bring the child's feet to the right level. A small seat can also be placed over the larger one.

If your kiddy uses a nursery chair, let him use it only in the bedroom or lavatory and not in the kitchen or living-room. It is not too soon for the toddler to learn that certain things, though perfectly natural and ordinary, are not done or talked of in public.

If your child is to learn bladder control he must be given frequent opportunities to urinate. Children of under two often need to visit the toilet every two hours. (Note that allowance has been made for these visits in the time-tables on page 68.)

Finally, as an aid to clean habits, comes suitable clothing. Both boys and girls should wear knickers that they can easily unbutton themselves, since it is your aim to teach them independence as early as possible. A little one of four-and-a-half should be able to look after himself quite well.

Hygiene

HAVING discussed what we might call "Internal affairs," we must now turn our attention to the external care of the child's body which will keep him the fresh, sweet-smelling, attractive little person you love to see.

No less than in babyhood the child of "Nursery" age needs a daily bath and he should help to bath and dry himself. Even in homes which have no bathroom, a very successful tub can be given in a small footbath in a warm room.

Each child should have his own face flannel and towel and use no one else's, and he should be taught to wash his hands after every meal and every visit to the lavatory. His teeth should be brushed at least morning and evening—ideally after every meal. His hair should be washed once a week. Teach him to use a nailbrush and to take a pride in keeping his fingernails nice. Keep them cut short and he will not be tempted to bite them. Toenails should be cut straight across.

Genitals. In a little boy who has not been circumcised, the foreskin should be pushed back several times a week so as to expose the glands and allow of proper cleansing. Little girls should be washed morning and evening to prevent the redness and irritation of the parts which sometimes occur.

Nose. Let your child have his own handkerchiefs marked with his initial and teach him to blow his nose regularly, but if you hold the handkerchief for him, be careful not to press on the nostrils, and remember that hard blowing may do more harm than good by carrying infection into the ears.

Ears. Wash the outer ears daily with soap and water and dry them thoroughly, but don't poke hairpins or other instruments into the ears in the hope of removing wax that is beyond the reach of the facecloth. Such wax will work its way to the surface in time, but you may injure the delicate drum by impatient probing.

Teeth. If your child is to have good, strong, permanent teeth, his baby teeth must be kept in good condition until the permanent ones are ready to come through. The permanent teeth will themselves be influenced by the food your child eats during the early years and the care taken of his milk teeth. Do not give your child soft and " pappy " foods ; do not give him sweets and chocolates between meals. Remember that no food must be given after the teeth have been cleaned for the last time at night. Soft, sweet biscuit crumbs, for instance, which become wedged between the teeth, are an active source of decay. It is a good plan to give children either three sections of an orange or a quarter of an apple after every meal : the juice of either of these fruits acts as an excellent cleanser.

See that you use a suitable brush for cleaning your little one's teeth and that it is replaced at regular intervals ; you can obtain excellent toothbrushes at your local clinic. Rinse the mouth thoroughly after each brushing. The little one should, of course, be encouraged to learn to brush his own teeth, but you will have to see that they are done properly.

When he is two years old (or earlier if necessary) he should begin his regular quarterly visits to the dentist. If he begins these visits simply for inspection, he will never dread the dentist, and at the same time any decay can be dealt with before there is time for serious damage to be done.

As you prize your child's health and appearance, do not neglect this most important care.

Clothing

A LITTLE child should never be " clothes conscious." His garments should be so planned that he does not feel any restriction or awkwardness in wearing them. He ought to be able to manage them himself when dressing and undressing and going to the toilet. Then, of course, they must be warm enough without being too warm, and the practical mother will choose materials and styles that are easy to launder and will stand hard wear.

From the point of view of warmth as well as freedom, the garments should be as loose as possible, provided that they fasten snugly at wrists and neck. It is a scientific fact worth remembering that several light, loose layers of clothing are warmer than one tight heavy one, since the air in between the layers keeps in the warmth ! Another very practical reason for looseness of clothing is, of course, to allow for growth.

In regard to warmth, more

Thumb- and finger-sucking habits are ugly and they can spoil the shape of the jaws and interfere with the development of the teeth. If your tiny sucks in bed at night, make a cardboard cuff to prevent her from bending her elbow.

If your little one masturbates at night, try to get him to go to sleep with his hands folded together, or keep his arms outside the bedclothes or give him a toy to hold.

mothers err on the side of over-clothing than the reverse. Much depends on the child's physical condition as well as on the weather. A robust, active child needs less clothing than a frail child who does not play so energetically.

In very hot weather, the less your little one wears the better, provided always that the back of his neck is protected from the sun. A cellular cotton vest is the best type to wear next to the skin, since it is porous. A woollen jersey or cardigan can easily be slipped over the suit or dress for extra warmth when necessary.

In winter three layers of wool are the regulation clothing. Out-of-doors a little child needs overall leggings, and a coat that keeps out the cold wind. (For this reason, a knitted coat needs lining.) A hat or cap need only be worn in the coldest weather.

Finally, since your child's feet have got to be his faithful servants for many years to come, do see that his shoes are well-fitting and well-shaped and that his socks are long enough not to cramp the little toes. A host of foot troubles that are having to be treated among the adults of this generation are due to unwise choice of shoes in childhood.

Some Bad Habits

WE have discussed the training of your child in good habits, but perhaps your little one has already contracted some bad ones, and you want to know the best way to cure him.

First I would say in general that it is easy to take too serious a view of these bad habits and a great deal of harm has been done in the past by over-correction on the part of anxious mothers. By correcting the child in such a way as to draw his attention to what he is doing you may give the act an added fascination for him which will make it all the more difficult to cure. The best way to break a bad habit, therefore, is to replace it by a good one. Patience and calmness on the part of the parents are essential, and so is co-operation between them. It is no use mother trying to cure little Johnnie of nose-picking if dad quite freely allows it !

Now let us consider a few of these habits in detail.

Bed-wetting. A child of three or over should not wet the bed at night. If he does, the doctor should first of all be consulted to find out if there is some physical cause. If he finds no such cause, you must begin training on the lines I have suggested for the younger child (*see* page 73).

Appeal to his pride in being a big boy (or girl) and you may find it helpful to introduce some system of marks with a small reward for a certain total at the end of the week. Don't let him think he has any weakness which cannot be conquered, don't punish him for failure, and don't shame him by discussing the subject with others before him.

A child who wets the bed should be given plenty of fluid to drink during the early part of the day, but very little towards evening. Always rouse him to pass urine before you yourself retire for the night, and make sure that he is sufficiently awake to know what he is doing. Otherwise the habit of relieving himself unconsciously will only be strengthened.

Thumb-sucking. Sucking habits are not only ugly but they also tend to spoil the shape of the jaws, and interfere with the development of the teeth and of the nasal passages. For this reason, as soon as the little one starts to put his finger or thumb in his mouth, you must quietly distract his attention by giving him something else to do with his hands. If a small child sucks in bed at night, you may make a cardboard cuff deep enough to prevent him from bending his elbow.

A child of four or five years is old enough to be made to *want* to overcome the habit, and he should be given the same sort of encouragement suggested in the case of bed-wetting.

Nail-biting. The same thing applies to this habit. The child must be encouraged to take a pride in his hands and a small girl might well be given a tiny manicure outfit and shown how to take care of her nails. Needless to say, a child cannot be expected to overcome this habit if he sees one of the older members of the family doing it!

Masturbation. This is the medical name for the habit of getting pleasure from handling the genital organs, but it is by no means such a serious matter as some people would have you believe. Most children outgrow it if their attention is not drawn to it by over-correction. It is a great mistake to tell the child he is doing something "nasty" or "bad". Simply say, "I shouldn't do that if I were you," and give him some toy to play with.

If he masturbates at night, encourage him to go to sleep with his hands folded together, or keep his arms outside the bedclothes or give him a toy to hold.

Some children start the habit accidentally as a result of the sensations produced by too tight clothing, and, of course, lack of cleanliness is another possible cause.

What Can the Matter Be?

A MOTHER'S eye is quick to notice the slightest sign of sickness in her child, but if she is inexperienced she is not always able to distinguish between symptoms that are serious and those that are not. When in doubt the safest plan is always to seek medical advice. Here is a list of symptoms and what they may point to.

Fever. If the child's face is unusually flushed, or if his forehead and limbs feel hot to the touch, you should take his temperature (see Appendix).

Drowsiness, irritability, and refusal of food. All these are indications of sickness if they are not due simply to over-tiredness.

Sore throat. This may herald a simple cold or an infectious disease such as diphtheria or scarlet fever.

Vomiting, diarrhoea, constipation, or "tummy-ache" may be due to some digestive disturbance or to some general infection.

Pain, tenderness, redness, or swelling in any part of the body indicates infection or injury of the part.

A rash points to a disease such as measles, to skin disease or to digestive disturbance.

A discharge is a sign of infection or irritation.

Childish ailments will be dealt with more fully in Chapter XI and with the nursing of children in the Appendix, but here are some of the ailments common in little ones under school age.

Adenoids and Tonsils. Enlarged tonsils and adenoids are very common in children. The adenoids are a small gland at the back of the nose, composed of the same material as the tonsils, which guard the entrance to the throat. They have a moist, sticky surface which entraps and kills numberless microbes from the air as it travels over them on its way to the lungs.

If the air the child breathes is impure and laden with dust and germs from close, stuffy rooms, then the adenoids and tonsils, in their effort to cope with the extra work thrown on them, become enlarged until they almost block the passages.

When unhealthy tonsils and adenoids are neglected, the child's appearance develops certain marked signs such as a pinched look about the nose, dropping of the lower jaw, and " rabbit teeth." Deafness, mental dullness, mouth-breathing, and susceptibility to infection are among the other results of this trouble.

In regard to treatment, it is best to be guided by the doctor. If he advises an operation for removal of the adenoids and tonsils there is no need for alarm, for it is a very simple matter, will cause the child very little discomfort, and will only necessitate his being in hospital for a few days.

Sore Throat. A little child may not complain of a sore throat even when it is inflamed, but he may refuse his food or vomit or he may be feverish. At the first sign of such symptoms, put him to bed and send for the doctor. A red-looking throat may be merely inflamed, but if white spots or patches appear, the trouble is serious and may mean tonsilitis or diphtheria.

Swollen Glands should never be neglected, for they are generally due to some infection—often from the tonsils—or to some general disease. A doctor should be consulted without delay.

Colds and Coughs. The best antidote against winter colds and coughs is plenty of fresh air, for germs flourish in stuffy, hot rooms. Secondly, if you build up your child's resistance by means of the right diet and clothing, he will be less likely to catch other people's colds. Remember that iodised salt contains very valuable properties, and should be used in cooking your little one's food.

Do not overclothe the child. It is not wise to muffle up the neck and chest ; it is far more important to see that the thickness of clothing is evenly distributed all over the body. For this reason, pay particular attention to stockings, shoes and gloves.

Cold sponging is an excellent way of hardening a child against colds. After the usual morning wash, sponge the child's throat, chest and back with tepid water and dry with a rough towel till he glows all over. Gradually reduce the temperature of the water until the little one can stand it quite cold.

A good winter cold preventative can be made at home by mixing 4 tablespoonfuls of cod-liver oil and malt, the same amount of honey, 1 tablespoonful of glycerine, and the juices of 1 lemon and 1 orange. Give a teaspoonful of this with a teaspoonful of lime-water night and morning.

A child who shows any tendency to chest weakness should be given two or three drops of halibut-liver oil two or three times a day, and the chest and back should be rubbed with olive oil at bedtime. This is absorbed by the skin, and so gives protection against chills.

If the child is actually suffering from a cold, keep him in bed with the windows open until the temperature has subsided.

Give him plenty of water to drink and see that he has a daily motion of the bowels. To avoid spreading the cold to all who come in contact with him, teach your little one to cover his nose and mouth when he coughs or sneezes and never let him use anyone else's handkerchief.

Bilious Attacks. An occasional bilious attack in a child is generally due to some digestive upset, and the best treatment is to keep the little patient in bed for twenty-four hours or until the attack subsides. No food should be given during this time, but the child can have drinks of soda water, Imperial drink or Vichy water, flavoured with lemon juice. At night give a $\frac{1}{2}$ or 1 grain calomel powder, according to age, following this up in the morning with half a Seidlitz powder. A morning dose of salts should be continued for the next few days. Keep the diet light until all signs of the trouble have gone.

Periodic bilious attacks which occur at more or less regular intervals are generally due to acidosis, and a child who is subject to these should be under the care of a doctor, who will restrict the amount of fatty food taken. The child will be allowed plenty of fresh and dried fruit, vegetables, salads, brown bread, porridge made with very little milk, fish, lean meat in small quantities, jellies, honey. Glucose is useful in helping to get rid of the partially digested fats which set up an attack. It is best given in lemonade, in the proportion of 1 tablespoonful of powdered glucose to a tumblerful of water.

As a preventative, twice a week give bi-carbonate of soda in minute doses—a pinch in every drink during the day, amounting to about a teaspoonful in all.

Constipation. If you follow the diet and routine of strict bowel training already suggested, your child should not be troubled with constipation. If he occasionally goes a day without a movement or with only a very small one, there is no need to worry unless he seems otherwise out of sorts. He will probably have a large motion the next day. If he goes forty-eight hours without a motion, however, the best thing to do is to give him an enema or a dose of mineral oil (not castor oil, which is constipating after the first dose) or magnesia mixture. An excellent laxative for occasional use can be prepared at home in the following way. Lightly stew 6 figs, 6 dried apricots, 6 prunes, 10 dates and 2 tablespoonfuls of raisins in a very little water, passing them through a hair sieve to extract all the pulp and juice. Then add 2 tablespoonfuls of liquid paraffin. Mix all together and keep in a wide-necked bottle. The dose for a child of four is 1 to 2 teaspoonfuls before breakfast and again in the evening if necessary. Never let a child get into the habit of relying on laxatives to obtain bowel regularity, however.

A child who shows a tendency to chronic constipation should take not more than $1\frac{1}{2}$ pints of milk (boiled or pasteurised) daily; he should have at least 3 glasses of water a day, at least 2 green vegetables a day, raw fruit at least once a day, cooked fruit such as prunes, apples, apricots and rhubarb once a day, wholemeal bread and cereals.

Diarrhoea. Frequent loose movements of the bowels may be a sympton of some infection or of stomach upset. It is always safest to send for the doctor and in the meantime keep the child in bed. Give plenty of boiled water to drink but no food. No medicine should be given except by doctor's orders.

Croup sometimes comes on during or after a cold, and you will recognise it by the long, crowing intakes of breath.

Temporary relief for the difficulty in breathing can be obtained from moist air. Prop the child in his cot, bolt upright, undo all the clothing round the chest and take away all but the lightest of blankets. Throw the window open wide, so that the maximum of fresh air can enter, and then boil a kettle of water as speedily as possible. The steam from this will provide a moist atmosphere, and if you can improvise a kind of tent by means of draping a sheet round the sides of the cot, you can keep the air round the child as moist as required.

Ipecacuanha wine, given in doses of ten drops on a lump of sugar every hour till the sufferer is sick, is a valuable aid in croup, but this should only be resorted to if the doctor lives at a distance.

Earache may be due to some affection of the ear itself, or to a decayed tooth, or even to unhealthy tonsils. On the other hand, a small boil in the outer canal will cause acute pain in the ear, as will a plug of wax against the drum, or eczema of that part. When a foreign body gets into a little one's ear, the only treatment which the mother should apply is to pour in a little olive oil. If this is not successful a doctor must remove whatever is lodging in the ear.

To relieve minor earache an excellent plan is to pour hot water and borax, in the strength of a dessertspoonful of borax to a pint of water, into the ear. It is not advisable for an inexperienced person to use a syringe, however. Great pain and harm will be caused if the solution used is too hot

(99 degrees Fahrenheit is the correct temperature). As it cools during use, a little more hot lotion can be added to maintain the required heat. The ear should be thoroughly dried out afterwards with a little cotton-wool.

Dry heat in the form of common salt, which has been heated on a shovel and put in a little flannel bag, is also very soothing.

Rickets is caused by unsuitable food during the first two years of life, and sometimes by lack of sunlight and fresh air. In most cases there is a deficiency of fat in the diet. Milk which has been boiled too long, condensed milk, mother's milk after the ninth month, are all deficient in fat.

The symptoms of rickets are definite. First, there are changes in the bones. The long bones of the arm become enlarged at the wrist and the ribs get depressed, causing the condition known as pigeon breast. The leg bones are bent, producing bow legs. Knock-knees begin at a later stage, whilst the forehead is enlarged, the sides of the head protrude, and the fontanelle does not disappear as it should do by the time the child is two years old. Considerable tenderness of the bones may be present, so that the child cries when handled and cannot bear any degree of pressure upon the bones.

The rickety child is generally subject to constipation or diarrhœa and other digestive disturbances. Teething is delayed, and the child is restless and subject to attacks of sickness or diarrhœa under the strain of cutting the teeth. The abdomen is generally round and flabby. Sweating of the forehead is nearly always present, and there is often a tendency to convulsions.

In the early stages rickets is quite easily cured, *provided the child is under the care of a doctor,* who will instruct the mother as to proper diet and other measures.

The diet is perhaps the most important part of treatment. Cows' milk diluted with barley-water, according to the age of the child, must constitute the chief food. Daily bathing in warm water is soothing, whilst the child should be warmly clad and kept in the fresh air and sunshine for as many hours of the day as possible.

Sea air is one of the best medicines.

Ringworm of the scalp is very common amongst young children, and is highly infectious.

It usually starts as a small, semi-bald, pink patch, which soon shows a powdery appearance with broken hairs. The red ring enclosing a central patch dotted with black dots of broken hair is very characteristic.

Treatment will have to be undertaken by a doctor, as the malady is very difficult to cure and requires careful and regular treatment. The mother will probably have to clean the part carefully every day with a special mixture, and to apply proper ointment. Sometimes X-ray treatment will very rapidly cure the disease, but such treatment must of course, be undertaken by a doctor.

A clean linen cap should be worn to prevent the disease infecting the pillow-cases and the clothing, and in most cases shaving the scalp will be found necessary.

See that the child uses his own hairbrushes, towels, etc., and sleeps in a bed by himself.

Worms. Threadworms are quite a common complaint in children, but fortunately are easy to cure by the right methods. The symptoms are varied. There may be nervous irritation, digestive upsets, fretfulness, loss of appetite, restlessness at night, or the development of such habits as grinding the teeth, nose-picking and so on. The worms, which resemble tiny threads of white cotton, will be seen in the child's motions.

The usual treatment is an injection of salt and water into the back passage after an ordinary soap-and-water enema, twice a week for six weeks.

Be careful to guard against re-infection. The eggs may lie around the back passage, and as the child is liable to scratch himself, the eggs may get under the finger-nails and thus be transferred to the mouth when food is taken. The child should therefore be washed after each motion with soap and warm water, to which a few drops of lysol have been added. Then apply a little ammoniated mercury ointment. This will kill any eggs.

See that the child's hands and nails are well scrubbed before meals, and as a further precaution let him sleep in cotton gloves, which should be well boiled every day.

CHAPTER VIII

Pattering Feet

QUITE early in your life as a young mother you will find, probably to your astonishment, what a strongly marked little character of his own your baby has. He may be placid or restless, amenable or stubborn, happy or peevish, emotional or stolid, but he will certainly show signs of definite traits, surprisingly distinct in anyone so young and tiny and physically helpless. And as he grows into the toddler stage these traits will become even more clearly marked.

Some of these characteristics may be partly due to physical causes, to reasons of health. As a rule, a healthy, comfortable child is a happy, contented child, while a tummy weakened by wrong feeding in early infancy will make him peevish; a nervous system that has been over-excited by mistaken " fussing " in the first months of baby's life will cause moodiness and " tantrums." But generally speaking, baby's character was to some extent formed before these influences affected him. He inherited certain tendencies from his parents and forbears. Not even at the very beginning is his mind a blank sheet of paper on which you can write what you please. This is a fact to bear in mind.

There are many mistaken ideas about heredity. It is not easy to say which traits are inherited and which are not. Practically every child as he grows resembles his parents in character—his mother in some respects, his father in others —but no one can be sure that this is not partly the result of imitating the people with whom he passes his early life. But when little Tommy has quite plainly the happy-go-lucky disposition of his granny, which neither of his parents possess, it is pretty plain that the trait has been inherited and not acquired.

Some mothers find this a depressing thought. They are afraid that because young Peter shows signs of taking after Uncle William, who was the black sheep of the family, he is destined to become the same unsatisfactory type of man.

Not a bit of it. The inherited tendency may be there ; it may never be possible entirely to remove it ; but it can be reduced, restrained, and diverted into useful channels by environment, by good example and wise training.

That is the keynote of success in bringing up a child : not trying to change his entire character from what it is into what you would like it to be, but taking it as it is and directing it, encouraging the more desirable qualities and curbing and diverting the less desirable ones.

" Mother Knows Best "

HOW is this to be done ? Every young mother suffers something of a shock when she first finds that the tiny, sweet being she has brought into the world, of whom she has had such sweet dreams and upon whom she has lavished so much love, can be deliberately disobedient and, with astounding courage, actually defy her. She wonders, despairingly, how she can cope with this pronounced character, for the training of which she is responsible.

The old idea of " breaking a child's will " was cruel and mistaken. It often produced timorous, spineless characters incapable of thinking or acting for themselves. But, on the other hand, a great deal of nonsense has been talked about " self-expression." The idea seems to be that parents should not exercise any authority over their children, that even the tiniest ones should be allowed to do exactly as they please, lest their characters be spoilt by restraint. This method, if a child survived its obvious dangers, would result in a selfish, wilful young person who would be neither popular nor successful, nor even happy.

Parents *must* influence the development of their children's characters, not for their own personal convenience but for the little ones' own good. Parents *must* have authority, or family life is impossible. It need not be the authority of fear, but wise, tender, loving yet firm authority, guiding the child along the path that is best for him.

Tiny children cannot know what is best for them. They have no experience, and they have not the instinct that is given to young animals. Mother knows best, and therefore mother must be obeyed.

But don't expect too much of your tinies. Their little minds are quite incapable of grasping, or holding, ideas that to you are simple and obvious. A toddler forbidden to twiddle a gas-tap will do it again and again. His distracted mother will feel that he is a deliberately disobedient child. He is nothing of the kind. He merely does not remember. His mind cannot yet retain a memory of being forbidden to touch that fascinating tap.

Some people say that whenever you give a child a command you should explain your reason. The principle is a sound one, especially when applied to older children, and in time it will have an effect, but don't expect too much from it in the case of toddlers, because the reason that to you seems obvious and satisfactory is completely out of reach of the child's understanding.

Little Tommy dawdles over his breakfast. You may say " Hurry up, dear." He answers " Why ? " because to him time has no value whatever. " Because mummy wants to clear the table and get on with the day's work." Again Tommy will ask, exasperatingly but quite honestly, " Why ? " He cannot understand the necessity for clearing the table and getting on with the day's work. Sooner or later you will have to close the discussion with a final " Because mummy says so." That, to a tiny, must be reason enough.

Don't expect from your little ones a grown-up standard of behaviour. Don't, in dismay, regard little Winnie as a born thief because she persistently helps herself to things that are not hers. Children are not born honest ; that is to say, they are not born with any respect for the rights of property. They see no reason why they should not take what they want. By all means explain why they shouldn't, but don't expect them to understand your explanation. Merely insist that they mustn't, because mummy says so. And go on insisting patiently ; once, twice, three times is not enough.

Early Tussles

SOONER or later you will have your first real tussle with Sonny or Girlie. It may come as early as his babyhood, when he refuses to go to sleep ; it may not come till the toddler stage, but sooner or later it is inevitable. And in that tussle mummy *must* win. You may feel a bully, pitting your will against the will of a tiny, comparatively helpless creature. But you must be firm : you must maintain discipline, not for your own sake but because the child needs discipline.

Having once decreed that Tommy must put away his toys before bedtime you must insist that he does it. It may take time, he may be late to bed, your own supper may be late, your whole domestic time-table may be thrown out of gear, but it is worth it. That single incident may have a vital effect upon the child's whole life ; he will learn, and may remember, that mummy's " no " means " no " and not " Oh, very well, just this once, if you're going to make a fuss about it." In dealing with children, " anything for the sake of peace " is a disastrous policy.

Children have no respect for a shilly-shallying parent, for one they can " get round " with pleading or defeat by obstinacy. They are very quick to take advantage of weakness, but they love best the parent they respect most.

You will have painful " scenes " that will make you feel a brute. But remember that a child is not so heartbroken as he may appear. He is probably not play-acting, but he has not yet learnt restraint. Grown-ups control their emotions ; they seldom give way to them entirely. A child does, and the tears and sobs that in an adult would indicate a broken heart, in a child merely signify a deep but temporary distress. Five minutes later the child will be laughing happily, his grief or anger forgotten.

But don't keep telling a child he is a " naughty little boy." He'll believe it, you know, just because you've said it. Repeated too often, it may brand him in his own mind, and he may feel all his life a sense of moral inferiority. Or—so strangely do toddlers' minds work—he may come to regard it as a distinction, something to be almost proud of. Or, worst of all, he may develop an " I'm made that way so what's the use of trying to be different" feeling. Always reprove the sin rather than the sinner. Say " that was a very naughty thing for a good little boy to do." The difference may seem slight, but it is important.

Don't reprove a child more often than you must. Nagging defeats its own ends, for the little fellow grows used to it and becomes indifferent. Let him do as he pleases so long as he is doing no harm to himself or anyone else. When he is risking his own life and limb, or damaging the furniture, try to suggest some other outlet for his activities rather than merely say " don't do that." It is not always successful, for forbidden fruit is always the most tempting, but it is a wise principle.

Punishment

AS a rule, with a tiny, a reproof is sufficient punishment. Unless he is unusually unemotional, the fact that he has grieved mummy will make him sorry for his misbehaviour—not for very long, mind you, but for a little while. Don't however, affect intense grief at his naughtiness. Sooner or later he will find out that you are play-acting, and you will fall heavily in his estimation.

But if he persists in misbehaving, punishment of some kind becomes necessary. Not necessarily corporal punishment ; " spare the rod and spoil the child " is a discredited maxim nowadays ; it often defeated its own object by making a child resentful and callous. Out of date, too, thank heaven, is the deplorable habit of giving a tiny a small slap every now and then—often mechanically, by way of a reminder to the little fellow to mind his p's and q's, and often in irritation. This was perfectly useless : the child became accustomed to it and took it as a matter of course.

A better form of punishment is depriving him of some favourite delicacy—*not* any portion of his real food—or some little treat. If you can " make the punishment fit the crime "—for instance, by stopping his Saturday chocolate till you have paid for the cup he smashed in sheer temper—so much the better. The child mind is logical enough to appreciate the justice of this, and it teaches him that all actions inevitably bring their own reactions.

But, quite honestly, there are some children upon whom nothing but the infliction of pain has any lasting effect. A good sound smacking is the only possible remedy. It is a remedy to be used as seldom as possible, and when it is used, it must be sufficient to make a real impression that the young rascal will not easily forget. Remember the small boy who said : " My daddy hardly ever spanks me, but when he *does*—Ooh ! "

Try not to punish a child in anger or in haste. Ask yourself first : " Do I want to punish him for his own good, or to give vent to my own annoyance ? " If you can't honestly say " yes " to the first question, it is unjust to punish the child at all. When the punishment is over, forgive instantly, take the little sinner in your arms and love him, and never refer to the incident again. All children resent the raking up of old scores.

Never threaten a child unless it is fair to give him a warning of what his misbehaviour will lead to, but if you *do* utter a threat, carry it out inflexibly.

Be fair to your toddler. Give him a chance. Don't pounce on him when he is in the middle of an entrancing game and say " Come to bed at once." That is simply inciting him to rebel. Tell him a few minutes before—not longer or he will forget—" Very nearly time for bed, darling. Finish that game quickly and don't start another." He probably *won't* finish quickly, but at least he will have been warned, and he will realise it.

What *is* Naughtiness ?

WHEN you feel a toddler is naughty, ask yourself the reason for his naughtiness. As has been said, a disordered tummy may be responsible for a fit of tantrums. The obvious remedy for this is not punishment, but an aperient. Hunger, thirst, tiredness, boredom, often unrealised by the child himself and unsuspected by his mother. will make him tiresome. Sudden and unaccountable naughtiness is often a symptom that the tiny is sickening for some ailment.

After all, what *is* naughtiness ? It is very seldom deliberate. More often it is the result of a perfectly sound instinct expressing itself in a way that is inconvenient to yourself. When little Tommy crawls into the coal-cellar and emerges looking like a nigger minstrel ; when he wanders out into the road, perilous with traffic, he is not being naughty ; he is merely satisfying the urge of his developing mind and strengthening muscles to investigate and explore. When he pulls the cat's tail he is not being cruel ; he does not realise that it is painful to the cat ; he is merely interested in the curious fact that a pull at one end of the animal produces strange noises at the other.

Of course, this doesn't mean that Tommy must be allowed to play in the coal cellar to the destruction of his romper, run into the road at the risk of his life, or torture a cat. Nothing of the sort. For his own sake and the sake of the home he must be restrained from doing these things. But don't regard them as instances of youthful depravity. Even when, in spite of reproof and punishment, he persists in doing them, he is not being deliberately disobedient : the urge to discover makes him forget your previous reproof.

Be patient, be understanding, however trying his ways may be ; don't think of him as a naughty child but only as a healthy enterprising one whose activities only need guiding into channels that are safe for himself and not too destructive to the household.

This eager little mind is in your charge, not to thwart and frustrate, but to develop and encourage along the right lines. Your tiny looks to you to help him to make the most of himself in this rather bewildering and inexplicable world into which you have brought him. Encourage him to come to you with his troubles : never be too busy to listen to him ; try to understand and to solve the problems that puzzle his little mind.

Even when he has wrought domestic disaster, keep your patience. There is nothing more gratifying to a mother than to know that her little one will come to her, in remorse but without fear, and say " Mummy, I'm sorry, but I've been naughty : I've done so-and-so." That can only be achieved by being firm but just and kind, patient and understanding, exacting some kind of penalty for the offence, but making allowances for the strength of the tempta-

Children have no respect for a shilly-shallying parent, for one they can get around with pleading or defeat by obstinacy. You will have painful scenes that will make you feel a brute. But remember that the child is not so heartbroken as he may appear.

The imaginary playmate some children conjure for themselves often gives the mother anxious doubt as to whether the little one is quite normal and mentally healthy. There is no cause for worry. It is usually a lonely and imaginative child who creates a playmate in her own mind. The remedy is to provide a real one.

tion and forgiving the small offender.

It's a tragedy when a small child is afraid to confess his misdeeds to his mother, when he tries to hide them, or tells lies in an attempt to escape punishment. When this regrettable state of affairs exists it is almost always the mother's fault, for children are truthful by nature : lying is an acquired art. Mother has been hasty-tempered with them, punished them too severely, failed to make allowances, or frightened them. To find that your child is afraid of you is a dreadful thing.

When Toddlers are Afraid

WITH other fears, mummy can help so much. A very tiny child is seldom afraid, for he has not yet learnt that sharp things cut and hot things burn and cats may scratch. An exception is the fear of the dark that sometimes— though by no means always— seems to be instinctive. Never laugh at fears of this kind : never force a child to face them : don't make too ponderous an attempt to explain them away, for the child will probably not be convinced.

If little Winnie is scared of sleeping in the dark, let her have a nightlight. It will do her no harm ; it is not pandering to her. For her to lie in bed quaking with terror at the nameless horrors that she imagines people the darkness is far worse for her ; you cannot calculate the effect it will have on her nervous system, perhaps for life. Don't discuss this, or other groundless fears with a tiny unless he himself approaches the subject ; don't be scornful and call him a baby or a coward ; just say sympathetically : "There's really nothing to be frightened of, darling : mummy wouldn't let anything be here to hurt you."

But don't make a coward of your child. The little people are naturally courageous, because they have at first no experience of danger. They have to be cautioned against the things that may hurt or harm them, but if the warning is too horrific, the seeds of cowardice will be planted. It is quite impossible to lay down any rules for achieving the happy medium : you must discover it for yourself.

If an emergency arises, try not to panic before the child. If the heartrug catches fire, try to keep your head and deal with it calmly. To see mummy scared will have such an effect upon the little one's mind that he may have a quite exaggerated dread of fire for the rest of his life—a dread that the fire itself would never have instilled in his mind.

If for any reason your toddler has in some way acquired an unreasonable fear of some definite thing— water, animals, or something of that kind, don't force him to face them and don't laugh at him. Be patient, and little by little demonstrate to him that his fears are groundless.

Baby Explorers

"WHAT am I to do ? " many of you will ask, "with a child who wanders away from home ? " It is not an easy problem. Wandering is a sign of an adventurous, enterprising spirit that it would be cruel and unwise to thwart. Yet obviously a tiny cannot be allowed to roam about, exposed to dangers he does not realise and causing his parents agonies of anxiety. The only thing is to reprove him on each occasion, explain to him the pain his wandering causes you, and promise him that when he is bigger he shall be at liberty to explore. But don't expect him to be deeply distressed by the grief he has caused you; tinies are far from unfeeling, but they cannot really understand and share the emotions of grown-ups. Your tiny's lack of consideration for your feelings may wound you, but don't take it to heart; it is merely normal.

A wise precaution is to teach a child, as soon as he can talk, his own surname and address, and if he is inclined to wander, tie on him a label addressed by yourself. And you may be able to find an interest at home that will absorb his mind so that he will not be tempted to wander. Picture-books, in which he can wander in imagination, sometimes achieve this.

Just as we want to teach our children to face danger without fear, so do we want to train them to endure pain and trouble and disappointment with fortitude. But the mother who, when her tiny tumbles and hurts himself and comes to her for sympathy, steels her heart and tells him it's " nothing to make such a fuss about " is tackling the problem in the wrong way. The child will probably learn, in time, to bear pain in uncomplaining silence—but he will be deeply wounded by mummy's lack of sympathy—the one person to whom he naturally turns when he is in trouble. He will cease to bring his troubles to her, to think of her as a help and comfort; he will shrink into his shell and she will have raised between them a barrier very difficult to break down.

Even worse is the mother who gives way to that odd yet very common impulse to be angry with the child for alarming and upsetting her by hurting himself! Yet almost as bad is the over-sentimental mother who gushes commiseration and makes the child feel that the damage is far worse than it really is, and rather enjoy the fuss that is being made over him. This weakens the child's character.

Beware of saying, when sonny bumps his head against the door: " Bad door to hurt poor sonny." This makes him feel that the pain he suffers is not the result of his own carelessness, but due to a spite against him on the part of the inanimate things around him. He is liable to grow into the type of man who never believes that his failures are due to his own actions or inactions, but to bad luck or some vague enmity on the part of other people.

The wisest method, as in most things, is the happy medium. Be sympathetic, but cheerfully sympathetic. Explain that men endure far worse hurts without making a fuss, and he wants to be a man, doesn't he? Never neglect to praise fortitude. Affect sympathy for the poor door with which he collided, and sonny will probably forget his hurt in delighted amusement at the absurd idea.

The old " Don't let Cissie—or the cat—or the kitchen clock—see you cry " is a sound one. It inculcates the principle that grief is a private thing: that one does not indulge it in public but keeps a stiff upper lip before the world. So you help toward building up a fine, firm character that can take its troubles courageously, without exaggeration, and exercise restraint over emotion.

Apron-strings

A CONVERSE problem to the too-enterprising type of child is the too-dependent, shy one who is wretched away from his mother and scared of strangers. This more often, but by no means always, happens in the case of an " only " child. It is a failing that needs attention, for enterprise and sociability are characteristics needed in life. Its cause is difficult to analyse and its cure is not easy.

Something can be done by inducing the little fellow to play with younger children and, mildly, to " boss " them ; this will develop self-confidence. Take him out with you when you go shopping and meet with friends, but persuade them not to make advances towards him ; just let him get used to being amongst people and to seeing you talk easily with them. And ask yourself if you are as sociable as you might be. If you are very reserved and seldom have friends to the house, your toddler will naturally adopt the same attitude. Widen your social circle, chat with people when you meet them, with shop people and others, and it will dawn upon your tiny that the strangers of whom he is so frightened are not ogres, but quite as human as mummy herself.

Many mothers are alarmed because their little ones seem selfish. They have little conception of other people's rights of property, but they have a very keen one of their own. They become absorbed in their own pursuits and ignore their surroundings. These are not sinful traits to be wiped out if possible : a certain selfishness, an acquisitiveness, is necessary in the battle of life in which your tiny will later on have to take part, and absorption in the interest of the moment is a valuable quality when, later on, it is applied to a job of work.

But these characteristics need checking to prevent their becoming excessive. The obvious way is to encourage the child to play with other children, and to allow them to play with his toys. And don't expect very little people to play *together :* they won't. At first they will each play separately, in each other's company. This is good enough to start with : real playing together will come later, quite naturally and without any need for stimulation from you.

Imaginary Playmates

THE " imaginary playmate " some children conjure up for themselves often gives a mother hours of anxious doubt as to whether the little one is quite normal and mentally healthy. Actually there is no cause for worry ; it is a phase through which the child will pass without any ill-effects. It is usually an only and lonely child, and an imaginative one, who creates a playmate for herself in her own mind, and in this case the simple and obvious remedy is to provide her with real flesh-and-blood playmates.

When a child with brothers and sisters, or with plenty of little friends, creates an imaginary playmate, the case is rather different : it is a symptom not of loneliness but of something else missing in the child's life. It may be that she has not enough interests in common with her real playmates ; it may be that she feels misunderstood by her parents, that in some way, she is frustrated. Without realising it she is trying to escape from something in life as it is, and manufacturing a dream-friend to the pattern she desires, in whom she can confide her troubles.

The mere fact that she invents an imaginary friend is of no importance whatever ; the fact that she has felt compelled to do such a thing is very important indeed. Already, although so tiny, she is out of tune with life and her parents, and there is a risk that she may always be so, which means much unhappiness in the years to come.

The case needs the most tactful and delicate handling. Don't mention the imaginary playmate ; don't try to force the child's confidence, but be very loving and very sympathetic at all times. Sooner or later she will tell you, perhaps with great difficulty, the trouble that is preying on her mind. Probably it will prove to be something that seems to you both trivial and fantastic, but don't even seem to laugh at it or dismiss it as foolish. Very gently and patiently reason with her and show her how mistaken she is, and rejoice that you have succeeded in breaking down the invisible barrier that was rising between you and your baby.

One other word about toddlers' failings. If your tiny seems thoroughly naughty and intractable, don't envy too much the mother next door whose toddler is " always good " and " never any trouble." Honestly, a child like that is likely to be lacking in some way ; either his health is not good or he has a lethargic temperament that is not likely to achieve much in life. Often the child who is always getting into trouble grows into the man who makes his mark in life.

Preparation for School Life

IN another chapter the health of the pre-school child has been dealt with. The mental and psychological preparation for school life is not so simple. It is not very much use your trying to teach your tiny reading and writing and the other lessons he will learn at school. Methods of education are different from those existing in your own childhood. For instance, children no longer learn the alphabet as A, B, C, D, etc., but by sounds similar to those made when the letters form spoken words. They do not learn that C.A.T. spells " cat " : they call the letters by the three sounds that make up the word : they learn to recognise words as a whole rather than by spelling out the letters that compose them.

Whether you consider this method an improvement or not, you will realise that if, with the best intentions, you teach a child in the old-fashioned way, you are hindering rather than helping ; you will make things difficult both for the teacher, who will have to make the child *un*-learn something before he can start to learn anything, and for the child, who will be completely bewildered between " mummy's way " and " teacher's way."

But in other directions there is much you can do to give little Tommy a good start in his school life. You can encourage him to use his eyes and his hands and his brains, you can foster in him qualities that will make him successful in his lessons and popular with his teachers and his schoolmates.

Your greatest help in this way will be the choice of suitable toys and suitable games. Building blocks of various kinds are excellent. Most boys nowadays take easily to constructional toys, and though, of course, some of these are too advanced for tiny little fellows, and too expensive, there are many at a reasonable price that the fingers of a four-year-old can cope with. The making of models, however simple or crude not only trains little hands, teaches little eyes to judge size and symmetry, but develops the qualities of neatness, care, accuracy, and perseverance which are valuable in whatever occupation they may be used.

Games and Toys

EVEN without this special equipment, you will probably find little Tommy, with a hammer and nails and a few scraps of wood, constructing some object that to you may appear to have neither shape nor sense, but that stands to him for a definite object. And in one way this kind of thing is even more valuable than the putting-together of pieces prepared for the purpose : crude and mysterious though the result may be, the child used imagination to devise it and ingenuity to construct it, and these, too, are valuable qualities.

Nearly all boys have also a destructive instinct : the instinct that leads them to enjoy setting up a bottle and throwing stones at it. This is not a thing to be regarded with aversion and stamped out if possible ; it has its purpose in human nature ; but it often requires restraint. The best restraint is the encouragement of the constructive instinct.

Little girls too small to learn sewing and knitting can be encouraged to use their fingers in plaiting, easy weaving and similar simple things. Materials, patterns, and such helps as sewing cards can be bought if you like, but materials can be provided and some kind of pattern improvised out of the resources of the home.

Almost every little girl loves dolls, and though it cannot be said that playing with them is any help to school life, it is valuable for the larger, wider life that lies beyond. Every mother looks forward to her little girl, whatever she may do in life, eventually becoming a happy wife and mother, and many a sound principle of the art of motherhood can be instilled into the receptive mind of a tiny girl while she is mothering her doll. This kind of play, too, fosters and develops the protective mother-instinct.

Encourage your children to play these games but don't *force* them to do so. That is spoiling the happy hours of carefree enjoyment that are a small child's right, and that he will never be able to enjoy again. And it will make him dislike the very things that you want him to pursue with interest. And, as has been said, don't try to make him keep on at one thing too long ; don't think that because he soon drops one game and turns to another, that he is a scatterbrain. A tiny's mind soon tires of monotony, just as a kitten, busily chasing its tail, suddenly loses interest and turns to something else. Continued interest, perseverance, will come naturally by degrees as the child grows older.

And don't think, just because little Tommy only copies and imitates you, or other children, or the things around him, that he has no originality of thought. Originality must grow out of something, must be based upon experience of some kind. A tiny child has no experience of his own, at first he must borrow from the experience of others and adapt it to his own purposes.

Don't interfere with your child's play. Suggest things for him to do, show him how to do them, when he is in difficulty and asks for help give him just as much help as he needs and no more ; but otherwise leave him to get on with it in his

A sense of religion should be
instilled into a tiny as soon as
possible. Point out how
beautiful the flowers are, how
brightly the sun shines, how
the little clouds chase each
other so happily across the
sky. Tell your tiny that God
made all these things.

own way. He'll be happier, and the play will be more use to him. Sonny likes mummy to play *with* him, but he doesn't want her to play *for* him.

There are other " lessons " that the toddler is not too young to learn. Lessons in independence and self-reliance. Teach the tiny to put his toys away tidily when he has finished playing : it is not only a help to you but valuable training for him. Yet be considerate about this. If Sonny has, at a great expense of time, trouble, and patience laid out some sort of a model railway, and bedtime comes when he is just ready to play with it, he is justified in feeling aggrieved if he has to take it all to pieces again to rebuild next day. This doesn't mean that you should have the thing all over the sitting-room carpet all the evening ; that's obviously ridiculous. But if you can provide a corner where he could—not always but sometimes—construct anything of this sort and leave it till to-morrow without making the house look like a jumble sale, it will save him from a great deal of discouragement.

But he will need your advice. He, with his limited experience, will not foresee whether he will want the railway to remain in being : you will, and you should warn him : " If you lay that out here, you'll have to tidy it up before bedtime, but if you go into your corner it may stay till to-morrow."

Dressing Themselves

YOU have already been advised to teach your tinies, as early as possible, to dress themselves. You will waste an appalling amount of time at first—for a little one's fingers can take an incredible time to put a button into a buttonhole— but it will be well worth while. It will save you a great deal of time and trouble later on, and it is valuable training for the little one himself.

But buttons on garments and laces on shoes are difficult at first, and the Montessori schools have an excellent method of training tiny fingers in their manipulation. Material furnished with buttons and buttonholes, eyelet holes and laces, is hung on a frame, far more convenient to get at than garments on the child's own body. A handy daddy could easily knock up such a frame, an old waistcoat of his would provide practise in dealing with buttons, and mummy could probably find something with buttonholes through which shoelaces could be threaded. A tiny who first learns to manage these fastenings in this way will soon learn to dress and undress himself.

And, as has been said, tinies should be allowed, too, to wash and bath themselves. They will require supervision : they will be terribly slow ; the washing will be of a sketchy nature, and mummy will certainly have to dry the small body, but it will be well worth it in the end.

Let the tinies help you with your work. It will take far longer and be far more trouble than doing it yourself ; but they will enjoy it, and it is all useful training. But don't expect too much from them. When little Winnie dries the tea things you have washed she will leave them smeary. You will, of course, point out her shortcomings, but do it gently, not suggesting that she is careless but merely that she hasn't yet learnt to do the job as mummy does it.

Don't merely let her handle unbreakable things : she loses half the benefit of the lesson. When a tiny drops a cup that doesn't break it teaches her nothing ; when she drops one and it smashes, it teaches her to be careful. (This does not mean, of course, that you are to let her practise on your favourite tea-pot or your best dinner service !)

Don't keep a tiny at these house-hold tasks too long ; it isn't fair, and it turns what should be regarded as a privilege into drudgery. You may long to say " Stay and just finish the job; see it through." That's a sound prin-ciple to inspire. But it is too much to expect at first. Achieve it gradually by asking the child to do a *little* more than she wants to each time. And remember this : You sweep a floor to make it clean, little Winnie will sweep it for the fun of sweeping. So, although you will show her how the work should be done, don't expect her to make a thorough job of it at first.

You may possibly find that after a time she loses interest in helping you. If she does, there'll be a reason. It may be that you have been too exacting, or it may be that she is the independent, self-reliant type of child who prefers to do things herself rather than help other people to do them. Don't crush this spirit : it is an admirable one and none too common. Give her jobs to do on her own, praise her for doing them, and point out very gently how she might have done them better. In that way you are fostering a quality that will be invaluable to the child in after life.

Frank Words to Fathers

SO far, this chapter has been written from mother's stand-point. But father must play his part in bringing up the children from the very first. You may not find them so interesting, young father, while they are in the toddler stage as when they are bigger and you can enjoy sharing their games, but you must learn to know them well while they are tinies, otherwise you will not understand their natures when they are older.

Of course, a small child sees his mother and father in very different lights. Mummy is with him all day long ; she washes him, dresses him, feeds him, ministers to his needs ; it is to her he runs for comfort when he is in trouble, it is usually she who has to reprove or punish him when he is naughty ; he gets to know her very well ; he sees her not only at her best but at her worst, when she is tired and nervy and irritable—for she has little chance of escaping from the little fellow's sight when she is finding things a strain.

Father is, in the child's eyes, quite a different being, less often seen, more remote, comparatively un-known, something of a mystery. For this reason, the little chap has —at any rate at first—a great respect for daddy ; he may even stand in awe of him. It is for father, and mother, too, to turn this mental attitude to good account.

In the bad old days father was made something of a bugbear. It was so temptingly easy for a mother, when she felt that the children were getting out of hand, to say " I'll tell your dad when he comes home." It was easy for her, when he arrived, to tell him how intractable young Tommy had been that day and to insist that father did his bit in the child's upbringing, with a slipper. If this happened often, the child came to associate father with the idea of punishment, to dread his homecoming ; all through the rest of his life he thought of him, not as someone in whom he could confide, sure of sympathy, understanding, and wise advice, but someone who would punish transgressions, someone whom one kept in ignorance of one's weaknesses and lapses if possible.

Even if father were not so complete a bogey-man as this, he often demanded that when he was at home the children must be kept quiet, they must not disturb him, whatever he might be doing, and mother, as a dutiful wife, hushed the little ones' healthy high spirits and restricted their games while father was in the house.

All this was wrong, of course. But nowadays there is a tendency to swing to the other extreme. In stepping down off his uncomfortable pedestal, many a father has descended too far ; he has, so to speak, gone down on all fours with the children and become one of them. He joins in their games—which mummy hasn't time to do ; he is never irritable with them—he hasn't had to endure their noise, their incessant questions, their exasperating misbehaviour, all day ; he finds extra pennies for sweets that mummy cannot spare out of the housekeeping money ear-marked for wholesome nourishing food for them, he—sometimes in ignorance—allows them to do things that mummy has forbidden. In other words, he spoils them, and makes poor mummy, trying conscientiously to train them in good habits, seem an unreasonable tyrant.

This kind of thing is not only unfair to mother ; it is not fair to yourself, father, and it is not fair to the children. They will learn to take advantage of your good nature ; little by little you will lose your authority over them ; as they grow older they will think of you, not as a person who must,

on occasion, be obeyed, not as a person whose greater age, knowledge and experience make his advice worth asking and taking, but as one of themselves.

You want your children to love you, to look forward with delight to your homecoming, to enjoy being with you, to give you their confidence without fear. But you must keep their respect : you must maintain authority over them, you must not allow them to "get round you." All that has been said about mother enforcing obedience applies to you, too.

And you must not let mummy down. In many things husband and wife can agree to differ : they can hold opposing opinions without disharmony. But to the children they must present a united front. If mummy has said " No," daddy must never allow himself to be wheedled into saying " Yes."

If he does not agree that mummy is right, he can talk the matter over with her afterwards and they can come to a mutual decision, but before the children he must uphold mummy's decrees as firmly as he does his own ; he must not let himself seem, in their eyes, more tolerant, more generous, more sympathetic than she. There are times when it seems brutally unfair that two large grown-up beings should be allied against one small, rather bewildered child—but it is necessary for the child's own good.

A Warning to Wives

BUT a word to mothers here : some of you, anxious not to make daddy a bugaboo to your children, run the risk of making him a butt. You find fault with him, before their sharp eyes and sharp ears, as you do with them. You

" tick him off " for dropping cigarette ash on the carpet in exactly the same tone as you do little Tommy for spilling his milk. Don't. Even if only laughingly you call daddy a clumsy owl, the child will take it as a serious statement of your opinion of his father. He will look upon daddy as being, not on your side in enforcing authority, but as a fellow-sufferer with himself from your domination. The child's sympathies will be drawn away from you to his father.

Be very, very careful how you behave to each other before the children. Exercise restraint ; don't let yourselves go until you are alone together. Of course, you won't indulge in a real quarrel in front of the little ones, a thing that makes them utterly miserable and may give them all their lives a mistaken and warped idea of married life. But don't even be hasty, or sulky with each other, or mildly sarcastic at each other's expense.

And do remember, always, the terrific effect of example upon the receptive mind of a young child. Children are naturally imitative. If mummy is methodical and daddy is punctual, they may very likely follow suit ; if the parents are slipshod in their ways it is a thousand to one the children will be the same.

And in nothing is this more true than in the attitude of the parents to each other. If mummy is tender and gentle and kind with daddy, little Winnie will be tender and gentle and kind too—not only with daddy, but with other people and, in the years to come, with the man she marries. If daddy is polite, helpful and considerate with mummy, Tommy will be the same, and the girl he marries one day will be the lucky possessor of a good husband. For the seeds of happy marriages, as well as of worldly success, are sown in childhood, in happy, well-governed homes.

Baby Prayers

ONE aspect of the little one's training that no mother will wish to neglect is the religious side. But it is so difficult for tinies to understand the real meaning of religion that many a mother is tempted to leave the question till they are old enough to grasp its true significance.

This is a mistake, however. A sense of religion should be instilled into children as early as possible, so that they accept it absolutely naturally, and grow up with it— then, even though they may in later years question particular creeds and doctrines, they never lose their original belief in God's goodness and mercy, and in His divine plan for each and every one of us. A child of four, at the latest, ought to be quite able to say a simple prayer, and to understand something about God and Heaven.

Point out to her how beautiful the flowers are, and how brightly the sun shines on the grass, and how the little clouds chase each other so happily across the sky. Tell her that God made all these lovely things, that He made the whole beautiful world for mummies and daddies and little children to live in, and that He wants everyone to enjoy these wonderful gifts of His, and that as long as people are good they will be happy. Then tell her that God lives up in Heaven, in a land that is even lovelier than this, and that some day we will all go there and be with Him for ever and ever.

You can't teach a very young child much more than that, and at first she might only grasp half of what you say. But if you bring up the subject whenever suitable opportunities occur, then it will soon become fixed in her mind, and she will accept it as a matter of course. You will find that, as she grows older, she will begin to ask questions, and will insist on definite replies.

Don't be disappointed if at first the little ones have strange ideas of their own about what you have told them; if a tiny girl's Heaven is the seaside, with sand castles and paddling and donkey rides all day long, or a small boy's is to drive a sort of celestial locomotive in the Beyond. The childish mind can only interpret these immense ideas (which after all are far beyond any human understanding) in the terms of familiar, everyday experiences.

It is the same with prayer. There is no sense in teaching a child to repeat a long string of words and sentences, however beautiful they may be, if they convey nothing whatever to her mind. A few simple words each night, thanking God for her happy day, and asking Him to bless and take care of those she loves, is all that is needed. Then in the morning she can use much the same words again, and ask God to help her to be a good girl all through the day.

Christmas gives us an opportunity to talk about the Jesus in the manger, and at Easter we can say something about His death on the Cross. You can tell the tinies, too, how Jesus loved little children, and how they should all love Him and be good to please Him.

It is part of our duty as parents to instil the principles of Christianity into our children, more than ever in these days of doubt and indifference. All too soon they will come up against problems and difficulties, and if we have taught them a knowledge of right and wrong, and some understanding of God, and of the comfort of prayer, they will never be completely at a loss in Life's battles.

In the bad old days father was made something of a bugbear. It was so temptingly easy for a mother when she felt that the children were getting out of hand to say, "I'll tell your dad when he comes home". If it happened often, the child came to associate father with the idea of punishment.

CHAPTER IX

Baby Brother

MOST people would probably agree that the jolliest men and women, and those who own to having had the jolliest childhood, come of large families—families where the babies followed each other very quickly and grew up together, sharing their games and making their own little world within the home. This applies to the pre-war generation which is now in the thirties or thereabouts, and even more to the generation before it, which had its roots in more secure days than ours.

Things are very different now. The cost of living, the size of houses, and so many other conditions have changed so enormously that the large family is in many cases no longer " practical politics." The next best thing is the well-" spaced " family, by which is meant a family whose small members arrive at intervals long enough to give the busy mother " breathing space,"

yet not so long as to interfere with the happy companionship of the children themselves.

Two years between is a sensible space ; it means that all the children are at the stage of being constantly cared for at the same time. It means that they will be grown up and out in the world very closely together, so that you, the parents, have the chance of making a new start in life yourselves.

It is less satisfactory for a mother of children at school or just left school to have a tiny baby to care for again; she may be past the stage of loving to tend tiny, helpless things ; she has switched her mind on to the problems of older children and in homes where the family goes on spreading out for many years, the older children are often neglected for the new-comer just when, perhaps, they most need their mother's thought.

Moreover, the mother who has

spent twenty years of her life looking after children is fortunate if, when they go out into the world and need to stand on their own feet, she can take up some new interest and feel young again.

The question you young parents will naturally ask is, how can we be sure of spacing out our family according to plan ? That is a delicate matter and calls for the personal help of some experienced medical adviser. There are, of course, many methods employed, but some of them are definitely harmful and a great many are not always effective.

The best plan is for the wife to see either her own doctor or to attend one of the many women's advisory clinics which are springing up all over the country. It should be mentioned here that these are intended for people whose incomes do not exceed £5 a week, but they will always supply those who do not fall within this category with the address of a private doctor who will give the same advice for a moderate fee.

The Firstborn's Feelings

WHEN you realise that another little one is on the way, the thought is bound to come to your mind : " Oh, dear, I do hope little Tommy—or Winnie, as the case may be—will not be jealous ! " But remember that whether or not your first child is jealous of the new baby depends entirely on *you*. It is *your* attitude towards the little newcomer that will help Tommy or Winnie to love him—or hate him !

Right from the beginning you should let the first child into the secret. " Darling," you might say in the tone you use for a special treat in store, " what do you think ? There's a lovely little brother or sister coming for you to play with soon ! " And then set about making it a real treat, and keep it well in the child's mind by mentioning it at every opportunity.

Then, when the new baby has actually arrived, make a point of letting Tommy or Winnie help to bathe him, put him to bed and push the pram—let the first child fetch and carry as a special treat, learning all the while to be very careful of this precious new possession, to creep about on tiptoe, as a lovely game, when the new baby is asleep, and to play with him very gently when mummy is busy, and baby needs amusing.

Always speak of the children together, whenever possible, so that one does not feel left out. When people admire the new baby, draw Tommy or Winnie into the conversation, too, and say : " Aren't we lucky to have a new baby of our very own ? " Never mention the word jealousy, and it probably will not occur to the little first-comer.

Telling Children about Sex

AND the new baby, of course, gives you a splendid opportunity of introducing the facts of life naturally.

Remember that to a child nothing is " shocking " or " not nice," unless it has been labelled so to him by grown-ups—so you may talk freely to your little one and lay the foundation stone of honesty and frankness which is going to mean so much to you when you are bringing him or her up later on.

" Mummy," Tommy or Winnie is likely to say, " where are we getting

D

the new baby from ? Why must we wait ? Why can't we have him now at once ? "

And then, while you are getting on with the job in hand—whatever it may be—tell him or her, quite casually, but lovingly, that it is a tender secret you will share together—that the new baby is growing inside mummy, in a little nest within her—and that he's not quite ready to come into the world yet, because there is a cot to be prepared for him, and little clothes to be made—and so on, in a pretty little story that clings to the truth, and does not mislead by fairy-tales which will afterwards have to be contradicted.

If you find you are having to answer rather more than you bargained for all at once, answer what you can with comfort, and then say something like : " Mummy's busy now, darling ; we must get daddy's tea—but I'll go on with the story another day. Now, will you get mummy that little yellow cup over there—— ? " And so you take the child's mind off the subject and gently on to another, which will give you a chance to think out just what you are going to say when the next opportunity arises.

" How did baby get there ? " is a question that needs skilful handling, of course, for a little mind could not understand the truth, and you would do best not to try to answer that question direct— but to point out that every little baby has a mummy *and* a daddy, and it was because daddy loved mummy so much that the new little brother or sister decided that he would like to come and join their family.

If you have a " pigeon pair "— a boy and a girl—bath-time provides a splendid opportunity for them to learn the difference between a girl and a boy—and, if you have not, it is a good idea to invite a little friend of the opposite sex to stay with you occasionally, for it will give them knowledge of the facts without exciting much curiosity. If they do ask why they are made differently, all mother has to say is : " Why, darlings, if you were all exactly alike, you wouldn't be boys and girls—you'd be all girls or all boys." And then pass on to another subject.

Never make a secret of Sex ; always answer the kiddies' questions frankly—and you will not find that, later on, they will try and find out things for themselves because they tell themselves it is no good asking mummy !

Lessons from Nature

THE ideal way to give children sex instruction is to prepare their minds for the beautiful truth before they even ask any questions. Always think and speak of it as a beautiful truth and you will find it so much easier to explain.

The simplest and loveliest way to train your children towards the day when you want to tell them the truth is to teach them through the flowers. When they are quite tiny speak to them of daddy flowers and mummy flowers and the little baby flowers which are the seeds. One day you may ask the kiddies to help you shell peas and you can say, " Do your remember those pretty white flowers that grew on the peas when they first grew up ? "

The children will remember.

" Well, these are their babies. Now let us see how many babies there are in this little green nursery." And with your thumb you crack open the pea-pod and there lie the snug little green peas.

Tell your little loved-one that every baby has a mummy and a daddy and it was because daddy loved mummy so much that the little new brother or sister decided that he would like to come and join the family.

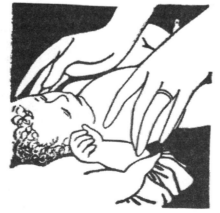

When the new baby has arrived, daddy can say: "When mummy woke up this morning, she found that your new sister had arrived and she was curled up in bed beside her."

You will call out in excitement:
" See, this mummy flower has got a big family this year, ten little green babies ! "

Another time you can take a flower, and open the little round or oval bulb, just below the bloom, where the seeds are formed. Show the kiddies the little seeds cuddled down close together, waiting to be born when it is time for them to fall to the brown soil. You can also show them the little stems or stamens at the top of each of which is a kind of pocket containing the golden pollen. Tell them that every daddy plant has this pollen.

It is only a step further from this to tell the children about " The Blessing of the Bees " who carry the golden pollen from daddy flower to mummy flower. You will thus be leading up to the idea that marriage is God's blessing and this is a lesson that should be learned by boys as well as girls. Every mother should realise that by bringing up her boy with the right idea of sex, she is going to make some little girl, now playing with her dolly, a happy wife and mother in the years to come.

From plant life you can pass on to the animal kingdom, explaining how the mother fish lays her eggs in the sea or river nursery she has chosen and the father fish lays the " pollen " over them to give them life and turn them into baby fish. And so to the birds who choose a mate in the springtime and build a cosy nest in which their babies are to be born and nourished.

If you make the children's minds perfectly familiar with the idea of motherhood and fatherhood throughout all life, it will not come as a shock to them when they learn the truth about human parenthood. What helps mothers very much is that knowledge dawns very slowly and sweetly in the intellect of a child. Information comes gradually. The child sees, what he sees is telegraphed to the brain, but the real person in the child's body takes a little longer to comprehend what he has seen. That is why children always ask " Why ? " This is the reason their " whys " should always be patiently answered.

No Nose out of Joint

SO now you have inspired your first child with the thought that he is lucky to have a new baby in the house, and you have done your best to explain how the little one arrived. The main thing to consider now is how to bring them up together to the best advantage.

Plan out your day, as well as you can, so that, when you have just finished doing something for one baby, you do not have to start something else for the other !

Help the elder child to become self-reliant, to put on his own clothes, and perhaps some of the new baby's, too. Find him little jobs to do about the house, for now Tommy or Winnie is going to take a great pride in being the elder— the little man of the family, or the little mother, and things should run smoothly if you encourage this attitude.

More and more as the little pair grow up, you will be able to trust the elder to look after the younger, and to take on responsibilities that would otherwise hinder you in the busy work of a day.

In a way, the first-comer is losing quite a lot by having a new brother or sister, for attention must be divided between them now, Father Christmas may have to bring smaller presents, and perhaps clothes have to last twice as long—and therefore it is well to make up to Tommy or Winnie in any way you can for the loss of such privileges, by letting them feel you do not know what you would do without them, for instance. But, of course, in other ways they are gaining immeasurably, the little Tommies and Winnies of the world—they are learning to share, to give and take, to be good sports, and not to be tell-tales, learning in a way they do not even notice—though they can only learn these lessons if the parents are sensible about dealing with the children.

Because Tommy is the elder, he should not be allowed to rule the roost, to bully and tease, and to expect the younger child to do everything it is told ! He should be allowed to feel that, now he is a little man with a real sister or brother, he is much too big to be naughty or unkind—and his better nature appealed to in that way.

And, in the same way, you must be careful not to give the younger child an inferiority complex because he or she has an elder brother. Each child must be made to feel that it has its own place in the family that could not be filled by anyone else, and must be brought up to respond accordingly.

It has been said, by people who have suffered in this way when young, that there is nothing quite so harmful to one's self-respect as always having to wear the cast-off clothing of an elder brother or sister—and one can well imagine the feelings of a child for whom this is a necessity. Therefore, if you find that you, like many other parents, must manage in this way, do try, just occasionally, to let the younger child have something new. It will give him a sense of importance, a feeling that he is

somebody, after all, and will wipe away any resentment he may feel at having to wear the rest of Big Brother's clothes. Always to have second-best will never bring out the best in anybody !

And you will find that, whereas you used to have one saving-box to slip pennies into, you now have two—and be very fair about that ! If the kiddies cannot have everything both at the same time, then let them take turns with the treats you can provide. Keep any inkling of resentment away with a cheerful thought about the joys in store— and help your bairns to look on the bright side of everything—make it into a game, if you like : who can see the bright side first when something particularly gloomy crops up !

Daddy Does His Bit

AND what should father be doing all this time ? Right from the moment when he knows he is to have another little son or daughter, he can help the wife by talking to Tommy or Winnie in the same strain as she does, and carrying on the good work. The most awkward question he is likely to come up against is when his wife is actually confined, and he is left with the youngster, who very naturally wants to know where she is. Of course daddy will say that she has gone to bring baby home, but the thoughtful child will immediately want to know why she has had to go to bed.

Perhaps the best answer to that is that mummy has been very busy just lately, and she is really very tired, and so the kind nurse and the doctor thought it would be best if she had a nice long rest in bed until baby came. Then, when the time comes to tell Tommy or Winnie that the new baby has arrived, daddy can say something like this : "When mummy woke up this morning, she found that your new sister had arrived, and she was curled up in bed beside her—wasn't that lovely ? "

It only needs the final remark that, in so many days, mummy will have had enough rest, to complete all the necessary explanation—and the rest of daddy's time can be taken up with telling Tommy or Winnie how he or she can help mummy when she comes home—and how both daddy and Tommy must save her all the trouble they can, and do everything possible for her. If baby has been born at home, the story must be altered a little to suit the different circumstances.

Then, when the happy pair arrive home—or downstairs, as the case may be—daddy must set about carrying out those plans. Remember, husbands, that the wife will be wanting your understanding love and consideration every bit as much now as she did when

Tommy or Winnie was born. Cast your mind back to her homecoming then, and, if there was anything that went wrong that time, resolve that it shall be improved upon now.

Because she has experienced motherhood before, she will not be very different ; she may know why she feels irritable all of a sudden, or weepy, or a little unreasonable—but she will probably feel it just the same. Before, when Tommy was born, you knew very little about what to expect, or how to help, and you felt very inexperienced, didn't you ? Now this is your chance to show how much you remember, and what a splendid husband and father you can be !

She will not have a lot of time for you at first, because she may be a little overcome at the prospect of managing two children instead of one—but she will appreciate all that you try to do for her, even though she may not always show it !

Prepare their minds for sex education by teaching them through flowers. Speak to them of daddy flowers and mummy flowers and the little baby flowers, which are the seeds.

Get them to help you to shell peas. When you crack open the pea-pod, call out in excitement: "See, this mummy flower has got a big family, ten little green babies."

CHAPTER X

Starting School

WHEN the toddler grows old enough to start school, his parents find themselves confronted with a fresh set of problems. Until now, you have principally ordered little Tommy's behaviour and shaped his character as it affected himself, yourself, and the home. Now he goes out into a world where he will mix with, and deal with, other people, and he will need your help in adjusting his outlook to his new surrounding.

School itself is, of course, a very different thing from school in your own childhood. Lessons are made far more interesting, discipline is less severe and more reasonable. Classes are smaller and teachers are able to take a more personal interest in each child, to learn his virtues and his failings, his talents and his deficiences. Nearly all children of to-day are genuinely happy at school. But much can be done to make them happier, and to see that they get the utmost benefit from their school life.

The ideal, of course, would be for each school-teacher to know well the parents of every child in his or her class. This is not easy; it would make greater demands on the teacher's spare time than he might be prepared to give, and parents are not always ready to welcome Tommy's class-master into their homes. But if it can conveniently be done, it is an excellent idea: you and the teacher will be able to work together to draw out the best that is in Tommy instead of, as so often happens, seeming to pull different ways.

That first day at school! You take your darling, with a shrinking feeling of apprehension, and hand him over to the keeping of a perfect stranger. You will try to buttonhole Miss Blank, and tell her that

Tommy is quite a good little fellow, but sensitive ; he can't bear to be spoken to sharply. And she mustn't be impatient with him if he is not very quick in the uptake ; he is slow but sure. And as he is apt to catch cold rather easily, will she please see that he doesn't sit in a draught. And will she please seat him next to a *nice* child.

Miss Blank will listen to you pleasantly and patiently, but she will have heard the same kind of thing from half a dozen other anxious mothers that morning, and will have to listen to it from at least half a dozen more. She understands the feelings of mothers, but she proceeds to study her small charges for herself.

Even if you have taught Tommy not to be a mollycoddle, dependent on you ; even if you have told him how he will enjoy school, and not allowed him to be scared at the thought of school-work and school teachers, he will probably weep at your leaving him among strangers. Even if there are in the class one or two slightly older children whom Tommy knows, you cannot feel sure that they will look after him and make him feel at home ; they have their own friends and their own interests. You see him standing there forlorn, and you feel that you are deserting and abandoning him. You tear yourself away—if you are wise you will tear yourself away quickly—and go disconsolately home to a silent and empty house, and all through the morning you wonder if Tommy is desperately lonely and unhappy and wanting his mummy.

At dinner-time you go to meet him—probably half an hour too soon—and at last he comes out of school, whooping and leaping, so taken up with his new little friends that he has hardly a word to say to you ! Not till he is alone with you at home will he begin to chatter excitedly about the interesting things he has been doing and the delightful games he has played with the other children.

Parents and Teachers

AFTER a little while, some of the gilt will wear off the gingerbread. Miss Blank, at first so kind and patient and charming, will have been obliged to enforce discipline, to insist on silence or application to the work in hand, and Tommy will be upset about it. Don't leap to the conclusion that Miss Blank is a bad-tempered tyrant who bullies the tinies in her charge. She is doing her job, and it is not an easy one. The children are given to her to teach and she has to teach them, and if they won't be taught she has to do something about it. After all, you know, you didn't find Tommy a perfect saint at home, did you ? And if he'd been one you'd have felt uneasy about him.

Very well. Explain to him that Miss Blank wouldn't have been cross with him without a reason ; ask him what the trouble was all about—though you'll probably get a muddled, garbled, and one-sided account of it—and tell him that if he does as he's told, he'll avoid such unpleasant happenings in future.

Of course, it may seem to you that Miss Blank really has been unjust or unnecessarily severe. But don't tell Tommy so. If the matter really seems serious, make an opportunity to see Miss Blank and have a little chat with her about it—not belligerently, but showing a reasonable desire that your child should have fair treatment. You will probably find that the teacher was quite in the right and that Tommy has traits that you have never suspected—naturally, because at home he was not in surroundings that brought them into play.

But don't despair. If the incident has brought out some unsuspected failing in Tommy's character, it is as well that it was brought to light ; now you and Miss Blank together can restrain it or divert it into a useful channel.

Playground Bullies

IT is rather more difficult when Tommy comes home crying because Joey Briggs has pinched him or Willie Turner has thrown his cap into the road. You'll probably seethe with indignation, but remember that while there are always bullies and tormentors among children, there are far more who are merely high-spirited and mischievous, inclined to tease a newcomer just to see how he will take it and how much he can stand.

Sympathise with Tommy—whatever you do, don't scoff at his distress—but don't say that Joey Briggs is a nasty little savage and that you'll tell his mother. (If you carry out this threat you'll run the risk of winning for Tommy the reputation of being a sneak, and he'll be unpopular at school.) No. Point out that Joey was only teasing, that it isn't really a serious matter, and explain that if Tommy takes that kind of thing in good part and doesn't get upset, Joey will soon leave off, because he'll get no fun out of it. Tell him that boys put up with that kind of thing bravely.

If you find that, after all, Joey Briggs persists with his pestering, it may be necessary to say a word,

not to his mother, but to the teacher. But don't do this unless it becomes really necessary. Tommy is only a baby, but he has to learn to stand on his own feet. He will never get on in the world if he feels, even subconsciously, that he needn't stand up for himself because mummy will do it for him. Even in those first schooldays he must find his own level, without your help. In fact, your intervention would not help, but only hinder.

Tommy will soon make friends, and quite possibly they will not be by any means the kind of friends you would have chosen for him. But don't interfere. If you say " You're not to play with Willie Turner. He's not a nice boy," Tommy won't understand. He finds Willie Turner congenial, or he wouldn't want to play with him. If he asks you to explain your reason for disapproving of Willie you will find it difficult, and Sonny will feel that you are prejudiced and unreasonable, and he will resent it. And to suggest that Harry Grant is a much nicer playfellow is almost worse ; you'll probably make him hate Harry Grant for life.

No, the only thing is to give Tommy time to tire of Joey. If you've brought him up on the right lines, installed the right ideas into his little mind, he will soon discover that his friend falls short of mummy's idea of a nice little boy, and in time he will drop him.

When he has been to school a little while, Tommy will probably, one day, make use of a word or an expression that will make you jump. It will certainly be rather a shock for you, but don't lose your head and be angry : remember that the little chap hasn't the faintest idea what the word means and has no intention of being naughty. He has heard a bigger boy say it, and he wants to copy the bigger boys. Just explain to him, quite quietly, that nice boys don't use words of that kind ; it isn't manly, or clever, or anything of the kind. If he argues : " Well, Bill Smith says it," you answer : " Bill Smith wouldn't if he were my son."

Good " Mixers "

MENTION has been made of children finding their own level at school. It is one of the most valuable things that schools teach, for a school is a miniature world, and in it a child learns to mix with others, as he will have to when he goes out into the world outside. These first years at school will give you a fairly good insight into how Tommy is likely to react to his surroundings later on in life.

Some children are naturally popular. They are " good mixers." They get on with others. This is a useful quality and should be encouraged. But if Tommy does not possess it, how are you going to develop it ? This is not an easy problem. The lack of the power to " mix " well may be inborn or acquired. The children of unsociable parents are often unsociable too, either by heredity or through following their example, and " only " children are frequently bad "mixers." In any case, you cannot force a child to be sociable, and it is difficult to persuade him. You can only encourage the quality in him by giving him every possible opportunity to play with plenty of other children.

Some boys and girls are " one-friend " children. Among their young acquaintances they find one particular friend whose tastes and ideas and ways are similar to their own, with whom they can play happily and contentedly for hours, and they practically ignore all others. In one way this is a good thing ; a deep, loyal, lasting spirit of friendship is a fine thing to foster. It is the spirit that makes a true-till-death husband. But it is not really, on the whole, a good thing for a child to be completely wrapped up in one playmate to the exclusion of all others : it is only one degree removed from absolute solitariness. A wider sociability is better for his character ; and if for any reason he should lose his one friend for a time, or altogether, he is going to be very unhappy.

But don't be in a hurry to try and change this trait in the child's character. Telling him not to be so wrapped up in Ted and to play with other friends as well, will probably only make him feel resentful, make him feel that you do not understand his need. And trying to introduce one or two other children into that exclusive game for two will probably only cause trouble. So be patient, and later on let Tommy join the Wolf Cubs or some similar organisation where team games and team work are strongly featured.

Leaders and Followers

IN school life as in the wider life of the world, there are leaders and followers : boys who seem born to command the others in games, in mischief and everything else, and boys who meekly follow where the others lead. To a certain extent this gift of leadership springs from a vivid imagination that visualises a game or a prank, an enthusiasm that infects others, and a resourcefulness that wins

D *

their admiration. But a child may possess all these qualities and yet not be the leader who keeps discipline without effort and whom the others obey instinctively. This latter is a type of character that will succeed in life, and will have the power to do much for his fellow men.

People used to believe that "leaders" were born, and that if a child was born a mere "follower" there was no help for it. But this is not so. A natural "follower" can sometimes be made a "leader" if he is taken in hand early enough and in the right way.

The main ingredient of leadership is self-confidence; faith in oneself and faith that what one is doing is the right thing and that one is doing it in the right way. Not many small children have this quality developed to any extent. When you consider how big the world that surrounds them, and the grown-ups that people it, must look to their eyes it is surprising that any of the little people have any confidence in themselves at all!

But it can be cultivated, and the best method is to let Tommy play now and again with children younger than himself, at some game at which he is more adept than they—brick-building, perhaps, or something else of a constructive kind. Soon he will be teaching the tinies, and finding that there are, after all, people in the world who know less than he does, who look up to him as a big, clever boy and not down on him as an infant.

After a course of this treatment you will find him holding his own with elder children, possibly taking command of those duller and less imaginative than himself. He may even become a "leader"—but don't be disappointed in him if he doesn't, for, after all, we can't all be leaders. There must be some followers. But at least you will have given your child confidence and faith in himself—a quality he will need in the life that lies ahead of him.

" Bossy " Boys

AS a contrast to the diffident, "follower" type of child, there is the aggressive, dominating kind who boasts and brags and "bosses" all the others who will let him. This kind of small boy is *not* the born leader; he is more often suffering from an inferiority complex and is trying to make up for it by an over-done self-assertion.

It is almost always other people's children who suffer from this obnoxious defect: we seldom recognise it in our own offspring! But if you should discover it, deal with it carefully. Merely repressing the small offender, "taking him down a peg or two" on every occasion, won't do: it will not cure the subconscious sense of inferiority that is the real root of the trouble, but will intensify it. He will probably become resentfully meek in your presence and unbearably assertive when away from it.

No. Praise him generously for the things he really does know and really can do; when he brags, say gently and with amusement—never in anger or irritation—"Of course, you don't really mean that, do you? We can't believe it, you know."

So far as his treatment of other children is concerned, the only thing is to try and insist on fair play. Explain that certainly he shall have his own way sometimes, but it is only fair that the other children shall sometimes have their own way, and he must give in to them in turn.

This subject naturally leads us to the question of training tinies in social behaviour. To a very great extent they teach one another to play fair, to give and take, not to be quarrelsome or selfish, better than any grown-ups can. The child who does not play the game according to the rules earns the logical punishment of unpopularity, as he will in adult life. It is only when Tommy comes crying to mummy because the others won't play with him that it is wise for her to step in and try to discover what his fault is. You can quite well ask the other children what Tommy has done to offend them, and then very gently, quite sympathetically, point out to him that he has brought his ostracism on himself, and show him how to win his way back into favour.

Manners for Tinies

BUT a mother can do a good deal in teaching a child to be a good host or hostess to little guests. This is not merely training for correct behaviour in later life; it encourages unselfishness, consideration for others, restraint, and other qualities that may be considered conventional but that do undoubtedly help towards popularity and successful social life.

Teach little Winnie, when her little friends come to the house, to look after them, help them off with their hats and coats and hang them up for them, to take them to wash their hands for meals, and so on. Teach her that she, as hostess, must allow her guests to play with her toys, must play the games they fancy, and that she must be polite to them and keep her temper with them. Teach her, too, to observe the same spirit of politeness and consideration when a guest in others' homes.

Of course, you will be faced with posers. Do you know the story of the rather pugnacious little boy who often quarrelled with another little fellow who was really his best friend ?

" Mummy," he complained, " you say I mustn't punch Ted in this house because he's my guest, and I mustn't punch him in *his* house because he's my host. But wait till I catch him in the road : I'll knock the stuffing out of him ! "

Never mind. You're inculcating into your tiny the right ideas for living, guiding him on lines that in after-life will make him liked, respected and — since character counts for so much in winning success—reasonably successful in life.

In the ways mentioned in this chapter you will be helping powerfully with your child's education, teaching him the things that he will not learn from his schoolteachers or his schoolfellows—things that in some ways are more important than book-learning. And if the advice sounds rather solemn and earnest, don't think that you need to spend all the time you have with him in carefully teaching him these " lessons," anxiously watching his behaviour and continually checking it, fussing and worrying over the development of his character. Good heavens, no ! You'll make both him and yourself wretched !

Let the little chap enjoy his childhood : he'll never have another. Enjoy these " little boy " days of his ; they'll never return. Let yourself love him all you want to, he needs every scrap of love he can get. Encourage him all you can ; encouragement to a child is like sunshine to a plant ; under it the mind and character open and develop in healthy, happy growth : discouragement and reproof are like icy winds nipping back the promising growth and making the child shrivel up within himself. Surround him with as much happiness and laughter as you can.

This character-training you have undertaken can usually be given painlessly and without tears ; the pill can be well coated with sugar.

But every now and again an occasion will arise in which you must be firm and talk seriously to the little chap. Don't shirk these occasions, but rise to them. After all, it's your job, and if you do it well, in after-life your son will thank you for shaping him into the kind of man he has grown to be.

When you leave Tommy at the school gate on his first day, you see him standing there forlorn, and you feel that you are deserting him and abandoning him.

CHAPTER XI

Health in the School Years

NOT all mothers realise what an exacting period in a child's life school days are. During those years, when the greatest physical and mental changes are slowly taking place, the youngster must be fit and able to undertake strenuous study and games in an atmosphere of keen competition. He has to face all weathers, and many children in country districts have to travel considerable distances by bus or bicycle twice or even four times a day.

Perhaps the greatest menace that all mothers of school children are up against is the exposure to infectious disease—those common ailments of childhood which invade most households sooner or later.

Because few children escape measles and chicken-pox once they start going to school, however, there is no need to take up a fatalistic attitude and leave these complaints to do their worst! The fitter your child is, the greater will be his resistance to disease germs, and even if he does catch the complaints he will not suffer from them so severely as a weakly youngster may.

In her campaign against illness and ill health, the mother of to-day has a most valuable ally in the school medical authorities. If the school doctor advises that Jack should have his tonsils removed, he is very likely to be right and Jack will probably have fewer colds next winter if you follow his advice.

None the less, the chief responsibility for the child's health rests with the mother, and her first care must be to guard her child from the particular dangers of each season of the year.

All-the-Year-Round Health

THE most critical season for most children is the spring. After the long struggle against our winter climate, the resistance is lowered and it needs a strong dose of sunshine to build it up again. Children also feel the strain of growth, and since we often get spells of very inclement weather in February, March, and April, they need the protection which well-chosen, nourishing food and suitable clothing will afford.

Milk and cereal foods, butter, sugar, fresh fruit, and green vegetables are needed in plenty. Cod-liver oil or halibut-liver oil is also valuable for the sake of the vitamins it contains.

In regard to clothing, don't let your children be too eager to " cast a clout " at the first spell of sunshine. There may be a treacherous cold wind. At the same time, as pointed out in a previous chapter, over-clothing is harmful and the chief thing is to distribute the warmth as evenly as possible, making sure that feet and legs are properly protected against wet as well as cold.

Finally, don't forget that fresh air is your greatest ally in the prevention of disease.

Most children love the summer, but hot weather brings its own dangers against which mother should be on her guard. If they come home from school pale and limp and irritable, their systems are being over-strained and they should be encouraged to take life a little more quietly.

When you send your children out to play in the sun, don't forget the risk of sunstroke, and insist that they keep the backs of their necks covered, as when they were tinies.

In hot weather none of us require heat-giving foods and therefore sugars, fats, and starches can be cut down. Make up the balance with fruit, salads, and milk (which should be very carefully kept cool and free from insects).

The approach of winter, though not a pleasant thought, has this consolation : After the long days of open air and sunshine that summer has meant for the children, their resistance to disease is at its highest, and you can preserve it by wise forethought.

First of all, have their winter underclothing ready in good time. A loosely woven woollen vest and pants or knickers make a good foundation, and good stout shoes and warm socks or stockings are a safeguard against chills.

Don't rely on heavy clothing to give the necessary body heat, however. The fats, sugars, and starches which were largely ruled out of the diet during the summer now come into their own. Porridge and milk, fat bacon, soups, and apple dumplings made with suet make excellent " fuel." The child who shows a tendency to chilblains and cold feet requires more calcium and this may be given in the form of calcium lactate powders or tablets. He also needs extra milk.

A child who has plenty of heat and energy-giving foods will always be ready for a stimulating game in the open air, and this is a tonic in itself. Let your children make the most of the sunny, frosty days, and only keep them at the fireside when the air is damp and full of fog.

On the opposite page you will find a diet sheet which will show you at a glance the general rules for school children's meals and also offers some valuable suggestions for menus. If you base the catering for your growing family upon this you cannot go far wrong.

DIET FOR THE SCHOOL CHILD

ONCE a child reaches school age he requires a great deal more food in proportion to his weight than he has needed hitherto. Not only is he using up a tremendous amount of energy that must be maintained, but also he is growing very rapidly and developing in every way. Providing his food is plain and wholesome, he should be allowed to eat until the appetite is satisfied.

The child should be called sufficiently early in the morning to leave time for a substantial breakfast and a regular visit to the lavatory before setting off for school.

A hot well-cooked supper is necessary for every child over eight years of age, but it should never be given at a late hour.

Here are some suitable menus :

ON WAKING.—The juice of an orange or tomato or half a grapefruit sweetened with sugar or glucose in a tumblerful of water.

BREAKFAST.—Cereal course. Porridge or any other cereal with milk and sugar. (Never satisfy the child's appetite with this course.)
Rasher of crisp bacon with tomatoes, or fried bread or potatoes browned under the grill, *or* a lightly boiled, poached, or scrambled egg *or* white fish *or* smoked haddock simmered in milk.
Toast or wholemeal bread-and-butter with marmalade.
Milky tea to drink at the end of the meal. All solids should be eaten first.

MID-MORNING.—Bottle of milk at school unless the child has any tendency to fat-dyspepsia or is in the habit of making a poor dinner. In that case it is much wiser to substitute an apple or a banana for the milk.

DINNER.—Small portion of broth or milk and vegetable soup. Fresh, lightly cooked meat, *or* lightly cooked liver, *or* rabbit or tripe with plenty of well-cooked green or root vegetables and potatoes.
Milk puddings with stewed fruit or a home-made fruit, treacle or lemon curd tart ; a batter pudding or a light suet pudding.
Water to drink.

TEA.—Sandwiches of brown bread-and-butter with either vegetable extract, lettuce, mustard and cress, sliced tomato, crushed banana, or cream cheese.
Rusks with honey or good jam.
Small piece of plain cake.
Milk or milky tea to drink.

SUPPER (for children of 8 years and over).
Macaroni or spaghetti with tomato sauce *or* a fresh herring *or* a little white fish or an egg dish.
Bread-and-butter or toast.
Cocoa made with half-milk and half-water or home-made lemonade.

NOTES

Boiled sweets or a piece of chocolate may be given at the end of meals (not between), after which the teeth should be well brushed. A quarter of an apple or a few sections of orange should be given after each meal to act as a natural tooth-brush.

Small doses of cod-liver oil emulsion or cod-liver oil and malt or a few drops of halibut-liver oil should be continued daily throughout the year except in the hottest weather.

Sleep

SLEEP is just as important to the growing schoolboy and girl as to the toddler. Children between six and fourteen need from ten to twelve hours' sound sleep in a quiet, airy bedroom every night. On no pretext should mother be wheedled into letting them stay up "just ten minutes longer."

Of course, the ideal arrangement is for each child to have a room to himself, but where this is impossible at least they should have separate beds placed as far apart as possible.

Bedclothes should be light and porous, and it is better to use three thin blankets than one thick heavy one, because between each of them there is a layer of warm air which holds in the heat, keeps the body at an even temperature, and prevents uncomfortable perspiration through lack of air reaching the skin. The fewer pillows the better ; one pillow with no bolster should be sufficient for the healthy child.

Except in very foggy weather, the window must be wide open.

If, in spite of all your care, one of the children falls ill, the following hints will help you :

Infectious Ailments and Other Childhood Troubles

Chickenpox. Since chickenpox is such a mild, childish ailment, mothers rarely suspect it, unless there is an epidemic of the disease in the school or neighbourhood. The little patients never feel really ill at any time during the infection, and doctors are not consulted about what appears to be merely an irritating rash, with no other serious signs.

Chickenpox is infectious from the moment the child begins to "sicken" for it, and you must consider it infectious until the last scab has fallen off. By "sickening for it," I mean that a child who is developing the germ in his system may be a little feverish, out-of-sorts, and crotchety for a day or so before the spots appear. But in mild cases there are no symptoms of illness at all before the rash comes out.

The spots of chickenpox are rounded or oval in shape, and the first crop always appears on the trunk of the body. Each spot goes through the same changes—from a red, raised pimple to a tiny, watery blister, which finally becomes discoloured and dries up into a scab.

One crop comes out after another, mostly on the trunk, face, head, upper arms and thighs. Take a peep inside a little patient's mouth and there also you will see the pimples. In a well-marked case, all stages of the rash can be found at one time, from the first red spot to the mark left by the scab.

The two main principles of treatment are : (1) Keep the child quiet ; and (2) keep him from scratching. The spots are extremely irritating, and little finger-nails can scarcely resist tearing at them to ease the itching. However, if you keep the little patient in bed, on a very light diet, and watch that the bowels are well opened daily, you will reduce the tendency to irritation a very great deal.

The spots themselves should be lightly powdered over with a dusting powder made of zinc oxide, starch, and boric acid. This is antiseptic and very soothing, and can be used plentifully and often. Keep the child's finger-nails short and clean, and so lessen any tendency for the spots to become septic through scratching.

Conjunctivitis ("Pink Eye").
This is an inflammation of the
delicate membrane which protects
the eyeballs, and is very infectious.
The first symptom is a sensation of
having particles of hot grit in the
eye. The following morning the
child wakes to find the eyelids
literally stuck together with dried
matter and after bathing has
enabled him to open them, his
eyes are very sensitive to light.

During an attack of conjunctivitis the best treatment is to drop
boric acid lotion (1 teaspoonful to a
pint of boiling water) into the eye-
sockets every hour. You should
press the eyelids well apart while
doing this and make the child move
the eyes all the time. While his
eyes are sore let him wear dark
glasses. Be **very** careful to keep
towels, etc. used by him away from
other members of the family.

Styes. A stye is an inflammation of the canal in which an
eyelash is held and is a sign either
of poor general health or of the need
for glasses. The young sufferer
should have his eyes tested. Local
treatment for the styes consists
of hot fomentations and the boracic
applications described for conjunctivitis.

German Measles. Children are
liable to catch this complaint in the
spring and early summer months.
It is the mildest of infectious
diseases, the two chief symptoms
being the rash itself and some
swelling of glands, mostly at the
back of the neck.

You may not be able to see these
enlarged glands, but if you gently
run your fingers down the back
of the child's neck, they can be felt
like chains of small shot, just under
the skin. This peculiar swelling of
the glands is quite marked for
several days before the rash
appears. A doctor, called in to a
case where he suspects German
measles, quickly diagnoses it when
he feels them. Other glands, such
as those under the chin, in the arm-
pit and the groin, also swell in
some cases, but they are never
tender unless they are pressed.

The rash appears first of all on the
brow and behind the ears, and it
quickly spreads all over the body,
arms, and legs. Within forty-eight
hours it has gone again, leaving no
trace behind it.

A German measles rash is a cross
between a scarlet-fever and an
ordinary measles rash in appearance—that is, the spots themselves
are small but not very closely set
together.

No child suffering from German
measles ever feels very ill, in spite
of the brilliant rash and no
troublesome complications need be
feared.

Beyond keeping your little patient
indoors until the rash has faded,
and seeing that his bowels are kept
open, you need not worry about
treatment.

Then there is the question of infection. Isolate the little patient
for one week after the rash has
appeared.

If you have reason to fear that
your children have been in contact
with a case of German measles, you
must wait until between twelve
and twenty-one days after exposure
to infection for the rash to appear.
The eighteenth day after exposure is
the commonest time for the rash to
show itself. If you have several
children in the family, it is useless
to isolate them when one develops
German measles. If the others are
going to develop it, they will have
caught it long before the first signs
of a rash in their unfortunate
brother or sister. In fact, German
measles is such a mild, harmless
complaint, that it is the *only* one

Early symptoms of measles can be mistaken for a violent cold, with continual sneezing, eyes and nose streaming, and a tendency to feverishness.

Startings are due to an irritable condition of the nervous system. They may amount to night terrors, the child starting up in fright, in fear of some unknown evil. The cause is often bad digestion.

in which you can safely be advised to " let all the children have it together and get it over ! "

Growing pains. Actually there are no such things as growing pains and when children complain of aching limbs they are really showing the first symptoms of rheumatism. Every care should be taken to check this unpleasant complaint in its early stages. The child's clothing should be warm but light. A loosely-knitted woollen vest should be worn next the skin, and a little girl should wear long, woollen stockings in winter. See that the shoes are roomy and strong, with good thick soles, and a change of shoes and stockings should always be provided on a wet day. Nightly bathing in salt water is very helpful. Add about a cupful of sea-salt, which can be bought in packets, to two quarts of hot water. Do not rinse afterwards, but dry with a rough towel.

If, after five or six weeks of this treatment, the child shows no improvement, the doctor should be consulted. He will probably prescribe a course of medicine containing some form of iodine.

Measles. The first symptoms of measles may be mistaken for a violent cough and cold—with eyes and nose streaming, continual sneezing, and a tendency to feverishness. This may last for several days. Then a thick rash comes out suddenly. The child goes to bed with quite a clear skin at night, and in the morning he is covered from head to toe with little raised spots. Some of these are crowded close together, but others leave patches of clear skin in between, which show up oddly against the bright red blotches.

Measles is an ailment which a child rarely escapes having at some time or other in his early years. But never treat measles lightly. No other complaint is so likely to be followed by severe troubles, such as bronchitis or pneumonia, if the little patient is neglected in the early stages. It is always safest to call in a doctor.

After two or three days the rash fades, the temperature falls, the cough and cold improve, and the child clamours to get up. Then comes the danger. It is just at this stage that bronchitis or pneumonia is liable to appear. Therefore, however well the little invalid may seem to be, always keep him in bed for a full week after the rash has appeared.

The principal part of the treatment is to keep him warm in bed, but at the same time to see that the room itself is airy and fresh. For a child who rather easily gets " chesty," make a light cotton-wool jacket.

Feed him on a light milk diet, and allow plenty of cooling drinks, such as water and lemonade, to quench the thirst. When the temperature is normal, more solid food can be given.

The eyes of a child suffering from measles require great care. They are so sensitive and inflamed during the first few days of illness that the bedroom is better kept almost dark. Bathe the eyes regularly every two hours with very weak boracic or glycerine and thymol lotion.

Isolate your little patient from other children for a fortnight. However slight the illness, the old idea of putting others deliberately in the way of catching measles, " to get them over," is a dangerous practice. A very slight attack in one child may develop very seriously in a little brother or sister.

Mumps. Children frequently develope swellings on the neck as the result of septic throats, sore places about the lips, nose, or chin, toothache or ulcerated mouths.

However, it is always wisest to consult a doctor about any suspicious swelling of the neck, unless you are quite sure in your own mind what is the matter.

The very first sign of mumps may be the conspicuous swelling which appears first on one side of the face and neck. After two or three days the other side also swells. Very often the child complains of earache, a sore throat, or he may feel a trifle shivery.

In a well-developed case of mumps, the two swellings get so enormous that they nearly meet under the chin. The worst discomfort occurs when he tries to open the mouth or to move the jaws. The swellings themselves are also very tender if they are handled. However, mumps is soon over, and in a week or ten days the face has shrunk to its ordinary size.

Much can be done in the way of simple home nursing to relieve the patient. Keep him in bed as long as there is any fever, and you need have no fear of complications. Swallowing is the one great difficulty, but if you feed him on thick liquids, such as gruel, milk porridge, and bread-and-milk, you will find that he readily gets his meals down.

For the pain in the neck, the best plan is to heat strips of dry flannel by the fire, or in the oven, and apply them like poultices. As soon as one gets cool, have another ready to replace it.

Sometimes, in addition to the local pain in the neck, a little girl with mumps may complain of pain in the stomach. This is due to swelling of the ovaries and, to relieve it, you must apply hot flannels wrung out of boiling water.

Little boys may get swelling of the testicles, in which case you should call in a doctor.

A child is not considered free from mumps until eight days after the disappearance of the swelling.

The complaint is spread by the nasal and throat secretions. If the sufferer sneezes, coughs or breathes into the face of a child who has never had mumps, then it is extremely " catching " to that child ; but it may be anything from a fortnight to a month before he begins to develop suspicious symptoms.

Nettle-rash. This tiresome trouble is an eruption of the skin, consisting of circular patches, accompanied by acute itching. Children are subject to it if they are being improperly fed, especially by excess of food. The rash usually appears suddenly, and may pass off in a few hours, or it may persist for a long time, coming and going without any apparent reason.

Treatment consists principally in discovering and avoiding the foods which have caused the trouble. A dose of salts should be given at the beginning of the attack. Magnesia mixture or cascara, or syrup of figs are the most suitable aperients. The itching can be dealt with by sponging with calamine lotion, or a lotion of half a teaspoonful of bi-carbonate of soda dissolved in a pint of water, or the child can be put into a warm bath to which has been added a teaspoonful of calamine powder stirred up in a cupful of water.

Scarlet Fever. The typical first symptoms of scarlet fever are a very sore throat, headache, high temperature, loss of appetite and sickness.

About two days after the rise of temperature the rash appears— first on the chest and later on other parts of the body. It appears as little red pin-points with small patches of clear skin in between.

The tongue is bright strawberry red at the tip and sides, with a white centre of thick fur.

After about four days the bright, scarlet flush which gives the disease the name of " scarlet fever " has died away from the chest, and only the remains of it can be seen on the arms and legs.

The doctor should be summoned as soon as the first symptoms appear. Only by the sore throat, the vomiting, the headache, the strawberry tongue and the rash can he diagnose scarlet fever. Remember that any child, untreated in the early stages, may already have developed serious consequences by the time the " peeling " makes you seek medical advice.

As a rule, a child with scarlet fever has been infected about four or five days before he begins to show any signs of it. Infection can be carried by a healthy person on the clothes, and even books and toys have been the source of an outbreak.

All cases of scarlet fever must be notified to the local Public Health Authority. Steps are then taken by them to see that the child is being properly isolated. If you have a small house, with other children in it, it is best for your little patient to be removed to an isolation hospital, there to be skilfully nursed back to health.

If you do keep a scarlet fever case at home, carry out thoroughly every order given you by your doctor, for much depends on careful nursing and attention.

The " peeling " of scarlet fever, to an inexperienced eye, is never so complete as most mothers expect. Some folk think that shreds of skin will fall off over all the body and limbs. This is not so. A very thin, powdery appearance is all that the chest or back shows. Only on the hands and feet does the average scarlet fever case " peel."

Tuberculosis. Mothers dread the very word tuberculosis or consumption, but since complete cures can so often be effected by timely treatment, it is important to know the chief sources of infection and the symptoms.

The disease may affect almost any part of the body and it may show itself in a failure to gain weight, a chronic cough, swollen glands, unaccountable fever or attacks of abdominal pain, or by pain or stiffness in a joint which cannot be otherwise explained. A mother who notices any of these symptoms in her child should consult a doctor immediately.

The chief sources of infection are contact with a consumptive person, and the taking of milk from tuberculous cows, or milk products made from it. That is why all who can afford it should buy Grade A, T.T. (tuberculin tested) milk.

Whooping cough. Whooping cough begins with just an ordinary cold, about a week or a fortnight after the child has picked up the germ.

The early cough of whooping cough is short and dry and very painful ; there is obviously difficulty before the child can cough up any phlegm. It may be only a few days, or it may be fully a fortnight after the cough has started, before the whoop is detected.

The child begins by giving ten or twenty rapid, short coughs. He is then forced to stop for breath, and the rapid filling of the lungs with air makes a strange crowing noise. This is caused by the blocking up of part of the bronchial tube by a tiny lump of phlegm. The process described is repeated several times, until at last a small round piece of yellow phlegm is coughed up. Another frequent ending to a typical whoop is for the child to vomit.

Children vary greatly in the severity with which they take whooping cough. Babies suffer most, and for this reason try to keep tiny toddlers and babies away from elder brothers or sisters who have contracted the complaint.

As long as there are no signs of feverishness, keep the little sufferer out of doors as much as possible, but alone, of course. Keep the bedroom warm and airy.

To get the piece of phlegm away as quickly as possible, make the child bend his head and chest well forward, whilst you support his forehead with your hand. Tiny children should be held literally upside-down.

Another important point in nursing whooping cough is that of meals. Give very light, nourishing food which can be easily digested. Lightly-cooked eggs, milk dishes, soups, and similar foods are best.

If a child has many attacks of whooping in a day, and brings up his food each time, feed the little one always about ten minutes after a whoop. In this way you will ensure that some, at least, of his food will have time to be digested.

Nervous Troubles

" Fidgets." Amongst young children, certain spasmodic movements of the muscles of the face or limbs are fairly common. The child has a habit of twitching his eyelids and making peculiar grimaces or spasmodic movements of the arms.

In nearly every case the child's general health is not very good. He may be out of sorts or growing too quickly, and sometimes he is of a nervous disposition. In no circumstances should the child be found fault with, as this simply increases his nervousness, and the habit becomes more marked. The best thing for such a child is to give him plenty of outdoor life, with simple diet and regular sleep. Heavy lessons should not be permitted, and every effort must be made to get the child into a good state of health. Physical culture exercises will do a great deal to counteract these spasmodic muscular movements.

" Fidgets " are often associated with adenoids, so that in every case the nose should be examined for any growths, which must, of course, be removed. Another common cause of spasms is defective eyesight, and sometimes all that is necessary is that the child should be fitted with glasses.

It is never wise to leave a child to " grow out " of this ailment without extra care and treatment, because the presence of any such condition indicates that the nervous and physical health is below par. A course of cod-liver oil should be given if the child shows such evidences of poor nutrition as excessive thinness, pallor, or lassitude. Simple, nourishing food is, of course, important.

Stammering is a spasmodic affection of the muscles that have to do with speech and breathing. It is most evident in pronouncing words commencing with such letters as B, D, P, T, K, or G. There are several varieties of the condition.

There may be difficulty in commencing to speak, or the stammer may be in the form of " syllable stumbling," in which one letter or syllable is constantly repeated before proceeding to the next. In severe cases the spasm may spread to other muscles of the face, with the result that the face is screwed up or the mouth kept open before any sound can be uttered.

The condition is in a sense a bad habit, but there is generally some nervous condition to account for it. Stammering is, however, infectious. A child will contract the habit from association with a friend who is given to stammering. Except in bad cases, stammering is not evident when singing or whispering. It is when the sound of the word is uttered in ordinary speech that the affection is noticed.

The child should be made to read aloud slowly, to recite verses, to sing. He should be given deep breathing exercises and taught to speak very slowly and distinctly, and stop whenever stammering begins. A sing-song method of speaking is a great help until better habits are acquired. In the case of nervous and delicate children attention to the general health must form part of the treatment.

Startings in sleep are due to some irritable condition of the nervous system. They may amount to night terrors, the child starting up in fright, in fear of some unknown evil. In many cases the cause is irritation of the central nervous system by bad digestion. Another cause is adenoids.

In every case the cause should be found out and dealt with. The child may require to be properly dieted, or he may need treatment for adenoids.

St. Vitus' Dance is a fairly common nervous disorder, which produces awkward spasmodic movements of the limbs and other nervous symptoms. The movements generally affect the muscles of the face and hands, but any group of muscles may be affected. True St. Vitus' dance, chorea, must be distinguished from mere " fidgets." It is far more serious, being associated with disease of the valves of the heart. It very often follows rheumatism or scarlet fever, but fright or sudden emotion may bring on an attack. It generally lasts a few months, and the important point is to watch for any evidences of heart disease or rheumatism. The child should be removed from school and treated by a doctor. A quiet life must form part of the treatment, and fresh air, moderate exercise out of doors, and plenty of sleep must be given.

Good management will help considerably to prevent a return of the trouble. As in the case of rheumatism, the child must be guarded from damp. The strain of too much work at school is certainly a factor in producing the disease. The bright, intelligent child, who is encouraged to apply himself too closely to lessons, is only too apt to break down with an attack of St. Vitus'. Early symptoms of the condition, such as restlessness, emotional disturbances, night terrors, headache, should receive every attention. When they occur in children of a neurotic family, mental and bodily quiet must be ordered, and the child should be kept lying down in bed. These measures are often sufficient without medicines.

CHAPTER XII

Schoolboys and Schoolgirls

AS your children grow out of the "tiny" stage into real boys and girls, you will find their characters developing and strengthening. The traits they revealed as little ones will persist —though perhaps modified by your early training—and they may surprise you by suddenly exhibiting some characteristic you had not known they possessed. But don't be mistaken; it was there all the time, but the conditions surroundthe child hadn't brought it into play. Whatever it may be, it demands your attention; your care in developing or restraining, guiding and shaping it.

The time has come for you to alter a little your methods in bringing up your children. You must still maintain discipline in the home, you must still demand obedience—but no longer the blind, unquestioning obedience of early childhood. "Mummy knows best" is still true, but "because mummy says so" is no longer good enough.

The child is now a thinking, reasoning being and his instinct is to challenge commands and prohibitions. His mind wants to know the "how" and "why" of everything he encounters, and the matter of obedience is included. And can you in fairness deny him the right to know your reason for insisting upon this or that? (Actually "she" would be a better word to use than "he", for little boys are usually fairly amenable; it is more often the girls who are born rebels and "don't see why" they should do as they're told.)

There are parents who argue that it is better for a child to be taught to obey implicitly and without question.

"Suppose," they say, "your child is in danger; is, say, stepping into the road in front of a car. You call out, ' Tommy, come here ! ' If he has been taught to obey promptly, he will respond instinctively ; if he has been encouraged to question whys and wherefores, he will hesitate—and be run over."

That argument is plausible, but not convincing. To begin with, the child who is treated as a reasoning being is less likely to put himself into a position of danger than the one who acts blindly as told. And don't you think that if Tommy has learnt by experience that when Mummy says " do this " or " don't do that " she has a good reason, his mind, which is better than his instinct, will prompt him to obey ?

So when you command or forbid, give a reason ; say " Tommy, if you're going in that wet grass, put on your gum boots, or you'll catch a bad cold and be a perfect nuisance to yourself and me too."

Tommy Wonders Why

IF you don't give reasons in this way, the children will want to know them. They may ask you, and it will sound rather like impudent rebellion, though it may not be meant in that way. Or they may ask themselves, and not be able to find the answer. Tommy may be tempted to disobey because your demand seems to him unreasonable.

He has, you see, reached the age when he thinks things out for himself. Don't discourage this. It is exactly what you will want him to do, if you are wise and far-seeing. So treat him as a reasonable being, make him understand your perfectly good reason for commanding this or forbidding that. If he disobeys and suffers the natural consequences, there's no harm in saying " I told

you so. I knew best, you see." But don't rub it in too hard.

There are times when you can leave the decision to him, when you can say : " Do as you please, and take the consequences " and let let him learn his own lesson. But never do this in matters of any importance, such as things that may affect his health, and don't do it often. After all, he can't visualise consequences as you can ; he looks to your experience and judgment to guide him ; he may jib at the rein now and again, but he likes to feel it is there, holding him up from stumbling. So don't let him down.

But don't label your children " naughty " if they are not always obedient, even to your explained orders. The child who never disobeys has a vein of weakness or meekness in his character ; the little rebel has at least a will of his own. You want your children to be live, individual personalities, not human jellyfish. Even when a child deliberately decides to do something you have forbidden, and take the consequences—well, he has made a decision for himself, and you want him to be able to make his own decisions and stand by them. There are too many people in the world who don't know their own minds.

Think of their other failings in this way. A philosopher once said : " Vices are virtues run to seed." Your children's faults are not so much bad qualities as good ones that are going astray though excessive development, or through being expressed in the wrong way.

The boastful, aggressive child needs " taking down a peg or two," but, at any rate, he has plenty of self-esteem, and that is a necessary quality in a world that takes a person at his own valuation. The man who has no self-confidence, however clever he may be, finds it difficult to inspire others to have confidence in him.

It is unpleasant to have to admit that one's own child is greedy and selfish, yet these undesirable qualities are only an overgrowth of an acquisitive instinct that is needed in the battle of life. The too-generous child, who gives away his possessions and is always ready to give in to others, is charming—but is not likely to make much headway in the world.

It is very little use *forcing* a selfish child to give to others. He will only resent it, and obey under protest, clinging more tightly than ever to his possessions when you are absent.

The better plan is frequently to praise the generosity and unselfishness of other children before him—not too pointedly or in their presence, or he will merely be resentful—but quite casually. When possible, demonstrate that those who give, receive gifts in return. Let the child see that you and daddy enjoy giving to each other, and giving in to each other.

In this way—and helped by the experience he will undoubtedly have, that selfishness does not make him popular among his small friends—he will little by little become less greedy. It will be a slow process but a sure one.

Then there is the " grousing," discontented child. He's a trial, and has to be taught not to cry for the moon—but after all, the child who is content with what he has and never asks for anything better may grow up into a placidly happy man, but not into one who gets on in life.

Be patient with all your child's over-developed tendencies and restrain and direct them quietly but persistently. If you can, find out their cause. Some, as has been said before, are inborn and can never be eradicated, others are acquired for some reason or other.

Naughtiness and Nerves

THE reason may be physical ; one of health.

Such defects as bad sight, bad teeth, slight curvature and other definite disabilities that adversely affect the development of a schoolchild's character and his capacity for being educated, will almost certainly have been discovered at the school medical examination, and you will have been advised to take steps to remedy them. But there are other physical causes, less easy to discover, that may be poisoning the child's nature and clogging his brain.

The boy who is " lazy " and inattentive at school and sullen at home may be suffering from malnutrition—not lack of food, but lack of the right kind of food for him—for the proverb about one man's meat being another man's poison is very true of children's diet. Study the information in the diet chart given you in Chapter XI. Or he may be subject to constipation : it is not so easy for mother to be sure that a schoolchild's digestion is functioning regularly as it was when he was a tiny.

He may be sleeping badly, and actually be needing more rest. The fact that he may have plenty of energy for play does not rule out either of these physical causes : running about in the open air is one thing : sitting still at a desk in a warm schoolroom, trying to concentrate on lessons, is quite another. Whatever the cause, a

Little boys are usually fairly amenable. It is more often the girls who are born rebels and don't see why they should do as they are told.

The girl up to twelve or so is physically quite as strong as her brother. The girl who would once have been called a tomboy is nowadays regarded as healthy and normal. She often beats the boys at their own games and is all the better for it, for she learns the lessons of sportsmanship and fair play that boys' games teach.

child who is half-asleep during school hours is not only wasting valuable time and opportunity, but will become disheartened by his inability to cope with his work, and by being accused of laziness, and will acquire an inferiority complex.

Lack of proper sleep, malnutrition, and anæmia may affect a child in an almost opposite way; they may make him nervy, irritable and restless.

It is a sad fact that our natures are very much at the mercy of our bodies. We know, of course, of chronic invalids who are astonishingly sweet-natured and bear their sufferings with patience and fortitude, but these are the notable exceptions. As a general rule, a disordered liver, a weak digestion or a bloodstream poisoned by some such ailment as pyorrhoea will in course of time warp a naturally sweet disposition and sour a happy and confident outlook on life. Give your children's characters a chance to express themselves by removing all the physical hindrances you can.

Mistakes Mothers Make

SOMETIMES the cause of a regrettable trait lies, not in the inherent nature of the child, or in his health, but in some mistake the parents have made in his early training.

Many a mother is hurt to find that her child is secretive, that he never talks to her about his doings, and seems to resent any interest she takes in them. Depend upon it, this is your own fault, for any normal small child is frankly confiding, anxious to chatter about his little doings and projects. Perhaps, unintentionally, unknowingly, you snubbed him when he was a tiny, made remarks about his doings that wounded his sensitive little soul. Children of this type are always very "touchy" and deeply hurt by what seems to them a slighting remark about their play, or by mother being too busy to listen to them when they are eager to confide their ideas to her.

Come off Your Perch

AT all costs you must win back his trust. Don't try to force his confidence by asking what he is doing, or what the article he is constructing is meant to be. However kind your tone, he will shrink back into his shell. But remark brightly and casually: "That looks nice, dear," or: "Aren't you a clever little lad?" —even when you don't understand in the least what his play is meant to represent.

He will respond to this—perhaps not at first, but later—and oh, how gladly and eagerly he will pour out to you all the ideas and imaginings in his busy little brain. Listen to them all, mother; listen though the milk boils over and the household time-table goes completely astray, for this is an opportunity that you must seize, or you will regret it all your life. Miss it, and it may never come again, to your future sorrow and your son's.

If you suffer from the old-fashioned idea that it is beneath a parent's dignity to try to win a child's confidence, that you should demand it as a right and the child give it as a duty—forget it! You have no right to sonny's confidence unless you deserve it, and if you have lost it, it is for you to win it back, for it is too precious to lose. Don't be afraid of losing your dignity ; you won't. But if you refuse to come down off your perch, you run a risk of losing a good deal of your child's love. Which is worth more to you ?

But if you never quite succeed in curing sonny of the reticence he has acquired, don't despair about it. At least he will not grow up to be the kind of man who babbles everything that comes into his head and can't keep his mouth shut when he should.

Mention has already been made of a child's fears, of physical cowardice. More serious, and even more difficult a problem is the moral coward, the child who lies or deceives in an attempt to escape punishment.

It is not too much to say that the child is not to blame for this. He wasn't born like it. Through some mistaken treatment when he was naughty once, he has become afraid of someone—of his parents, if the incident happened at home, of his school teacher if it occurred at school—and his poor, scared lie is the grown-up's fault. Anger at his adding a lie to his original offence will only make him worse ; more frightened than ever, he will persist with the wild, pitiful stubbornness of desperation that he is telling the truth.

The only possible course is to talk to him gravely but gently, pointing out how cowardly it is to deny his wrong-doing in an attempt to escape the punishment he deserves, and explain that this grieves you far more than mere disobedience. Let him see that you are not angry so much as hurt and disappointed in him, that he is falling in your esteem. Unless he is a downright callous little boy —and these are scarce—he will melt, burst into tears, confess his faults, and plead for forgiveness.

Be gentle with him ; explain to him that a boy who has been disobedient should take his punishment like a man. Let him feel that your punishments will not be excessive or unjust ; and by degrees you will drive that feeling of fear out of his poor, scared little heart.

Some faults in children's characters seem quite intractable ; nothing you can say or do seems to have much influence upon them. In these cases console yourself with the thought that many failings inevitably go with other very desirable qualities.

The untidy, happy-go-lucky child is an example. If he hasn't a methodical mind, nothing you can do will give him one. You can make him a little tidier, but not much. But remember that almost always this very fault goes with a very lovable disposition, generous, tolerant, self-sacrificing and affectionate, and often with a talented mind. The very prim, fastidious child—more often a girl than a boy —has seldom so charming a nature.

Brother and Sister

WHEN there are two or more children in a family, one of mother's tasks will be to keep the peace between them. You must expect them to squabble frequently ; they would scarcely be human if they didn't.

You may have in your mind a picture of a saintly little brother and sister who are inseparable chums, always affectionate toward each other, sharing each other's toys and amusements and interests, the boy chivalrous and protective towards the girl, the girl devotedly worshipping the boy. It's a pretty picture, but it is not in the least likely to come true. And if it did

An eldest brother of a family usually remains all his life a good deal of a hero to the younger ones. But an eldest sister who has been put in charge of the others often becomes a petty tyrant whom the others grow up to dislike.

—it would be a little sugary, wouldn't it ?

As tinies, a little boy and girl will play together very happily, but as they grow older, different sex temperaments will make themselves felt. This may not be as marked nowadays as it was in previous generations : the old notion of woman being the weaker sex is in many respects no longer true.

Certainly the girl up to twelve or so is physically quite as strong as her brother, able to play most of the active games that he does and enjoy them. The girl whom our grandmothers would have frowned upon as a tomboy is nowadays regarded as naturally, healthily normal ; she runs and jumps and climbs and swims with her brothers, and often beats them at their own games. And she is all the better for it, not only physically but morally, for she learns the lessons of sportsmanship and fair play that boys' games teach.

Nevertheless, when a fellow goes to school and mixes with other boys, he acquires the undying tradition of contempt for girls. His sister may be a demon bowler and a hurricane batsman, but he will refuse to admit that she is really his equal. Even if a little girl, fired by the example of a big brother, shows a decided bent for mechanical and constructive toys, he will only look at her as a promising pupil, no more.

And she with her school friends will regard her brother and his friends as rough, untidy creatures, useful on occasion, but not really civilised or suitable for polite society !

When brother and sister play together, it will probably be a little shamefacedly, probably with protests to the outside world that it is only because there are no other playmates available. And ten to one they will squabble with each other as they never would with outside friends. And often a boy will almost neglect his brother, or a girl her sister, for school friends.

Home Truths

DON'T let this distress you. It is perfectly natural. Brothers and sisters know each other so well, you see. They've known each other all their lives and there's no novelty about them. Also, there is a subconscious undercurrent of —not exactly jealousy, but of competition for their parents' notice and attention. This keeps them slightly on the defensive against each other, ready to " score off " each other when opportunity offers. This expresses itself in gibes and sneers and occasionally blows, but it really means very little.

Tommy will call Winnie a " mutt." He will jeer at her efforts at painting, or at best tell her that it is " not so bad, for a kid." Some odd kink in human nature will prevent him from praising it to her face. But to his schoolmates he will brag about his sister's painting as if she were a born genius, and if any other boy should dare to call Winnie a mutt, Tommy will be ready to knock his head off.

Winnie will probably call Tommy a clumsy bully—but the tone in which she will speak to other girls of " my brother " will be one almost of hero-worship. Against a common enemy the two will unite in an unshakable loyalty.

Often this very loyalty gives rise to quarrels, when Tommy feels that Winnie is in some way " letting the family down " and tells her so. Really, this is all to the good.

Candid criticism is good for all of us, but we don't always get it from our friends—or if we do we suspect them of spite or jealousy—or from our parents—or if we do we regard it as the "interference" of old-fashioned people who "don't understand." But when brother Tom tells sister Winnie that she's making a little ass of herself, she knows that there is no question of spite or jealousy or lack of understanding; his disapproval is honest and well meant and probably justified. She will probably dislike being "taken down a peg or two," but Tom's remark will do her all the good in the world.

So don't expect your children to behave to each other like a couple of sugar saints; don't be distressed if they squabble and slang each other in moderation.

Of course, constant petty bickering is bad: it's exceedingly irritating to the parents who hear it, and not a good sign. Yet how to keep the peace? That's one of the most difficult problems of parenthood.

The logical thing, no doubt, is to hold a court of inquiry, discover who began the quarrel, and punish the culprit. Oh, yes! And you will almost certainly find they are equally to blame. Winnie teased Tommy beyond the point of endurance, and Tommy lost his temper and smacked her, good and hard. There is only one thing to do. Separate them. Send Tommy up to his bedroom, and Winnie up to hers, to simmer down: tell them you will not allow them to play together until they can do so without squabbling. In about ten minutes two tearful, repentant little people will be begging forgiveness from you and each other and promising they will never quarrel again. And they won't—till next time !

Don't make too much of these incidents: they're a trying but inevitable part of family life. But seize the opportunity of giving Tommy a little homily on keeping his temper, on being patient and long-suffering with those younger than himself—especially girls, who can't stand up to him as boys can. And give Winnie a similar talk on playing the game, on not taking advantage of the fact that she is a girl and so immune from the punch on the nose she would certainly have received had she been a boy.

" Sneaking "

HEAVEN help you if little Winnie comes running to you forty times a day bleating that Tommy has pinched her, or cut the hair off her doll, or something else. It is not a thing to encourage, and yet the child looks to you for justice and protection. If her complaints are justified, you cannot allow that kind of thing to go on. What are you going to do about it? As before, investigate the complaint, give the culprit—or both of them—a little lecture, and separate them for a while.

Rather different is "sneaking," when Winnie joyously runs to tell you that Tommy has upset the milk, or is playing with matches and is about to set the house on fire. You may be grateful for the information, but you can't approve of your small daughter's motives in giving it to you: ten to one she is only doing it to be in favour with you, to make herself seem, in your eyes, a better behaved child than her brother.

The only thing is to ignore the tale if you can. Say coldly, "Thank you. I shall find that out for myself," and so discourage sneaking. But you will have to take steps to " find out for yourself " so that the offender does not get away with it scot free. Try to behave, however, as you would if there had been no small sister to give young Tommy away.

It is in some ways easier, in others more difficult, when one child is three or four years older than the other. They will play together less, they will squabble less, but on the other hand you will be very tempted to put the younger one in charge of the older, to make the elder more or less responsible for the younger one's behaviour. It is convenient for you, and up to a point it is good for, at any rate, the elder child. It teaches him, or her, responsibility and control of others.

Elder Children in Charge

BUT there is a risk that Tommy will either resent being held responsible for little Winnie, over whom he has no real authority, or that he will bully and dominate her.

This latter is not good for Winnie, for it may either turn her into a human doormat or fill her with a smouldering resentment against her big brother that will last all her life. And it is still worse for Tommy. He will acquire an exaggerated idea of his own importance and will try to " boss " and dominate everyone with whom he comes into contact. Many a promising character has been spoilt by being given authority of this kind too young.

Curiously enough, it happens more often in the case of girls than of boys. An eldest brother of a family usually remains all his life a good deal of a hero to the younger ones ; an eldest sister who has been put in charge of the others often becomes a petty tyrant whom the others grow up almost to dislike. Sometimes, if she never marries, she becomes that objectionable type of grown-up daughter-at-home who bullies her ageing parents.

A Child's-eye View

SO much for the children's behaviour towards each other : there still remains their attitude towards yourself and their father.

When they were tinies, they thought you wonderful ; in their eyes you could scarcely do wrong : if you seemed to fail them, they felt it was their fault rather than yours. Now they are beginning to find out the truth about you ; they know you are not perfect ; they are beginning to criticise you. How well can you stand up to their criticism ? What do they ask of you ?

First of all, they ask you to love them, and to show your love. Mothers are busy people, fathers often are late home from work in the evenings and preoccupied with other interests at the week-ends. But however busy you may be, spare time now and again for a kiss and a caress, and never, never rebuff with a " don't bother me just now " a child who comes to kiss you.

Secondly, they expect you to be just and consistent. If you forbid a thing on one occasion and allow it on another, if you permit one of them to do a thing and forbid the other, they don't know where they are with you.

They expect you to play fair. They don't expect the same standard of behaviour to apply to themselves and to you in all things. They quite understand that " it's

If you answer your little one's questions saying "Ask daddy", he may see daddy as someone who knows everything until he asks something daddy doesn't know. It can be a crushing disillusion.

different for grown-ups." But in some things they expect you to do as you'd be done by. If you, father, borrow young Tom's fret-saw without his permission, you've no right to complain if he helps himself to your screws without asking.

And never be tempted to be funny at young Tom's expense. That's taking an unfair advantage, for he can't retaliate, and he will resent your not playing the game.

Thirdly, they look to you to help them, to listen to their childish confidences, to take an interest in their doings, to give them praise and encouragement when they deserve it—even if they only deserve it for trying—and to advise them where they have failed, and to answer their questions.

There are times when you really are too busy; you cannot be at a child's beck and call every moment of the day. But don't rebuff the poor child; don't be irritable. Just say sympathetically: " Darling, I'm too busy just now, but I'll come and look at your sand castle, or answer your question, when I've finished what I'm doing." And *don't forget*—because he may be too proud to remind you, and he'll reproach you later, either to your face or in his mind; he will feel you've failed him.

Parents on Pedestals

AS for children's questions—well' of course, they're a standing joke. The little people ask so many, and so often they're quite un-answerable. But never dismiss a child's question as " silly " or you'll wound his feelings deeply—unless, as occasionally happens, he really *is* asking meaningless ques-tions, teasing you through a per-verted sense of humour. But you can usually tell this.

Of course, the little ones will ask you all sorts of questions you can't answer, and it's a great temptation to say: " Oh, ask daddy when he comes home." This is really rather hard lines on daddy, unless he is likely to know the answer, and it gives him a good deal to live up to. The children will regard him as a wonderful being who knows everything—until the time comes when he has to admit that there are things he doesn't know. And that is really a rather momentous incident in the family life, when daddy has to step down off his pedestal. It may mean a crushing disillusion for the child who has idolised his daddy.

The solution, father, is to see that your pedestal is not too high. You want the children to think of you as a wonderful being; it's very flattering; and it is quite right that they should do so, even if you don't altogether deserve it. To begin with, they'll put you on a pedestal, in spite of yourself. Do your best to be worthy of it, but don't build it any higher than they have done, then you won't have so far to fall.

If Tommy asks a question you can't answer, don't pretend you know, however tempted you may be to keep his good opinion of you by false pretences. Say quite frankly, " I'm sorry, old chap, but I don't know." But if you can find out; if you've a book of reference in the house that may hold the answer, add : " Let's see if we can find out," and together you hunt for the required information. In this way you will be teaching him to find facts himself—and don't think you'll lose " face," because he will still think it clever if you know where to find the answer to his question.

And while on this matter of pedestals, when you've made a mistake don't be afraid to admit it. You may think this is lowering yourself in the child's eyes, but it is nothing of the kind. He will admire you all the more for it; if he is a sensitive child, he will be quite embarrassingly overcome by your magnanimity.

What else have our children a right to ask of us?

They ask us to have dignity. They like us to be a " pal," to play their games and enter into their interests, to be someone in whom they can confide without fear—but not to try to become one of themselves. They want to respect us, and if we do anything that weakens their respect we are letting them down. Especially before other children you must remain, however good a " sport " you are, someone who enforces discipline firmly and whose decisions are accepted without argument, someone who won't put up with impudence or unfair play.

They expect you to be reasonable, to see their point of view as well as your own, without permitting argument over your commands. Above all, they will admire in you qualities that they know they lack.

They know they have very little restraint, that they give way to feelings of temper, fear, hastiness, jealousy and envy. If they see you always balanced and restrained, impartial in your judgments, a good loser at games and a generous winner, playing for the sake of the game and not out to win at all costs, they will admire you immensely, and will try hard to follow the example you set.

Of course, father, while the children are young, you won't see much of them except at the week-ends. Only then will you have much opportunity to play with them, talk with them, and learn their ways and their ideas. You have your own interests at the week-ends—but make the most of your chances to learn about your children. Only in this way will you understand when, later on in life, they bring to you problems that really matter, and trust you to be able to solve them.

Pocket Money

THE question of pocket-money becomes a serious one at the school age. It is your only way of giving the children first lessons in the value and management of money.

Don't make the mistake of giving them odd pennies when they ask for them—if you can spare them, and refusing if you can't. Let each child have a definite sum each week, and teach him to make that do—except of course on special occasions like an outing. Encourage them to buy wisely and to save some, at least, of their money to buy some definite thing they want and that costs more than a week's pocket-money.

But on the other hand, don't interfere too much with their spending. To you, they may seem to squander their money on sheer rubbish, but if the thing they buy gives them the pleasure they expected, if it fulfils the purpose for which they bought it, can you honestly say it was rubbish or a waste of money? What more could your own purchases do for you?

When Tommy proposes to make a really bad bargain, the best attitude is : " I wouldn't buy that,

PLATE 9

HAPPILY TO SCHOOL

M O S T children are happy at school nowadays. School life is so much better in every way than it was a generation ago. But it can be made happier still if mother makes friends with the teacher. Together they may solve problems about the child's character that would baffle each of them separately. Some of the troubles of early schooldays are dealt with in Chapter X.

PLATE 10

HAPPY AND BUSY

TOYS that teach are worth more than those that are merely playthings to pass the time. Even for tinies there are toys that exercise little fingers and eyes and brains, yet are thoroughly enjoyed. For bigger children there are things that encourage the creative instinct, constructional toys for boys, household ones for girls. See Chapter VIII.

PLATE II

THE HEIGHT OF HAPPINESS IS FOUND IN HOMES WHERE LOVE AND PEACE ABOUND

PLATE 12

GROWING UP

IN a few short years the tiny toddler grows into the strapping schoolboy on the threshold of manhood. Adolescence is a trying time, when boys and girls are stirred and made restless by urges they do not understand. Encourage them at this time to find an outlet for their energy in sports and games and creative hobbies. There is much sound advice on the subject in Chapter XVI.

old chap : I think you'll be disappointed in it." If Tommy persists and the article does not come up to expectations, he will have learnt a lesson for himself, worth more than all your advice. And you can rub it in just a little by remarking casually : " You hardly got your money's worth, did you ? I should think twice before I bought anything like that again."

Of course, some children are born with a money sense and some are not ; some buy wisely and save easily, some squander and fritter away their pennies. Being cross with them for foolish spending is little use ; they must buy their own experience. When Tommy realises that he has wasted a week's pocket-money on some trumpery trifle and that he is penniless till next week in consequence, it's a better lesson than all the lectures on thrift you could give him.

More than ever, during schooldays, must both mother and father set the children a good example in the way they treat each other. Mother, not only tell the children that their daddy is a fine man, but show them by your manner towards him how much you love and admire him and respect his rights and his wishes. Father, let the children see that you think mummy the most wonderful woman in the world, someone to be loved and cared for, protected and helped in every possible way. They will respond eagerly, and so you will have a united family and a home that, however poor it may be, is full of love and happiness.

CHAPTER XIII

Married Life in the Thirties

IF you married fairly young, by the time you reach the thirties there will not be very much left for you to discover about each other. You will have got over those little attacks of " marriage measles " which are often so amusing to look back on, and you will probably know just what to expect from each other.

Now this state of affairs can be ideal, but it can also be a very big danger signal, so pause a minute and see which it is for you!

The first thing to take into consideration is the fact that love and life never stay completely still, and human nature will revolt against sameness if it continues day after day. The life-blood of marriage is its little adventures and surprises.

In many cases, unhappily, the couple fail to realise this, and they plod on in the same groove, year after year, earning a living, bring-

ing up the children, and exchanging matter-of-fact kisses that have lost all flavour of romance. If a pang of regret ever crosses their minds, they console themselves with the thought: " Oh, well, we've been married a long time. You can't expect to be newlyweds all your life, and, after a while, solid companionship must take the place of romance." And they leave it at that.

Now the great point to notice is this : When such a transformation takes place, and neither of you notices it, but both feel perfectly happy, the state of affairs is ideal —but when there is need to explain away the situation to yourselves and each other, then something is missing, and danger is at hand. You are taking each other and life and love for granted—and the novelty has worn off.

What are you going to do about it ?

No self-respecting wife would think of neglecting her home, and you, her husband, would be amazed if anyone suggested that you were slack at work, wouldn't you? Well, it is every bit as important that you should both take care of your love, polishing it with a little touch of romance now and again that not only brightens its appearance, but strengthens its endurance, too.

Husbands, do remember that, in the thirties particularly, a woman needs you to be her lover as well as her husband. The first flush of her youth has gone, leaving behind it a woman instead of a girl—a woman with a family and a home to occupy her attention, with responsibilities and duties—in fact, everything about her may have grown up, except her heart; and that is as young as ever. She likes to hold your hand at the Pictures, and to get a surprise kiss now and again—she wants to hear how much you love her. Yes, of course she knows it, just as she did in those early days, but why should you think it is any less necessary to tell her so now than it was then?

Keeping Love Alive

DO all you can to keep love alive. No matter how bright and warm a fire may be, it needs attention, doesn't it? So does the fire of love. Don't let work or worries always take the first place in your consideration, with the wife as a pleasant background. She will understand the importance of your work and be willing to take a back seat sometimes—she will share your worries, too, of course—but do make a point of *telling* her how much she means to you, and remember that, if you want her to provide the romance in your everyday life, you must let her know she is succeeding.

Remember that she loves you, and she proves it every day in a hundred-and-one different ways. Your slippers warming by the fire, your favourite meals, an odd packet of smokes now and again, the way she runs to meet you and waves you off to work—what are these but outward expressions of her inner love for you? She might let herself get too busy to wave you off or to meet you, she might choose her own favourite food instead of yours, and she might spend her pocket-money on sweets for herself instead of buying you smokes. But she doesn't, does she?

And what about you? When she has been out do you put *her* slippers to warm? Do you make her welcome when she returns, or do you casually greet her and then go on reading the paper?

Just take a good look at yourself and see if there isn't room for improvement. You'll find there is a good deal more fun and happiness in life if you can remain her sweetheart—and she yours—until the very end.

It is not necessary to have a lot of money to spend, or to enjoy one round of pleasure after another, to avoid monotony. All you need is a lot of love and a great deal of thought for each other's comfort and happiness, together with a few surprises now and again, a determination never to take love for granted, and the thrill of hearing often—not just knowing—that you are making each other the happiest people in the world.

Yet sometimes it is difficult to save a marriage from that sense of boredom which is apt to creep in because nothing seems to have gone wrong that could be put right;

You may be happy
enough together with
just a feeling that life
itself is rather flat. Try
to take a honeymoon
holiday together – or a
trip to the scene of some
tender memory; the
bluebell wood where
hubby proposed, or the
park where you had
your first picnic.

the couple just don't seem to agree any more; they don't want the same things at the same time. Down underneath it all, they know they still love each other, but the romance has all gone, and they are feeling a little bewildered.

If this happens to you why not try spending a short time apart? "But," you are probably saying already, "we have never been parted in the whole of our married life." Then perhaps it is time you tried the experience. Persuade hubby to go home to his people for a week-end's holiday, or take the children away somewhere yourself. It need only be for one or two nights. You will each have the chance of seeing what life is like without each other, without those little habits of each other's that have become so irritating. You will get a rest and will come together again refreshed and happy, longing for the chance to make up for the recent past, with new topics of conversation, and a fresh interest in each other. You will have had time to think, time to long for each other, and to miss each other. Life will seem better just because you are together again—and no doubt you will find the experiment well worth while.

Or perhaps you are in need of another "honeymoon." You may be happy enough together with just a feeling that life itself is rather flat. Then don't sit down and wait for something to happen. Take the bull by the horns and see that something *does* happen. Try and take a "honeymoon" holiday together—or a trip to the scene of some tender memory: the blue-bell wood where hubby proposed to you, or the sandy beach where you met; the park where you had your first picnic. Who could possibly feel that life is drab in the presence of so much beauty and so many happy associations?

Women are romantic creatures. They love flowers and pretty little compliments, wonderful scenery and moonlight strolls. And romance in itself usually costs practically nothing in actual hard cash, so it is a poor husband who fails to provide it in one way or another.

Don't Grow Dull

MEN need change, excitement and freshness, too, for most of them are adventure-loving. So it is equally true to say she is a poor wife who cannot provide these things for her man.

If you are the type of wife who leaves everything to her husband to decide—where you shall go for your holidays, and what you will grow in the garden this year, for instance—turn over a new leaf, and surprise him by making a few suggestions of your own. He will be pleasantly surprised to discover that there is a side of your nature that he does not know quite so well as he imagined he did.

If you always go to visit the old folk on Wednesdays, change the day occasionally, so that you do not get into a rut—spend the evening with hubby, and jolt him out of the feeling he may have that he knows what you are going to do and say next!

There are so many possibilities in life, so much to be had for just a little thought—so many changes one can ring, and adventures one can meet right inside one's own front door—that no marriage need go stale if the partners have a spark of individuality in them.

Perhaps he has said he likes you in blue? But that does not mean that he *always* wants you to wear it, for then he comes to take it for granted, and to forget to remark that it matches your eyes or reminds him of the first time you met.

In the thirties, building for the future cretainly takes a lot of a husband's time, and caring for the kiddies occupies the wife's attention —but never lose sight of the fact that this is your life, and that each of you is all the other has to provide romance and happiness, so the more you can fill it the happier you will be—still a fine example of what married happiness can mean, both to your growing kiddies and to your single friends who are eagerly watching to see if, after all, marriage is all that it is cracked up to be !

Hubby's Hobbies—and Yours

AS the years go on, both the husband's and the wife's interests should widen out. Always in the background there is the safe anchorage of each other's love and the satisfying expression of it probably at lengthening intervals, so that the life-force, when it has done its work of parenthood, is very naturally directed elsewhere— into the building-up of the husband's business, into local politics perhaps, or some keen interest in sport ; in the wife's case, into interest in the children's pursuits, charitable work, or some kind of activity in social directions. Both of you should keep up-to-date with the other's interests, while broadening your own, and so make an outlet for the pent-up emotions that once went exclusively into the sex-life.

Don't be jealous of each other's hobbies. Share them if you can— or be friendly rivals, vieing with each other—and remember that a healthy occupation which keeps you at home together, or a more adventurous one that takes you out and about, giving you a wider outlook and fresh topics of conversation, is a friend to be welcomed rather than an enemy to be feared. It keeps boredom at bay and ensures that husband and wife are not wholly dependent on each other's presence for their amusement— which can be a great relief if, for any reason, you cannot always be together during your spare time.

But hobbies should be kept within bounds and not allowed to turn into obsessions, for there is nothing quite so boring as a man —or woman—who insists on discussing his favourite subject with all and sundry, whether they are interested or not. Keep your sense of humour, then, and a sense of proportion, and make your hobby a pleasure and recreation rather than a taskmaster.

The " Thrilling Thirties "

THE " thrilling thirties," as one might well call them, need be no less exciting than the twenties, for there is still the glorious future to spur you on, with the added help of experience to back you up—but there is a great tendency to get in a rut during the thirties, to sit back and think, " Well, here I am and here I stay ! "

That attitude is all right so long as you are both perfectly happy, but there may come a time when one of you gets a little restless— and then you will need to take yourselves well in hand to make sure that you are keeping each other interested, for restlessness is but a short step to finding attractions elsewhere—and nothing is more disillusioning than the discovery

When a man reaches middle age, it is not uncommon for him to imagine that he is in love with a little slip of a girl, young enough to be his daughter. Treat it as a little illness that men contract in the course of growing up.

In the meantime, plan your campaign to win him back. Make the best of yourself. Find a new hairstyle and buy a new dress in his favourite colour. If he goes dancing with the other woman, suggest going to the theatre or even to watch his favourite football team with him.

that your love, the home, and the kiddies are not enough to hold the beloved.

If, by any chance, you are called upon to meet this problem, face it squarely, and think well before you do anything about it. Look into your lives, just recently, and see what has been going on.

Perhaps you, the husband, have been working hard, and the wife has found the company of the children and the work in the home insufficient to fill her life ; perhaps you, the wife, have been too occupied with the children, or the home, and hubby has felt that you no longer need him ? Whatever the reason may be, you may be sure there is one, so determine to find it.

Husbands should ask themselves why they should be a failure as a partner. You love her—and she loved you in the same way, once— so take a pride in winning her back again as completely as before. Don't make a scene, or become jealous or suspicious, for that will drive her further away from you. Just try and put yourself in her place for a moment and see how you would feel—try to understand just what it is that is lacking in her life —then take her in your arms, and let her know that you are the same old you that she fell in love with, and that you intend to be even nicer from now onwards !

One thing that so many wives forget, and so many "other women" remember, is that husbands—like their wives—can do with any amount of " flattery." Think back to your courting days and remember the joy you took in telling him what a good fellow he was, how clever you thought he must be at his work, how you loved his smile, and how handsome he looked. They were dear little, tender, intimate flatteries, sincere enough, but nevertheless complimentary—and, where they were not quite true, be very sure he did his best to live up to your flattering ideas about him.

But, once you were married and settled down, didn't you leave off telling him all those things ? Perhaps your compliments got fewer and farther between. You still thought them, but you did not seem to have the time to utter them. Isn't that so ? Then, just as you were jogging along in the rut that married couples often fall into in the thirties—along came the " other woman," with her smooth tongue that made your man feel at once the romantic hero, instead of perhaps rather a tired husband and father.

Philandering Husbands

IF a wife discovers that her husband is becoming attracted by another woman, she either tackles him with it and demands that he stops the affair at once, or else, because she loves him so much that she is afraid of losing him, she turns a blind eye to the affair in the hope that it will naturally come to an end soon.

It is certainly good to pretend that you have noticed nothing wrong, if only for the fact that you will be doing the other woman out of the satisfaction of knowing that you are hurt—and the less importance you appear to attach to the whole thing, the more chance it has of fizzling out. But neither of these courses is in itself the best way—for one gives the other woman a free pass to your husband's time, and the other brings matters to a head with no satisfactory assurance that the real way out has been found.

As we shall see in a later chapter, when a man reaches middle age, it is not uncommon for him to imagine that he is in love with little slip of a girl old enough to be his daughter, simply because of her extreme youth—and in somewhat the same way, when a young couple settle down together, after the novelty has worn off, sometimes the husband allows himself to be flattered by a woman old enough to be his mother mainly because she is a woman of the world, and he feels " somebody " to be worthy of her attention ! Both these are really little " illnesses " which men contract in the course of growing up—and the wise wife treats them as such.

Holding Your Man

HAVING discovered the reason your husband's affection is wandering, you will know what part of his life the other woman is managing to fill, and can set about doing it yourself. But first you should try and decide just *why* she has chosen to fill that part for him. Is she just after the good times he can give her ? Is she young and genuinely in love with him ? Has she been setting her cap at him just for the pure joy of making a conquest, or has she been to blame in letting her think his marriage has not been a success ?

Having decided this point, plan your campaign to win him back.

Make the very best of yourself— find a new hair style, if you like, and buy a new dress in his favourite colour—and then appear to take it for granted that it is you he wants to be with. But do not try and beat the other woman at her own game. You know your man better than she can ever hope to do, and you must occupy his attention attrac-

tively in your own way, not hers. Perhaps he is having a " good time " with her—the good time you would have shared with him if you had not had the kiddies to look after. Well, get someone to take care of them for you—get grandma in sometimes, or ask a neighbour to keep an eye on them in exchange for your doing the same for her when she wants you to—and suggest to hubby that you go out together a bit more.

If the other woman accompanies him to dances, then you suggest going to the local theatre, or even to watch his favourite football team with him. Prove to him that you are still the same woman who fell in love with him years ago— and with whom he fell in love—and that you can be as good a companion as anyone else, *and* that you admire him, too.

Make his home particularly comfortable, and encourage him to take an interest in the kiddies—perhaps the mere fact of his finding that the time has come for him to tell your sons the things they ought to know about life will shame him, when he thinks how far away he is from the ideals he will naturally want to bring out in them. After all, it is the little homely links that bind a man to his wife and family —and any one of those may suddenly turn him from the arms of the usurper to the shelter of his wife's love. Then the less fuss you have made about it, the greater will be your victory, and the easier it will be for you two to go on where you left off.

Of course, each wife knows her own man, and she must decide for herself which is really the best way of dealing with such a situation should it arise—but usually you will find that if you make it plain that it has never occurred to you that your man intends to be disloyal, in most cases he will respond to that trust and shake himself into his senses.

The wife holds all the trump cards in her hand if only she can school herself to wait—she is his wife, the woman he really loves, and the mother of his children. The other woman holds no rightful place in his life, and in nine cases out of ten it is only infatuation that binds him to her—and, when that has worn off, he realises what a fool he has been.

The Perils of Pride

"YES," you may say; "that's all very well—but I'm proud; I don't want my husband when another woman has finished with him, or he has tired of her. Why should I suffer disillusionment and heartbreak at his hands, and then say nothing, but gladly take him back as soon as he wants to come?"

Some wives do say that, and they make a scene as soon as another woman attracts his attention. Perhaps the husband gives up the other woman and comes back to his wife—but there will always remain a romantic notion in his heart about her rival. Or he may even feel goaded into saying: "Very well, I'll go. I love her and I'm going to stick to her." And the wife is left none the less disillusioned and heartbroken because she has put her pride first, and now has practically no chance of winning him back again.

But where there is true love, the wife will stand by her man to the very last—thinking of him, even while her heart is breaking, as the naughty little boy she promised to care for when she married him.

She is proud, too—but her pride is in all that they have built up together. Perhaps, also, she is too proud to admit that the other woman has the power to steal her man. So long as the wife stands firm, her belief in their future happiness unshaken, so long as she makes it plain that she regards the affair as a passing infatuation, what headway can the other woman make?

You may still say: "But why should I take him back gladly as soon as he wants to come, and say nothing about what I know?" The question really answers itself. Say something if you really want to, but first picture the consequences. The man may have just parted from the other woman —who, no doubt, has made a pathetic and tearful scene. He hates himself for having hurt her, but he comes back to his wife, determined to give her a better deal. While the trouble was on she kept quiet and said nothing—but, when it is over, then she starts to tell him what she thinks of him. Would it be any wonder if he forgot all about his good resolutions at once?

If you have kept quiet all along, then don't break the silence just when victory is in sight. You can let him know well enough, without words, that a new chapter in your life is beginning—and he will be heartily grateful to you for your understanding—for most men hate "scenes," and are thankful to be spared them.

But don't imagine that when you reach the thirties your man is necessarily going to run after other women. Not a bit of it. We have been talking about a situation that does sometimes arise, but it is the exception and not by any means the rule.

CHAPTER XIV

Bending the Twig

" SEVEN years of childhood, sport and play.
    Seven years of school from day to day
Seven years a trade, or college life——"

runs the old rhyme. And though it is sound in principle, nowadays it is not quite correct in detail. Children start school long before they are seven, and if the first year's lessons are really no more than organised play, the little ones soon begin to learn the real lessons that are to equip them for life.

Certainly by the time they are seven they are little schoolboys and schoolgirls, and long before they are fourteen parents are thinking seriously about what trade or occupation they shall follow when they leave school. Already we feel that their education should be rather specialised, instead of including subjects that will be no use to them, and we are anxious that their home life shall help, so far as it can, towards training them for the calling they are to take up.

In the old days, far too many boys were pitchforked into occupations that did not in the least appeal to them. A father who had some sort of business of his own wanted his eldest son to come into it, and carry it on after him. A mother thought it would be so " nice " for Tommy to be a clerk in an office, rather than a carpenter or a mechanic.

These feelings were very natural, but they put many a square peg into a round hole. It is positive cruelty to force a boy to sell groceries, for instance, when he is pining to go to sea, or to sit on an office stool adding up figures when he is only happy making something with his hands. Many a boy with brains and character has done well in a calling that he disliked and for which he had no aptitude, but he

E *

would almost certainly have done better if he had been allowed to follow his natural " bent." And he would have been far happier, and we want our boys and girls to be happy as well as successful. There's a great joy in doing well a job of work that one likes, a joy that is becoming scarcer in these mechanised days. Don't deprive your children of it.

Of course, you cannot always let children do the things they want to do. When they have passed through the childish phase of wanting to be engine-drivers or cowboys, they may hanker after an occupation that is already terribly overcrowded, or one that holds no hope of success without an expensive training far beyond the parents' means. But apart from that, let your boy try, at any rate, the job he fancies, and give him your help and encouragement, however much you may prefer that he had chosen another line.

His Natural " Bent "

BUT more often the problem is not that Tommy wants to be something you'd rather he wasn't, but that he hasn't the faintest idea what he *does* want to be. He leaves it to his parents to choose for him, and unless they have studied him carefully through his childhood, and know him very well, they can only have a hazy idea of the occupation he is best fitted for. But at any rate you know that a boy who doesn't care for books of any kind will be no use in a clerical job, that one who has no head for figures will be miserable in a post that involves keeping accounts, and that a boy who is clever with his hands is wasted selling shoes.

The wise father of a boy of twelve or so will have a good talk with the lad's schoolmaster, and ask his advice about Tommy's future. The master may not know so much about Tommy's character and disposition as you do, but he should have a better idea of his particular capabilities, and he may know of suitable callings that had not occurred to you. Decide on the kind of work you think would suit Tommy, make sure that the boy does not thoroughly dislike the idea, and then ask the master to develop, so far as he can within the limits of the school curriculum, Tommy's aptitude along the particular line needed.

Not all schoolmasters will agree with this. They point out the advantages of a good general education, both for success and for leading a happy life full of interest. But after all, the vitally important thing is for a boy to make a good living—not too easy in these days —and other things must take second place.

One thing the wise father will not do ; he will not, if he can help it, let Tommy drift into a " blind alley " job, a job that leads him nowhere, merely for the sake of doing something and bringing home wages every week. Any boy can work a lift, for instance, and he will not earn much more at it when he is sixty than he did when he was sixteen. And girls can do such jobs as well as boys, and will usually do them for lower wages. The man who gets on in the world is the skilled man, skilled either with his brains or with his hands. Even in buying and selling there is a great deal to learn, and though perhaps most money is made in buying and selling, it is only done by men with a well-developed money sense and seldom without capital.

So make up your mind that it is

better that Tommy shall spend the first few years after he leaves school in learning a trade that will bring him in good money later on, even if his wages are very small at first, rather than earn good wages to begin with, but with little chance of ever getting much more. This may mean sacrifice for the parents, but one of the privileges of parenthood is sacrifice, and it reaps its reward in after-years.

In the next chapter you will find details of a number of occupations for boys and girls that offer good prospects for the future. In most of them the boy or girl will have to accept low wages while training; in some the training has to be paid for. But if you choose one that fits Tommy's or Winnie's tastes and aptitude it will be well worth while in the end.

Insurance for Education

AS for the cost of training, there is a method of insurance that will provide for this. At any time after a baby's birth—but the earlier the more advantageous the terms— you can take out a policy by which you pay in so much a year, and either draw a sum when the child is say, ten, to send him to a good school, or when he is fifteen or sixteen, to pay for his training for a career, or both. The actual sums, of course, vary according to the amount you pay in, but as in other insurances you not merely compel yourself to save the money, but you receive more than you pay in, since the insurance company have the use of your money, which they invest at a profit, during the years of payment.

This applies, of course, to girls as well as boys, and it is very nearly as important that your daughters should be trained as your sons. The old idea of " oh, the girls will get married " no longer holds good. With so many more women than men in the population of our country, thousands of girls cannot possibly marry; some of them don't want to; and even if they do marry, they are not secure for life. If misfortune of any kind should happen to the husband, it is a great thing for the wife to have a calling at her fingers' ends that she can turn to account. So if you possibly can, do as much for Winnie as you do for Tommy in the way of training for a career in life.

If you can do nothing for either, if you cannot spare the money for training of any kind, don't despair. Many a boy has made good by doing a " blind alley " job by day and learning a trade in the evenings at continuation classes or a technical school. Some of these are free and in none of them are the fees high.

And remember, too, that many a boy has been spoilt because his parents sacrificed *too* much for him, and spent their hard-earned money in educating him in the wrong way. They stinted themselves to send him to a good school and perhaps to college, and he merely absorbed extravagant ideas of living that he would never be able to afford, of being " too good " for most of the jobs he was likely to get, and mixed with lads who would never have to struggle in life and had no need to learn the gospel of hard work. The boy who expects to begin where father left off has been educated not well but unwisely.

So far as success in the world is concerned, the boy from a poor home is actually often more likely to get on in the world than the son of comfortably-off parents. He has learnt, early, the value of money. His food and clothes have not seemed to drop from the skies whenever he needed them. He has learnt to do without; if he has wanted any particular thing, he has had to save for it or earn the money for it; he has learned not to spend a penny till he is sure he is getting his money's worth. It's a hard school to learn in, but it teaches lessons that many a boy who seems more fortunate never has a chance to learn.

Training at Home

BUT apart from this actual matter of training for a definite career, there is much you can do at home to equip your children for life, and add to the education they are receiving at school.

The vexed question of homework leaps to the mind at once. Ought parents to help the children with their home-lessons? If they are working for marks, it is hardly fair to the other children in the class, who receive no such help. And after all, Tommy is not learning when you do his lessons for him.

The answer is—*Don't* do his lessons for him, but give him every help and encouragement to do them for himself. Give him the best conditions you can for working in. He needs a good light so that his sight will not be spoilt by peering at type he can scarcely see to read. He needs peace and quiet: he can't do his best if younger children are playing noisy games round him and distracting him. If, to obtain this, he has to work in his bedroom, see that he is warm; give him an oil lamp or even a fire. It costs money, but regard it as money spent on his education, one of the most valuable things

with which you can endow him. And see that he sticks to the job and gets it done; don't allow anyone or anything to interrupt him.

Then, while his lessons are within your own knowledge—for children nowadays learn a great deal that their parents have forgotten, if they ever learnt it—show him *how* to do them, if he doesn't know, show him how to find out information for himself. Check his sums, or teach him how to check them for himself, and insist upon his persevering until he has them right. Don't allow him merely to do them and hope he's got the correct answer.

In this way you are doing far more than helping with his lessons. You are teaching him habits of diligence and concentration, teaching him to be thorough and reliable. And in every occupation, in every walk of life, there's a need for men with just those qualities. "Old Reliability" is often a more valued person than the man who is highly talented but undependable.

Hobbies Help

ENCOURAGE your children to have hobbies. They have a very distinct value. They keep the little people happy, often they develop skill and ingenuity, and very often they provide you with an inkling of qualities in them that may help in choosing their careers. For instance, many a young man of to-day tinkered with wireless sets in his boyhood, and was regarded with no more than indulgent amusement—to-day he has turned his hobby to account and is doing well as a radio engineer or a wireless operator. Sometimes your children's hobbies will give you a better idea of their particular "bent" than the most careful study of their school work. And even if they never make their hobbies a paying proposition, they will give them lifelong interest and enjoyment. The man with a lasting hobby is a happy man.

Of course, it is not always easy to give a boy or girl all the opportunity they need to pursue a chosen hobby. There is the question of houseroom. You can't have young Tommy turning either the sitting-room or the kitchen into a carpenter's shop, and there are few houses where there is a room going begging that can be handed over to him. But why not let him use his bedroom, provided that he tidies up carefully every evening? Or what about a shed in the garden that he can make into a workshop? A suitable one can be bought, if necessary by instalments of a very few shillings a week, and will not only give the boy many hours of pleasure, and keep him at home, but may be the means of his finding his true niche in life.

Another snag is the question of raw material. Wood, tools, and appliances cost money, and at first Tom will probably waste much of the first and spoil many of the second. But do your best for him, make a little sacrifice to help him with his hobby; it will be well worth while.

Let the Youngsters Face Facts

THIS brings us to another point Many parents make sacrifices for their children without the children realising it. When Tom says that Will Jones has a bicycle and he wants one too, mother and father don't like to admit that Will Jones' father is just about twice as

well-off as Tom's. They deprive themselves of luxuries, or even necessities, to provide Tom with a bicycle so that he can be on equal terms with Will Jones, and Tom accepts it as a matter of course.

This is false pride and mistaken kindness. It puts quite wrong ideas into the boy's head. He comes to think, for one thing, that he is entitled to anything that any other boy has; he is started on a competition in possessing things that may prove disastrous later on. And he comes to expect that mother and dad will supply anything he asks for, and he will be disappointed in them, reproachful and resentful, when at last they are obliged to tell him that this time he is asking too much, he is demanding something they cannot afford to give him.

Of course, you don't want your children to be worried over money matters. Let their childhood be as free from that kind of thing as possible. But on the other hand, don't let them live in a fools' paradise and imagine that everything they ask for will always be given them. Sooner or later they will have to learn that it is not so, and if the revelation is delayed too long it will be a crushing blow.

Remember that children cannot be expected to have any real idea of people's incomes, of the cost of living, of the little money there is available for extra luxuries in the average home. Tom cannot possibly judge for himself whether dad can afford to buy him a bicycle or not.

Very well. Be frank with him. Tell him, "Will Jones' father makes twice as much money as dad. He can quite well afford to buy Will a bicycle. Your dad can't spare the money to buy one for you. It takes nearly all the money he earns to keep us fed and clothed, and with a roof over our heads. But suppose you save all your pocket money, and dad saves some money too, and then when you've enough you buy a bike ? ''

The boy will think far more of a thing that he has waited for, saved for, contributed towards, than one that has merely been given him. And he will have learnt the lesson that the material things of life don't drop from the skies : the money to buy them has to be earned, to be worked for, to be saved. It's a useful attitude of mind to cultivate.

And don't imagine that Tom will think less of his dad because he is not so well-off as the fathers of some other boys. Not a bit of it. If he has decent instincts—and he will have if he's *your* son—he will sympathise with dad, be drawn towards him in a bond of loyalty and common interest ; he will begin to understand dad—and it is nearly as important, and as difficult, for children to understand their parents as for parents to understand their children.

There are still too many young people who vaguely think of father as someone with an inexhaustible fountain of money that can be made to flow by wheedling ; there are too many young wives who, in spite of really knowing better, cannot help thinking of their husbands in the same way. It's the parents' fault, of course. Let your children realise that dad's income is as definitely limited as their own pocket-money, that though it may seem a great deal to them, it has equally large demands made upon it. Only so can you achieve a family who see the family income as something that, under dad's wise direction, is spent for the good of them all, and do not make unreasonable demands

upon it but are anxious to contribute towards it when they can.

But *don't* become the kind of mother who is always rubbing it in what sacrifices she makes for her children ; it merely makes them retort that they wish to goodness she hadn't !

Cheeky Children

AS for the children's characters at this age—well, they'll be pretty much what they always have been, but perhaps a little more so. Certain characteristics will have become strengthened and intensified ; others will have modified a little.

You will find them apt to be cheeky, to resent being reproved, possibly apt to sulk ; rather self-willed, imperious in their demands. Don't worry. These are phases through which almost every child passes. They'll grow out of them—though, of course, they need checking gently but firmly.

They're beginning to feel their feet. They are conscious of themselves as separate personalities, more independent than they were—though not so independent as they think they are. They have learnt many things, and think they know more than they do. They are making a very natural attempt to stretch their wings, to make elbow-room for themselves in a world they feel is trying to cramp them. All this is to the good, really : it is a sign of the right spirit—but it sometimes takes a rather objectionable form.

But remember this : they seldom mean to be as cheeky and defiant as they sound. Often a child who has been reproved for impudence will burst into tears and protest miserably that he didn't mean to be cheeky at all; he was only saying what he thought. Be patient with impudence: realise that it does not mean, to a child's ears, all that it does to your grown-up ones.

At the same time, teach your children good manners. True politeness springs from a consideration of the feelings of others, and that is an endearing quality. We always appreciate politeness, and everybody likes a well-mannered child. So teach your boys and girls to behave nicely to your friends, to rise from their chairs when grown-ups come into the room, to open doors for them, to act, in fact, as you yourself do to your guests. It will have a value both now and later on. The boy who is polite as well as alert and intelligent makes a good impression on a prospective employer. This social training, too, helps to cure a shy child of a trait that in later life may be a serious handicap.

At this age you will find them apt to be cheeky, to resent being reproved, possibly apt to sulk; rather self-willed and imperious in their demands.

CHAPTER XV

Careers for Boys and Girls

PARENTHOOD brings many joys, but it brings responsibilities, too, and one of the greatest is that of helping your boys and girls to find their right niche in life, and to choose the job that is not only going to get them a living, but in which they are going to be happy and content. So this chapter is devoted to giving useful information about various careers for boys and girls whose parents cannot afford to spend much money on launching them in life.

When you are helping your boys and girls in their choice of a career, remember they may have to stay in that particular job for the best part of their lives, and do not be in a hurry to make the final choice. So many parents, looking round for the particular niche their boy or girl is to fill, think only of the dozen

or so best-known jobs, they concentrate on shop or office work, or on one of the more familiar trades; but there are hundreds of ways in which a boy or girl may earn a living, dozens of lesser-known trades in which they might find congenial work and where, perhaps, the competition is not so keen. It is worth a little thought, and the trouble of making a few inquiries, to ensure that your boys and girls may find the work that is best suited to them, and where they will be happy.

Having studied your children's abilities, and their characters, too, take time and thought in helping them to find the right job. You may not do it all at once, but somewhere is the niche they will fill happily and in which they will earn a living and it's worth taking a little trouble to find it.

Let us take boys first. Although girls also need definite occupations, your son's career is really more important than your daughter's, since the majority of girls marry and give up their jobs. When boys marry, on the other hand, their need of well-paid employment is even greater than when they were single.

The Air Force.

Is your lad air-minded, as are so many boys at the present time ? The Royal Air Force offers him excellent opportunities of indulging his tastes in the best possible conditions. The easiest method of entry into the Force is as an aircraft-hand. The conditions of entry are changed from time to time, but at present the age limits are from seventeen to twenty-six, and at the end of a certain time aircraft-hands are given an opportunity of volunteering for training as pilots.

Applicants must have received a good general education, and particulars of the conditions of entry may be obtained from the Inspector of Recruiting, R.A.F., Victory House, Kingsway, London.

The Army.

Many boys still long to be soldiers, just as they have done throughout the ages, and the army of to-day offers a fine life with plenty of sport and variety to suitable lads.

The actual age of enlistment is eighteen, but boys between fourteen and sixteen years four months are taken and trained for various trades in the army, where they are not only paid, but are fed, clothed and lodged free, and are well looked after in every way.

Entry is by a simple competitive examination and these examinations are held periodically in every county in Great Britain. Parents who would like further particulars should get a copy of the booklet entitled " Careers for Boys," which may be obtained free from any recruiting office. The address of the nearest such office may be obtained from any post office.

Chiropody

is one of the more modern careers in which the demand for practitioners exceeds the supply, and the boy whose parents can afford the necessary training may be reasonably sure of success.

The necessary qualifications are a good general education, pleasant manners, and a liking for scientific subjects. Students—and it may be mentioned that this is a career for girls as well as boys—may begin training at the age of seventeen and this training takes from a year to eighteen months. The fees are from twenty to eighty pounds and particulars may be obtained from the London Foot Hospital School of Chiropody, 33 Fitzroy Square, London, W.1.

The Civil Service.

The Civil Service offers as good prospects— or even better—to the plodding type of boy as it does to girls. The conditions of entry are the same for boys as for girls and particulars of the examinations may be obtained from the address given on page 149.

Commercial Art.

Finding a career for the " artistic " lad is often a difficult task. He likes drawing and painting, he has an eye for colour and design, and would, you feel sure, be unhappy in an office, while he does not seem suited for any particular trade. Being sensible parents with a knowledge of present-day conditions, you realise that unless he is a genius he will find it very difficult to earn even a bare living at painting pictures, and though starving in a garret may sound very romantic it is in fact very uncomfortable—and even garrets have to be rented !

However, nowadays such boys may find congenial careers in commercial art, in the designing of posters, in preparing trade catalogues, in press illustration, or in designing for the pottery or textile industries.

There are art schools in various parts of the country and in most of these a training in commercial art is given. The fees are moderate, and the lad who has taken a thorough course of training should have no difficulty in finding a post suited to him.

Dispensing is another career for which the training is not expensive and in which there are reasonably good prospects. A good education is necessary, and the student must take the examination of the Society of Apothecaries. Training may be taken in various schools and hospitals, while classes for dispensers are also held in some polytechnics. The time of training is nine months, the fees about twenty pounds, and particulars may be obtained from the Society of Apothecaries, Blackfriars, London, E.C.4.

Engineering. Perhaps you have a sturdy son who is cleverer with his hands than with his head ? He enjoys making things and is happiest with a box of tools. Books don't make a very strong appeal to him, but he can mend the electric light, and enjoy doing it, while mother finds him a real " handy man " about the house. Such a boy would probably be a failure in an office, but might do well at engineering.

While a reasonably good education is necessary, it is not wise to keep the lad at school beyond the age of sixteen, for the earlier his practical training begins, the better.

The very best method of training is by apprenticeship to a good and well-known firm of engineers. A premium is usually required and sometimes, but not always, the pupil receives a small wage during his apprenticeship, which, as a rule, covers a period of three years.

Before paying such a premium you would, of course, be wise to make full inquiries about the firm, the kind of training it gives, and your lad's prospects when that training is completed.

Training is also given in many trade or technical schools, some of which offer the advantage of a National Certificate Course. The period of training is from one to four years, and the fees are moderate.

Farming. Many boys long for an open-air life ; they dislike the idea of being shut up in an office or workshop all day, and find their happiness in working in the garden or in some outdoor hobby. These lads, if strong and healthy, might find congenial work on a farm or market garden, but it must be borne in mind that such work is not very well paid, and unless the lad will have enough capital to set up for himself later on, or to go into partnership with a farmer or market gardener who is already established, there is little hope of advancement.

Many up-to-date farmers running their farms on scientific principles take pupils, and vacancies are often advertised in the agricultural papers.

Poultry farming attracts many

lads and the work is less strenuous than ordinary farming, also the wages are often higher than those paid to farm workers. The lad who aims at a job with a decent wage should take a diploma in poultry keeping. Particulars of the examinations for which diplomas are granted may be obtained from the National Poultry Council, 4 Vernon Place, London, W.C.I.

Handicraft Teacher. The lad who, unlike the budding engineer, is not mechanically inclined yet is clever with his hands, likes to make things and has, too, the gift of imparting knowledge, might well consider a career as a teacher of handicrafts.

Handicraft teachers who are recognised by the Board of Education are certain of well-paid posts, but to obtain this recognition it is necessary to take a three-years' course of training in a recognised training college, or to pass the special examinations of the City and Guilds of London Institute.

Librarian. Now for the studious lad who is always to be found " with his nose in a book." He is attracted by knowledge, yet not by an office career. He likes books, but not ledgers ; at school his best subjects are English, essay writing, and perhaps history, while it is plain that he is far more likely to be happy in a job suited to his temperament than in one where his principal object will be making money. Such a lad will probably do well as a librarian.

The best way to make a start in this career is to try for a post as junior in a public library. Such vacancies are often advertised in the local papers. He will then have the advantage of being able to take a correspondence course qualifying for the Diploma of the Library Association, which has its headquarters at the Carnegie Library, Herne Hill Road, London, S.E., and from which all particulars may be obtained.

The training includes work in different types of libraries, library law, literary history, and cataloguing.

Salaries are not high, but the posts are permanent. The junior will earn from forty to eighty pounds a year, while the salary of a fully qualified assistant will range from one hundred and fifty pounds a year to double that amount.

Policeman. Nowadays the police force offers an excellent career to suitable lads who do not care to spend their working hours between four walls, and who like a life of variety and interest with the opportunity for games and athletics.

Candidates must be between twenty and twenty-five, though exceptional candidates are accepted from eighteen and a half, and the minimum height is five feet nine inches. There is a medical test and an educational examination and the starting pay is three pounds a week. Young men may join for long service with a pension after twenty-five to thirty years, or for short service with a gratuity after ten years. Particulars may be obtained from the Recruiting Officer, New Scotland Yard, London, S.W.I.

Sailor. In every generation there are many lads who long to go to sea, and to those who are fitted for it a life at sea may be a very happy and healthy one. If your lad longs to join the Navy your best plan is to get a copy of the booklet entitled " How to Join the Royal

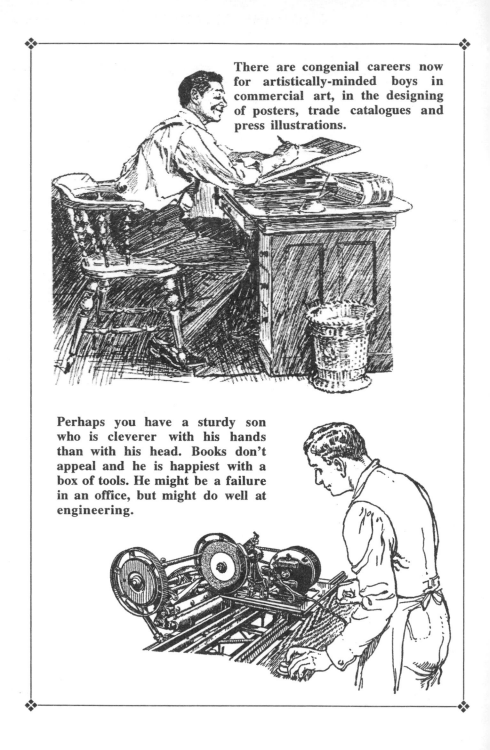

There are congenial careers now for artistically-minded boys in commercial art, in the designing of posters, trade catalogues and press illustrations.

Perhaps you have a sturdy son who is cleverer with his hands than with his head. Books don't appeal and he is happiest with a box of tools. He might be a failure in an office, but might do well at engineering.

Navy." This may be obtained free from any post office or from the Secretary of the Admiralty, Whitehall, London.

Perhaps your boy may prefer the Merchant Service, where his whole duty will lie in the navigation of ships. Entry into this service is by various methods. Some lads go straight to sea, others are trained at a sea school. Particulars may be obtained from the Secretary, The Gravesend Sea School, 52 Leadenhall Street, London, E.C.3.

Wireless Construction.

The boy who is keen on wireless construction will not hesitate if he is asked if he would like to take this up as a career.

The training can be taken at various schools and colleges throughout the country. The period is about a year, and the fees are moderate.

The student receives instruction in Morse, cable-slip reading, etc. He must also pass a medical examination.

Perhaps your young wireless enthusiast is attracted by the thought of being a wireless operator at sea. For this the training is much the same as that for a land operator, but before applying for an appointment at sea the operator must procure a certificate from the Postmaster-General.

Reliable information concerning vacancies may be obtained from The Association of Wireless and Cable Telegraphists, 194 High Street North, East Ham, London, E.6.

Trades with a Future.

The boy who prefers a trade to a business career may profitably turn his attention to printing, motor-body building, cabinet-making, or the building trades.

Entry into these trades is usually by apprenticeship, and in many towns and cities there are now Juvenile Advisory Committees which give most helpful advice on the question of apprenticeship. The address of the nearest such Committee may be obtained from the local Labour Exchange.

Attendance at a trade or technical school sometimes takes the place of apprenticeship, and the trades mentioned above, as well as many others, are taught at many such schools throughout the country. The fees are moderate, and the instruction is sound and very practical. A pamphlet on " Trade Careers for Boys and Girls " may be obtained from the Education Officer, The County Hall, London, S.E.1.

Careers for Girls

Beauty Culture. The quiet, " womanly " type of girl who is soft of speech and neat and dainty in her ways, but who does not care for clerical work or any job actually connected with the home, may like to take up some branch of beauty culture. She may decide to specialise in beauty culture alone, or she may prefer to take a training in hairdressing, which nowadays includes some of the simpler forms of beauty culture such as manicure and eyebrow plucking.

The training for beauty culture is shorter than that for hairdressing, but it should be borne in mind that the former is a luxury trade and there is naturally less scope, and fewer vacancies.

A thorough training in hairdressing takes at least two years, and apprentices are taken in all good-class firms. It is most important that a girl should take her training in as good a firm as possible, for this will be a real advantage to her when she looks for a paid post.

The Civil Service.

The Civil Service offers excellent opportunities to girls as well as boys who are attracted by clerical work, for the hours are easy, the pay good, and there is a pension at the end of service.

Girl Writing Assistants may sit for the examinations between the ages of sixteen and seventeen, and shorthand-typists at the age of nineteen. Entrance to all branches of the Civil Service is by competitive examination and there is also a medical test. Particulars may be obtained from the Secretary, Civil Service Commission, Burlington Gardens, London, W.1.

Girls who would like to enter the Civil Service, but who are not attracted by clerical work, may like to become telephonists. The age limits are from sixteen to nineteen ; there is a medical test and an educational examination. Particulars may be obtained from the Superintendent, Cornwall House, Waterloo Road, London, S.E.1.

Domestic Science.

The girl who loves helping mother in the home, who enjoys housework, but feels she would not care to become a domestic worker, will find full scope for her abilities and an interesting career in domestic science. For a girl who has taken a course of training in this subject there are many interesting jobs such as school matron or housekeeper in an institution. If the necessary training can be afforded a teacher of domestic science is sure of a good and well-paid post.

A domestic science course includes instruction in cookery, housecraft, needlework, and laundry. The usual period of training is about a year, but the girl who wishes to become a teacher of domestic science must be prepared to take at least a two-years' course of training in a training college recognised by the Board of Education. Particulars of training may be obtained from the Association of Teachers of Domestic Subjects, 29 Gordon Square, London, W.C.1.

Demonstrating patent cooking stoves and various electrical appliances for the home is a comparatively new career which may appeal to the girl who is interested in matters connected with the home, but does not wish to take up any kind of domestic work. The training is not expensive and may be taken at various colleges. Particulars may be obtained from the Secretary, Electrical Association for Women, 20 Regent Street, London, S.W.1.

Dressmaking, Millinery, etc.

What of the girl who is clever with her needle, who delights in dressing her dolls and who even as a child shows good taste in colours and skill in cutting-out ? For her there is a pleasant and profitable career in dressmaking, tailoring, and millinery, but it must be borne in mind that good health and good eyesight are essential for these trades, and the girl who chooses them must be prepared for hard work in the earlier stages and for a certain amount of monotony.

Apprenticeship with a good-class firm is an excellent way of entering any of these trades, and the usual age for " learners," as they are often called, is fifteen. They earn only a few shillings a week at first, but there are splendid opportunities for a keen girl to

Many girls feel that they would like a job that is really worthwhile. If your young one is a girl of this type, nursing offers many advantages, but she must remember that nursing is not only a career, it is a vocation.

Perhaps your lass is very fond of animals and would like to spend her time working with them. She may do well as a kennel maid. Vacancies and the addresses of training kennels may be found in the various dog journals.

get on, and a really skilled dress-maker or milliner earns good wages. One of the great advantages of the dressmaking trade is that in later years it can, if necessary, be carried on at home.

Dressmaking and kindred trades are also taught at various trade and technical schools, and a training at a trade school takes the place of an apprenticeship. Fees are very moderate, and there are evening classes at the technical schools, so that a girl who is engaged during the day, but wishes to improve herself, still has the opportunity of doing so.

Kennel Maid. Some girls are very fond of animals and feel they would like to spend their time work-ing amongst them. Such a girl would probably do well as a kennel maid. The training takes about six months and the fees are moder-ate, while it is sometimes possible for a girl to get her training in exchange for her services. Vacancies and addresses of training kennels may be found in the various " dog " journals.

Nursing. Many girls feel that when they set out to earn a living they would like a job that is really worth while, and in which they will be of some real use in the world. To a girl of this type nursing offers many advantages, but it must be remembered that nursing is not only a career, it is a vocation, and the girl who wishes to succeed as a nurse must not only have good health, sound nerves, and a strong constitution, but she must have sympathy, patience, and a real wish to help humanity, as well as the ability to work under the dis-cipline necessary in a large hospital.

At the present time when there is so much competition, and every worth-while job needs some kind of training—the cost of which it may be a struggle for parents to pay—nursing offers two great and very practical advantages. There are always vacancies for the right girl, and training is free, with free board, lodging, and uniform ; the pro-bationer is also paid a salary while training.

Training covers a period of three years, and it is important that the girl should take this training at an approved training school, and thus, at the end of the time, be entitled to put her name on the State Register, for this will be a real advantage to her in later years. A list of these approved schools may be obtained from the Secretary, General Nursing Council, 20 Port-land Place, London, W.1. The usual age for a probationer is eighteen.

While there is no fixed rate of pay for nurses, the nurse in a general hospital may expect from fifty to eighty pounds a year ; a staff nurse receives from seventy-five to a hundred pounds a year, and sisters from one hundred and twenty to a hundred and fifty a year. A matronship is, of course, the " plum " of the profession and is a responsible and well-paid post.

Midwifery is another career which may appeal to the older girl. Candidates must not be under the age of twenty-one and the training takes a year. This is not free, but is not expensive and the Ministry of Health will give a grant towards the cost of training to those who are willing to work as district mid-wives for a certain time after their training is completed.

Another branch of the profession which makes an appeal to a very wide circle of girls who are fond of children is nursery nursing and, there are excellent prospects for the girl who has taken a course of training at one of the nursery training colleges which are situated in various parts of the country. As a rule, this training covers a period of twelve months and the fees are from fifty to eighty pounds, but as this includes board and lodging it is not really expensive. One of the least expensive methods of training is at a crêche or day nursery where the fees are moderate and in some cases a girl may get her training in exchange for her services. There are day nurseries in various parts of the country, and particulars may be obtained from the Secretary, National Society of Day Nurseries, 117 Piccadilly, London, W.1.

Saleswoman. Shop life attracts many girls who prefer an active and varied job, and nowadays the girl who starts as a junior in one of the big stores has an excellent chance of getting on.

All large firms take apprentices, usually from the age of fifteen. These are paid a few shillings weekly, and are often provided with dinner and tea. In many of the up-to-date stores the new assistant goes to " school," where she attends lectures and learns how to deal with different accounts, how to make out all kinds of bills, how to deal with customers' complaints, and many other details of her work.

The girl who wishes to succeed in this job must have good health, for she will have to stand practically all her working hours, she must be business-like, have pleasant manners, and an even temper, for she will have to deal with all types of customer, and must never lose her patience.

In this, as in many other careers, it is wise to serve the apprentice-ship in a large, progressive firm. The experience is much more valuable, there are more opportunities, and the smart and ambitious girl who studies her work will aim at becoming an under-buyer and, in time, a buyer, where she will hold a responsible position and command a good salary.

Secretarial Work. Perhaps you have a girl to whom office work makes a strong appeal, and you think it will be easy to give her a training in shorthand, typing, and get her a job in an office. So it may be, but if you want your girl to get a worth-while job she must aim higher than this, for though it may be easy to get a job as a shorthand-typist this is work for young women only and may lead nowhere. Thus it is far better for the girl who likes this kind of work to aim at becoming a private secretary.

The qualifications are a good general education—some employers insist on at least a school-leaving certificate—the ability to compose a letter without dictation, and to interview callers with tact and discretion. Shorthand and typing are essential, while a knowledge of languages and of book-keeping is an advantage.

Secretarial training is given at many commercial colleges, where the fees vary from twenty to forty guineas. The keen and ambitious girl can also attend evening classes at various technical schools, where the fees are very moderate.

CHAPTER XVI

Adolescence

THE age of adolescence is a critical time for parents as well as for the young people. Physical changes bring changes of thought and outlook also; young girls especially are given to fits of moodiness and shyness, and the wise mother will need to study her daughter carefully so as to judge the exact form her advice shall take.

For it is very necessary that young people should be prepared for the changes that are to take place in their own bodies, and they should understand what they mean. If you have given your children some idea of the part sex plays in human life, as suggested in Chapter IX, you will not find it difficult to explain things in greater detail to your young daughter. Your husband will similarly take Tom out for a walk one day and tell him what his approaching manhood means.

The question arises in most parents' minds : How soon should they be told ? The answer in all cases is, *before* the changes take place. Some children mature earlier than others, but it is always better to tell them too soon than too late. Some girls, for instance, see their periods at the age of eleven and twelve, some not till fourteen or fifteen. If a girl shows no sign of menstruating during her seventeenth year, it is as well to consult a doctor about her. Boys reach the adolescent stage a little later than girls, usually between the ages of fourteen and sixteen.

It is a mother's duty not to let the first period come upon her daughter without warning. Such a happening can cause a sensitive, reserved child untold misery and sometimes serious shock may result. As soon as you notice that your little daughter is developing a womanly figure, her breasts filling out and hair appearing on the body, you may know that the change in her life, or puberty as it is called, is not far away.

You will already have explained to her how a baby is formed inside its mother's body, but now is the time to tell her of the little store-houses called ovaries which have been full of eggs since before she was born. Tell her that one of these eggs may one day be the beginnings of a baby of her own, but until she is old enough to marry, Nature will arrange a monthly " spring-cleaning " of the little nursery called the womb in which the baby will grow. Every month an egg will be freed from the ovary and will at last find its way into the womb, but until it is time for a baby to grow there, it will not want to stay in the womb and so it will pass out, together with a certain quantity of blood.

Tell her, when she first notices this loss, not to be frightened but to come straight to you (or to her teacher if she is at school) and you will show her what to do. She will be able to go about her ordinary occupations just as usual, only taking care not to get over-tired, and in four or five days it will all be over.

Telling Boys and Girls the Truth

DON'T let your girlie get it into her head that menstruation is an illness or that there is anything " horrid " or " disgusting " about it. Reasonable exercise is good for her and will counteract the tendency to pain which some girls

get. If she does suffer undue pain or if the loss is excessive, take her to a doctor or to the out-patients' department of the nearest women's hospital. They will advise treatment which may save her years of discomfort.

Let her take her warm bath as usual, impressing upon her the need for scrupulous care of the body which will one day be entrusted with the wonderful task of building a baby.

She may ask you how that task is begun, and it is unfair to let a young girl go out into the world without some knowledge not only of the sex relationship between husband and wife, but of the danger of meeting unscrupulous men or thoughtless lads who may ask of her what she has no right to give them.

In the same way let care and reverence for the wonderful powers of the body be the keynote of your teaching, father, when you have your intimate talks with your young son.

Explain to him that Nature is forming in the little bags called testicles the seeds of life which will enable him to become a father in years to come, when he is old enough and is in a position to marry. That time, of course, is a long way off and there are many things to be done and learned before he is ready to start a home and family of his own. In the meantime, Nature has to find some way of getting rid of the unwanted " seeds " and so they pass out of the body in a thick, whitish fluid which is sometimes lost during sleep. Explain that these emissions or night losses are quite natural and are in fact a sign of good health.

With puberty comes the dawn of interest in the other sex and now is the time to awaken a boy's sense of chivalry and that respect for himself which will never let him do anything unworthy just because "other fellows do it" or from curiosity. When a lad reaches the age of sixteen or seventeen, you may perhaps have a talk with him about the harm done and the disease and unhappiness caused among some people by the misuse of their bodies. Without going into grim details, you can make him see the seriousness of your warning.

In dealing with boys and girls alike at this time, do not let them dwell too much on the changes that are taking place within themselves.

The Difficult Age

THE age of adolescence is an awkward age and a difficult age. The young folk are no longer children and they are not yet men and women. New impulses and urges, only dimly understood if understood at all, are stirring in their blood. These, and the physical changes that have been mentioned, make them behave in strange ways; they cannot understand themselves, and beneath their outward independence and "touchiness" lies a dumb appeal to their parents, out of their ripened experience, to understand them and make allowances for them.

Perhaps at no other time of their lives do they more sorely need patient and sympathetic handling. Just at this period a wise and understanding mother can win from her sons and daughters a trust and friendship and love far deeper than the instinctive, dependent affection of childhood. The mother who is thoughtless and undiscerning can antagonise them to an extent that may leave scars for life on the affection that should exist between them.

Perhaps the first guiding principle is : Don't interfere more than you must. The young people's instinct —and a very right and sound instinct it is—is to buy their own experience. And experience *must* be bought, you know. It is one of the tragedies of parenthood that we cannot give our children the benefit of the hard lessons of life we learnt in our youth. They will very seldom listen to our advice ; if they listen they seldom believe that what was true for us is true for them : they feel that they are different : only their own experience will show them that they are not different at all, but at heart exactly the same.

Perhaps it is as well. Even we grown-ups seldom set much value on the advice of others—except on merely practical matters—until we have proved it true, at our own expense. The lessons we pay dearly for are the ones we remember best, they are the ones that guard us against making the same mistake again. Therefore we must, with sadness and misgiving, watch our sons and daughters buying their own experience, and only trust and pray that the cost will not be too high.

Our one consolation is this, that when an experiment has failed, a hope been disappointed, an illusion shattered, they will turn to us for comfort, for the soothing, encouraging words that tell them that it isn't really such a tragic matter after all ; that we, with our experience and ripened judgment, can tell them that failures are the stepping stones to success. We can give them the hope and the faith and courage to try again, and go on trying.

Take the matter of their friendships. Boys and girls will have friends so unlike themselves that you will wonder what they can see in them ; friends that you do not approve of, even friends that you consider bad companions. What can you do about it ?

To act the stern parent and forbid Tom to have anything to do with Bob Porter is perfectly useless. Tom, in the emotionally disturbed state of adolescence, will probably suspect you of having an inexplicable and unreasonable " down " on Bob : he will resent your criticism of the lad : Bob will seem to him a maligned and unjustly treated person, and the fervid loyalty, the passionate indignation against injustice, that are such a strong and such a splendid trait of youth will make him exalt the unpleasant Bob into a sort of misjudged hero. It is even unwise openly to criticise Bob's character and habits before Tom. It will have the same unfortunate result.

Friendships

YOU have to be wary and wily, for your son's good. Welcome the objectionable Bob to your house, encourage Tom to bring him in as often as he will—it is far better than their meeting at street corners. Possibly Bob may show up badly against the background of your home ; possibly he may not. But if he is the kind of boy you believe him to be, he will find you and your home life utterly uncongenial and sooner or later he will say so to Tom. And if the boy has any real affection for you, any loyalty towards you, it will leap up in your defence : he will tell himself that a fellow who can talk of you in such a way can't be such a fine chap as Tom thought him. You will have given Bob the rope with which to hang himself.

You may, too, be able to criticise Bob in indirect ways. You may speak, casually, of some other boy of Bob's type, and talk about his unpleasant ways ; you may, without making the slightest comparison, talk of another who is the pleasant opposite of Bob. But you must go carefully and not let Tom see through your smoke-screen.

Does this seem dishonest and deceitful ? It isn't, really. It is the only method of dealing with a serious situation that cannot be solved by direct action, a situation that may hold dangers for the son you love so well and for whom, and from whom, you hope so much.

Calf-Love

EVEN more serious, perhaps, are the boy-and-girl friendships that a little later on may ripen into that distressing and embarrassing complaint, calf-love. Even when they have sisters as an example of what nice girls should be, boys do become attracted by the most unsuitable and, you would think, uncongenial girls. Mother, looking ahead, visualises her boy married to one of them, and shudders. Or she foresees her daughter tied for life to some worthless lad, and she is aghast. Here, again, the same methods can be applied, usually with success.

And comfort yourself with this thought : Boys and girls rarely marry the object of their first passion. Calf-love is a complaint that cures itself in time.

Adolescence is a time of experiment, of trial and test. Because Winnie has developed a schoolgirl " pash " for that young hooligan Jack Stubbs, blushes at the mention of him, and hangs about in the hope of seeing him pass by, it

In your intimate talks with your young son, tell him about his little bags called testicles in which little seeds are forming which one day will enable him to be a father. Until then, unwanted seeds will sometimes come out of his body when he is asleep.

The boy who worshipped the beauty of a film star may a few years later be happily married to a girl with no looks whatever but with any amount of good qualities.

doesn't in the least mean that she has fallen in love with him. She cultivates the acquaintance of boys to find out what their natures are really like, to compare them with each other—and with an imaginary hero she has created in her own mind and heart. Neither Jack Stubbs nor any other flesh-and-blood boy will measure well against that imaginary figure, and in a very little while Winnie will be disappointed in him and look elsewhere for someone nearer her ideal.

Lost Illusions

BE careful not to scoff at her " crush " for the boy, and prevent her brothers from " ragging " her on the subject. Merely ignore it —unless she talks to you voluntarily about it. Then you can, without sermonising, give her a little wise advice. And if her disappointment in the lad hurts her, be very sympathetic and understanding. Don't condemn the boy too much or you will reawaken her interest in him. Merely say that people are often disappointing, and that we learn by degrees, as we go through life, to see them as they really are.

Very often, as a boy grows out of the stage of scorning girls as " silly," he will develop a worship of some woman old enough to be his mother—quite possibly one of your younger married friends. He will try to keep this a dark secret —and his pathetic pretences will be as transparent to you as a pane of glass. But don't appear to notice anything, even when you find that this hopeless passion of his is causing him what seems to be mental agony. These bouts of misery are emotional " growing pains," and in a way he is rather enjoying them, though the touchi-ness and moodiness they give rise to are extremely irritating to the rest of the family.

In a way, this odd " crush " for an older woman is a tribute to yourself. It is a symptom of what psychologists call a " mother fixation." He loves you so dearly, has such an admiration for you, that when his inward urgings make him want to pour out love on someone outside the family circle, he turns naturally to someone as like you as he can find.

But in a grown man this characteristic is a weakness. This type of boy, when he grows up, often marries a woman of the dominant type who " bosses " him and reduces him to a henpecked husband. And the very intensity of his love for his mother, his constant unconscious comparison of his mother with his wife, may cause a good deal of unhappiness in his married life.

What are you to do ? You don't want him to love you less, to think less of you ; you don't want to rebuff him. No, the only possible course is to try to throw him into the society of girls younger than himself who will look up to him and allow him to " boss " them, yet who are intelligent enough to satisfy his need for mental companionship. In this way you will cultivate his self-confidence and self-esteem, and encourage him to be a little more of the dominating male that every woman in her heart wants a man to be.

Schoolgirl " Pashes "

THE same emotional principle is at work when Winnie develops a schoolgirl " pash " for somebody like the drawing-master at school. She probably has an intense affection and immense admiration for her father, and she is seeking a man as like him as possible. There is less emotional danger here. She will pass through this phase and eventually—perhaps a little later than girls of other types—fall properly in love with a man of suitable age. But it is wise, if you can, to encourage a friendship with a boy of her own age who is mentally congenial—you will find that she scorns those who have, as she puts it, "nothing in them."

As for the phase in which boys stick photographs of actresses, and girls put photographs of film stars, on the walls of their bedrooms— ignore it with a smile. That kind of thing is normal, and doesn't last. The boy who worshipped the beauty of a film star will probably, a few years later, be in love with, and happily married to, a girl with no good looks whatever but with any amount of capability and good qualities ; a thoroughly satisfactory wife.

All this doesn't mean that you should *encourage* the erotic tendences of adolescence. It only means that it is no use thinking that they shouldn't exist, because they do, and no use trying to repress them. The thing to do is to try to divert them into other channels—to sublimate them as the psychologists say—because, as has been said, they must not be allowed to loom too large in the minds of boys and girls.

Games, of course, are good. In addition to giving health, they work off a great deal of the energy that is causing the adolescent so much unrealised discomfort.

And hobbies are good ; any physical or mental occupation of an unemotional kind acts as a safety-valve. You can't *force* your children to go in for games or take up hobbies, and it is unwise to try, but you can encourage them by taking a real interest in their doings and praising their achievements, however slight they may be.

This brings us to another, and quite different aspect of adolescence. You will probably find that your boys—and to a lesser extent your girls—will develop a fondness for "hanging about," for standing about at corners in groups —sometimes of boys or girls alone, sometimes mixed—talking by the hour. There is no harm in this ; it is a natural instinct to seek each other's company, and if they have been properly brought up, you need not be afraid that at this age they will come to any harm. But it is a waste of time, and a sound lesson to teach youngsters at this period is the intelligent use of spare time. They could, and should, be making each other's acquaintance in more suitable circumstances.

Keeping the Boys at Home

MAKE your boy's and girl's friends welcome in your home. If you haven't a room they can have to themselves—and you probably haven't—put up with the discomfort of having them in your sitting-room. It's worth it. Encourage them to play indoor games, to listen to your wireless, to have musical parties if you have a piano or they play musical instruments of any kind. They will not need entertaining, or much in the way of hospitality ; tea or coffee, a few cakes and biscuits will be ample.

" How to keep the boys at home " is one of the problems of parenthood. So often they want to go out—not anywhere in particular, but just out. It is not that they do not like or appreciate their own homes, it is because they want to foregather with companions of their own age and kind. Don't try to keep them at home by themselves or with only you for company : let them mix with congenial companions under your roof.

This doesn't mean, of course, that you should never let the boys and girls go out together. Let them go out to play games, let them go swimming, dancing, to picnics, so long as they are doing something. But the boy who spends his evenings just hanging about is apt to grow into the young man who spends his evenings at bars, and the husband who becomes bored at home. The girl grows into the kind of wife who feels caged in her own home, or the young woman who, frankly, gets into trouble through sheer idleness and lack of healthy interests. In adolescence there is plenty of energy ; half the troubles of youth spring from there not being enough to do. Find something for the boys and girls to do, suggest an outlet for that energy in healthy games or creative hobbies.

But you must advise and suggest rather than direct or dictate. You abandoned the " Because mummy says so " of toddler days for the " Mummy says so because——" of older childhood. Now you reach the phase when " If I were you I should——" is the attitude to adopt.

Adolescent boys and girls are so prickly : they so resent being told what they are to do in matters where they consider they should be free to choose for themselves. And they've a certain amount of right on their side. Even when they come to you for advice, the wisest line to take is not " Do so-and-so " but " Well, what do you propose doing ? " and when you've heard them, " No, I wouldn't do that : if I were you I'd do so-and-so, you'll find it best." In most cases they will take your advice, put in this way, because they have faith in your judgment and your experience. But they might flatly disobey a direct command, even if their own good sense told them it was a wise one, out of sheer rebellion against your authority.

Mother's Boy and Dad's Girl

ANOTHER thing that causes the parents of adolescent children a good deal of inward pain is favouritism—not the parents having favourites among their children, a thing they have always carefully guarded against, but the children having favourites between their parents.

When the boys and girls are tinies, mummy almost always has the first claim on their affections. She is always at hand ; she it is who gives them food, washes and dresses them, binds up cut fingers and bruised knees, hears their childish confidences, rejoices with them in their little joys, comforts them in their sorrows. Perhaps, too, some unconscious, instinctive knowledge remains in them that they are part of her in a greater sense than they are part of their father, and that their first food, in most cases, came directly from her.

Daddy is in a different position. They love him, of course ; but they don't know him so intimately ; they see little of him. He is possibly a wonderful being, but a remote one, not part of every hour of their daily lives, as mummy is.

As they grow older, and see something of daddy in the evenings,

When your boy grows out of scorning girls, he may develop a passion for a much older woman, maybe one of your young married friends. It will be his dark secret, but you will see through it like a pane of glass.

The same thing happens when your girlie develops a 'pash' for the drawing-master at school. She probably has an intense affection and admiration for daddy and she is seeking a man as like him as possible.

and he joins in their games at the week-ends, they get to know him better and consequently to have a greater, more conscious affection for him. They are becoming a little critical of mummy, a little apt to rebel against her ever-present authority : daddy, less under the necessity of keeping constant discipline, is apt to be indulgent, to sympathise where mummy blames. Yet still, in real trouble, real need for comfort, it is to mummy they turn. Daddy's knee may be a comfortable perch, but mummy's arms are still a haven of refuge. Their affection for both parents is fairly evenly balanced.

But at the adolescent stage the balance of these affections is likely to alter again, and no one can say beforehand which parent will weigh down the scale. So many things affect it. First there is the un-recognised, unconscious sex instinct that often leads an adolescent boy to love his mother more dearly and a girl to have a deep, almost passionate affection for her father. The youngsters themselves do not, of course, in the least realise the inward meaning of this attraction : it is pure blind instinct and can be nothing else.

But other factors influence it. Father and son may have common interests—football, fishing, a love for machinery or handicrafts—that mother and daughter cannot possibly share : they may be, as is often said, "more like two brothers." Tom may feel that he can talk to dad as man to man ; dad can understand a fellow's point of view as no woman can. The instinct of sex antagonism that is in all of us, oddly at variance with the instinct of sex attraction, influences him without his realising it. Yet he still has a profound—

and probably a very protective—love for his mother. This is a very happy state of affairs and fathers who achieve it have every right to congratulate themselves.

On the other hand, influences may turn the adolescent boy's affection rather against his father and towards his mother. For one thing, the easy-going father, who could never see much harm in the youngsters' small misbehaviours, becomes seriously concerned because Tom is not doing well at school, or gets into rather serious scrapes, or persists in making unsuitable friends. He feels obliged to turn into a stern parent, and probably rather overdoes it. The boy resents it, appeals to his mother, and she is tempted to plead for him and even shield him. Mothers are often very blind to the faults of their boys.

Cross Purposes of Affection

THE same kind of confused cross-purposes of emotion affect the adolescent girl. She may continue to love her mother better than her father, finding in her a similarity of thought and feeling and interests that the menfolk of the family cannot share. A woman, she feels, can understand a woman as no man can.

On the other hand, apart from that sex instinct that has been mentioned, she may find her daddy, if not more understanding than her mummy, at any rate more sympathetic and more reasonable. Mother may understand her *too* well for her mental comfort : mother may not be so easy to wheedle to win undeserved sympathy ; mother is a far sterner critic.

And between a mother and a growing daughter there is often

vague, unreasoning, and unrealised feeling of—not exactly jealousy, not exactly rivalry, yet something of the kind. A mother may rejoice in her daughter's beauty and accomplishments, yet deep down in her heart there is the knowledge that this same daughter is another woman, a competitor whose claims are ripening while the mother's are fading, a potential usurper of the throne of the home.

Well, what are you to do about all this muddle? Frankly, you cannot do very much. These leanings of the children's affections are rooted deep down in human nature, and cannot be entirely changed. You have to put up with them—but reassure yourself with the faith that they are to a great extent temporary : as the youngsters grow out of the emotionally unsettled adolescent stage, the pendulum of their affections will swing less and less until it settles down into a fairly even balance between both parents.

That is, provided the parents themselves give the situation the careful attention it needs.

Jealous Fathers

IN the first place, be very careful about your attitude towards each other. It may sound absurd to talk about a father being jealous of his son's affection for his mother, but the emotion does exist. And after all, to a slight extent, it is not unnatural and not surprising. A father does need his son's love. To feel that he has lost some of his share of it, even to the boy's mother, is painful.

But it is a feeling that must be hidden and repressed. If, father, you realise that you possess it, you are probably rather ashamed of it, and nothing would make you admit it openly, or say : "Why do you love your mother, Tom, better than you love me ?" But you may, without realising it, show it in other ways. You may be tempted to be unreasonably hard on the lad ; almost, God help you, vindictive. Or it may find its outlet, not in unfair treatment of Tom but in an irritability towards his mother, your wife, the woman you love. You may say this is nonsense, that you would not let such an unworthy motive influence you and make you unjust to your boy. Yet you must be on your guard. This kind of thing is so terribly insidious : it creeps into your mind unrecognised and before you realise its presence it has taken hold of you.

The same advice applies to the mother who suffers, however slightly, that feeling towards her daughter that has been mentioned —not jealousy of the girl's love for her father (mothers seldom feel that to any extent), but the germ of jealousy of the girl's attractiveness. Be on your guard against it.

Mother and father, at this stage in your children's lives, more than at any other, you need to exercise all your patience, all your tolerance ; more than ever you must be sympathetic and understanding and just : still firm, still exacting authority, yet concealing it as much as you possibly can. Do your best to achieve this, and your boy and girl will love you both equally only in different ways.

Hero-Worship

MENTION has been made of the adolescent boy's and girl's "pash" for older women and men, their distant and innocent adoration

PLATE 13

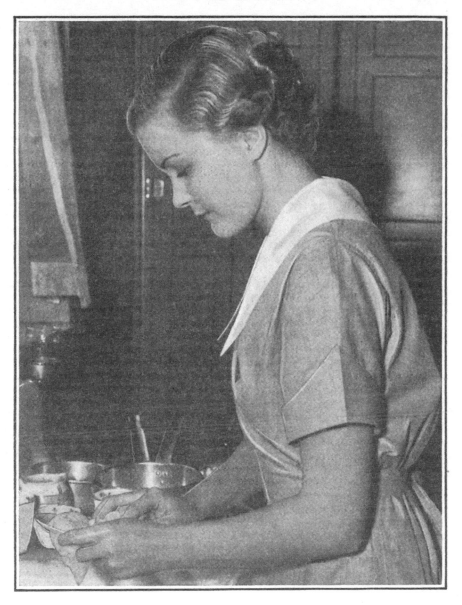

MOTHER'S RIGHT HAND

HAPPY the mother whose daughter gladly lends a hand in the house. Not only does she lighten the burden mother has borne for so many years, but the work is a safety-valve for the restless impulses of adolescence. (See Chapter XVI.) But aptitude for household tasks, and the willingness to do them, need to be encouraged and developed from very early days.

PLATE 14

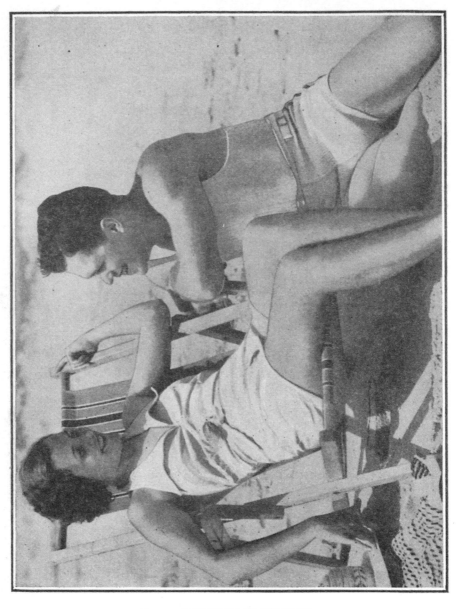

WHEN YOUR BOY'S A MAN

THE time comes when your son becomes a man and falls in love with a girl, as your husband did with you years ago. This often means anxiety for parents, for they cannot always see the lad being happily married to the girl he has chosen. This problem is dealt with in Chapter XVIII.

PLATE 15

" I LOVE HIM, DADDY "

IF anything, a daughter's love-affairs give the parents still more concern than a son's. She will be so dependent upon her husband for her happiness. Be the kind of father and mother in whom she will confide, telling all her hopes and fears, sure that you will understand and, even if you do not approve, will not condemn. There is good advice on the matter in Chapter XVIII.

PLATE 16

THE OLD FOLKS AT HOME

THE house seems strangely silent and empty when the young birds have left the nest. Yet there are letters and visits to look forward to, and still you can help the boys and girls in their troubles and difficulties. And father and mother can start life anew with a second honeymoon, and presently they will be " grandpa " and " granny "—a state which holds fresh joys all its own. The autumn of life is dealt with in Chapter XVIII.

of film stars and footballers. This hero-worship is not only natural, but it can be guided into useful channels.

The boy and girl will, of course, be attracted by the superficially attractive qualities of their hero and heroine—the beauty and emotional appeal of the film star, the physical fitness and skill of the prize-fighter. They will admire attributes that you do not in the least want them to emulate. And it is not easy to induce them to set up as an idol in their place a personality such as a successful business man or a noble philanthropist. To romantic youths these people are insufferably dull.

Yet quietly, insistently, you can drop words of wisdom that will slowly sink into their—possibly unwitting—minds. You can suggest that scoring three goals in a soccer international is not the greatest possible achievement in a man's life ; that the girl whose facial expression on the cinema screen can bring tears to millions of eyes is not necessarily the finest type of womanhood. You can speak admiringly of men and women who have done real things in life, real good in the world : humble heroes, people who have made sacrifices for their principles : you can steadily instil into your youngsters the idea that the thing that counts is not flashy attractiveness or showy accomplishments, but character, character, character.

And in the same way you can, without laying down the law or provoking argument, combat other false standards that youth is apt to set up. You can remark, on suitable occasions, that money is not everything, that beauty and dress are relative trifles, that life cannot, and should not, consist of " having a good time." You can gently expound the satisfaction that lies in good work well done, and equip your boys and girls with a sound, reasonable standard, an ideal of an honest, industrious, unselfish, and courageous life, that will bring its own reward of happiness and content.

CHAPTER XVII

Married Life in the Forties

MIDDLE age has its own special physical and mental problems for all married people. In the case of women a stage is gradually reached which is often called the " Change of Life " and which is finally marked by the ceasing to function of the sexual organs. What is not always recognised, however, is that men go through a similar stage. Just as the boy reaches the period of adolescence later than the girl, so men come to the changes of middle life a good deal later than women.

Probably the name which best describes these special alterations of middle life is the Greek one of " Grand Climacteric." The Climacteric denoted the step of a ladder and this is the Big Step; when that is taken we have passed from one stage in life to another; also, because of the changes involved, we have probably made one of the most important steps in our lives.

The fact that men reach the Climacteric later than women is bound to bring about a little adjustment in married life. Whereas the sexual side of her life no longer means so much to the wife, the husband is still in full possession of this side of his nature. Such a situation calls for tact and sympathy on the part of man and wife. During the months or even years when the Change is taking place there should be a definite forbearance on the part of the husband; he should be markedly patient and gentle. His is the part of a protector to the woman who is facing a difficult time in her life. Let him play the part in a calm, good-tempered spirit which will soothe jangled nerves and any tendency to depression on her part.

There is a big difference on one point where the Change in men and women is concerned. Whereas once the Change is over for the wife she can no longer conceive or bear a child, and the sexual organs gradually wither, the husband is not similarly affected. With him the Climacteric may be marked by lack of vigour and general sluggishness of mind and body, but he is still capable of becoming a father.

Until fairly recently the approach of the Change has been genuinely dreaded by most women. Gloomy stories of mental upset, of internal " growths," and of a general " breaking-up " filled their thoughts. Fortunately doctors are able nowadays to assure women that their fears are groundless provided they have paid reasonable attention to general rules of health during the earlier part of their lives.

The wife who has led a regular existence, has spent plenty of time in the fresh air, has taken regular daily exercise, and has generally had a sane, healthy outlook on life, has nothing to fear as the Change approaches. Admittedly she will be advised to take a few wise precautions—outlined further on—but, if that is done, any ill health or depression will prove to be a passing affair, after which she can hope to enjoy excellent health and vigour again.

Symptoms of the Change

IRREGULARITY in the periods is probably the first sign which will make you wonder if the Change is approaching, especially when such irregularities occur between the ages of forty-five and fifty— the commonest time for the Change. There is no hard-and-fast rule about age, however. The Change may easily occur at the age of forty ; sometimes it does not take place until well after fifty.

The irregularity is often attended by other signs such as hot flushes, dull headaches, indigestion, palpitation, and a general feeling of fatigue ; these are the physical signs. At the same time there may be depression, difficulty in concentration, forgetfulness, and a sense of foreboding ; these are the mental accompaniments of the Change.

In both sexes there is usually definite hardening of the arteries which leads to symptoms of high blood pressure—a bogey that need have no terrors, however, provided the life is arranged to meet it.

We may mention here that the Change in men usually appears about the age of sixty. It is marked by similar mental symptoms to those found in women. The man may confess that he is " not what he used to be." He begins to feel a lack of energy, a stiffening of the muscles, and a general heaviness and sluggishness.

People of both sexes have to face up to the situation coolly and sensibly. Every age has its compensations but, owing to the stress of modern life, undue exertion is sometimes demanded of middle-aged people nowadays and that is often where trouble arises. The woman who should have married early and for whom the hardest cares of motherhood should be over at the age of forty-five may find herself the mother of quite young children who are making constant demands upon her energy.

The man of sixty who should be thinking of retiring may have to face days of hard toil to keep things going for his family. It is no use rebelling against such circumstances ; all that remains is to make such readjustments as will help them to face the special strain involved. Extra rest must be obtained whenever possible, but when that cannot be, diet, exercise, and the general rule of life must be arranged to suit the temporarily weakened body.

Diet and Exercise

THE man or woman who has reached middle age no longer needs a " full diet " ; actually he or she will do far better on one that is light but sustaining and will not overtax the digestive organs. Red meat, for instance, need only now be eaten in very small quantities indeed, if it is not cut out altogether. Stimulants such as strong tea and coffee and all forms of alcohol raise the blood pressure and are therefore undesirable ; they should be avoided. Large quantities of starchy food which raise the body-heat are no longer needed and should be cut down.

A diet consisting largely of milk, green vegetables, salads, fresh fruit, white fish, and cheese is the one to choose. You should also drink plenty of water between meals so that the kidneys and bowels may be kept well flushed. In middle age you have reached the stage when three light meals daily, with a hot drink at bed-time to induce quiet sleep, are all that is required to keep you in bodily health. More than that is likely to tax the system unduly.

Precautions to ensure mental rest are perhaps of even more importance. Middle age is the time at which Mind has a particularly important influence over Matter. There is a tendency to become fanciful about one's health. The general feeling of fatigue and unrest often gives rise to the idea that some organ is seriously impaired ; the palpitation which is due to flatulence is mistaken for a faulty action of the heart ; vague internal pains, mostly due to faulty elimination, are thought to be due to some " growth." Thus do some husbands and wives on the verge of the Change torture their minds with undetermined but distressing forebodings until they may actually be driven into a state of definite ill health. All this could have been avoided by the exercise of a little sensible patience.

In the nature of things the man or woman who has reached middle life is expected not to be so easily swayed as the youngster. A philosophic, well-balanced attitude towards life should have then been reached which should make sudden anger or sudden emotion a rare occurrence. In other words the ideal for middle life is a well-regulated, balanced mind in a well-regulated and controlled body. Under such conditions the Climacteric will simply prove to be a very temporary upset ; once it is passed, brain and body will function smoothly once more.

Strain must be avoided, however, and here a word must be said regarding exercise. When you have reached middle age you cannot afford to subject hardening arteries, stiffening muscles, and bones that are gradually becoming brittle to sudden or violent movements.

It stands to reason, for instance, that a muscle that has begun to lose elasticity will not " give " as it once did ; instead the strain will come on the ligaments which attach it to the bone and they may be wrenched, causing a permanent injury. A bone that has become brittle by many years' deposit of lime salts may stand the strain of a jump on to a moving 'bus for many mornings in succession but one day the strain may prove too much and it will snap. Hardened arteries which no longer pulsate at every heart-beat are still perfectly useful as conductors of the blood-stream to the extremities of the body, but by taking part in some sport beyond his age, a man may cause a sudden rush of blood to the head through these non-resisting arteries and this *may* result in a stroke.

You still need plenty of exercise, but that exercise must be graduated to suit your years. Plenty of walking exercise at a reasonable pace, a moderate game of tennis, a game of bowls, all these are valuable adjuncts to good health during middle age and time should be found for them and also for the " daily dozen " which we all need.

Avoiding Troubles

IF you observe the rules for diet, exercise, and regular action of the bowels you are not likely to put on too much weight, though this often does occur otherwise and very distressing it can be. As already explained, after the Change of Life you can no longer cope with large amounts of food ; for one thing you are not having sufficient exercise to " work it off." If eating and drinking is balanced to suit the reduced bodily activity, there will be no undue increase in weight under normal conditions.

Sudden loss of weight must be viewed more seriously, however and a doctor should always be consulted when this occurs about middle life, because such a loss may be connected with gland troubles or with a deposit of free sugar in the urine.

The severe floodings from which some women suffer at the approach of the Change are always alarming and are bound to lead to much temporary weakness. This is a condition which often rights itself if the wife can be persuaded to stay in bed while the loss continues, but it is a matter that again should always be referred to the doctor, for in some cases special treatment is required to put matters right and so save great exhaustion.

In men the chief trouble connected with the Climacteric is difficulty and pain in passing urine owing to a certain condition which arises at this time. This again is a matter for the family doctor. In both this and the foregoing case safety lies in securing medical advice *early*.

Finally we come to the question of married relationships. Should they be continued ? Where the wife is concerned, much will depend upon her temperament. Occasionally one meets cases where the wife's sexual instinct is very much aroused ; more often, however, she has little or no inclination for this side of married life while going through the Change. Her wishes in the matter should be respected. As we have said previously, this is one of those special occasions in married life where great tact should be exercised by the husband, for her happiness, well-being, and peace of mind lie so largely in his hands.

It must also be remembered that some wives " meet the Change with a baby " ; in other words they are more liable to conceive, but it is not always desirable for them to have a child so late in life. It is *possible* for a wife to become pregnant as long as she is still seeing her periods, however irregular they may be.

The main point for both husbands and wives to remember is that the Change is only a passing affair, and that they are about to get their " second wind " as it were, before going on to years of further activity and happiness.

The Fascinating Forties

ONCE upon a time women dreaded to reach the age of thirty because they felt their youth had gone—and forty marked the beginning of old age ! Now, of course, we should laugh at such an idea, for we have learnt that a woman is indeed only as old as she feels—and what modern woman would think of suggesting that she took to cap and shawl and arm-chair at forty ?

It is, indeed, much better to think of them as the " fascinating forties," and to see they live up to their name.

In these days of moderately early marriages, it is probable that your " children " will have reached the reasonable age when they no longer need you to be forever at hand. The girls can do their own mending and sewing, and some of their brothers', too ; they are not dependent on you so wholly. They realise that you have a life of your own to lead, and that they must stand on their own feet. Besides which, they have their own interests which take them away from you more, and leave you with a little spare time.

So far you have done a splendid job in bringing the children up to be fine little men and women—you have devoted your life to them— and, without that necessity now, you may feel a little bewildered at first. Your eldest are probably out in the world, your youngest now at school. The home is still there with its insistent demands, and the mending-basket calls, but you miss the childish prattle that used to interrupt you so all day—the children's squabbles and cut knees, the hundred and one details that used to fill the hours with interest. Now life has taken on a humdrum appearance, and you are in danger of getting into another rut.

Think of " the thirties," and remember that you had just the same feelings then. Nothing ever seemed to happen, did it ? You had got into a rut. And so it is now. With every new chapter of life beginning, we must take stock of what we have become, improving on some things, letting many flow smoothly on, and disposing of others completely.

Married life, like a beautiful garden, must be planned and planted and watered and cared for, not only at first, when it is new, in the spring of the early twenties, but also through the summer of the thirties, and the crisp, dawning autumn of the forties.

It is not enough to say : " In the spring I planted excitement, adventure, love and happiness, and so they will come up year after year." They may not. Few of the flowers that grow in the Garden of Marriage are perennials—most of them need planting again at the beginning of each season, and need careful tending always. It is well to remember that.

The Fortieth Birthday

IF it is possible, every wife, on her fortieth birthday, should take a lazy " thinking " day. Perhaps someone kind will give you your breakfast in bed. Sit up and enjoy it ; read your birthday post, and open all your parcels. Then get up and take a lovely warm bath which will make you feel glad to be alive. Here you are face to face with the fascinating forties—what

Do not let the thought of growing old frighten you. If you have lived your life lovingly you will have around you crowds of youngsters who will be thrilled by your stories, and 'young marrieds' who will appreciate the tips you can give them.

are you going to do about it ? First of all resolve that for your own birthday gift to yourself, you are going to make yourself charming and shock that staid old husband of yours into realising that he has a wife who is not only an excellent wife and mother but a most attractive companion as well.

" Yes," you are probably saying : " I made up my mind I'd do that years ago—and it worked for a while, but, you see, it's worn off again."

Perhaps that was when the children had chicken-pox and you were extra busy—you forgot all your good resolutions and got back into the rut of domesticity again. Think back, and you will remember that something encouraged you to slack off. No matter what it was, it would still be rather fun to wake hubby up again, wouldn't it ?

Do your hair differently, and buy yourself a new frock—the same old tactics that came to the rescue before, yes, but they will bring you the same old success. Perhaps you have put on weight where you hadn't it before, or lost some of what you had ? Visit your doctor and ask his advice. A few easy exercises might soon put you right, and fit you for wearing your slim daughter's clothes !

But if Nature meant you to be generously proportioned, it is no use to fret about getting slim —and, if she meant you to be slight, why worry to put on weight ? The main thing is that you should be healthy and neat, attractive in your own particular way—with your good qualities studied to advantage, and your not-so-good ones overcome.

You will find it is fun, this taking a little trouble with yourself—and it is a privilege accorded specially to most of those who have reached

the fascinating forties, for only then do most wives and mothers get the breathing space to consider the idea.

And, having reached this stage, you will discover that there are a dozen varied interests waiting to occupy your spare time if only you will put your mind to them. Whist drives at the local hall for you and dad to win prizes at—social clubs where you can attend lectures, and learn about things that are going on in the world around you—clubs where you can become a leading light in no time, as you always wanted to, maybe, when you had so many ties before, and could not spare the time—dramatic societies, or welfare centres where you can help with the little, kicking bundles you have grown to miss just lately.

Make a place for yourself in the world outside your home ; take an interest in others, and they will take an interest in you. Life will become filled with excitement again. You will not be the woman who is " ageing so quickly, poor dear, now that her kiddies no longer need her." You will be the admired and popular Mrs. Modern who is " so much in demand now that she has a little free time to spare."

Hubby's " Last Fling "

UNFORTUNATELY, with increasing age, many husbands realise they have passed their prime and, unless they have very tactful and understanding wives, misery may result, for some little demon of madness seems to creep into their veins and urge them to have " one last fling." Madness it is, for it is capable of persuading an otherwise perfect husband that he has fallen in love with a girl half his age—a child young enough to be his daughter, and probably with no more brains than a babe.

He is flattered that anything so young and pretty can find him interesting enough to " fall for " —he is captivated with the idea of seeing how much charm he really has left ; he plays with fire, and usually gets badly burnt.

It takes a courageous wife indeed to stand by and watch this performance going on under her very nose —to keep her head when her heart feels disillusioned. She thinks of the years they have spent happily together, working, playing, suffering, sympathising, mates in every sense of the word ; she sees all that tossed aside—carelessly sometimes, but more often regretfully— for the madness that grips with a terrifying hold.

What is she to do ? How can she save their home, their self-respect ? How can she help the girl to realise what she has done and force her to give him up ? It needs very tactful handling.

First she must get herself into the state of mind when she can understand and sympathise more than blame ; remembering that all women, at some time or other, go through the physical " Change of Life," she must bring herself to regard this behaviour of her husband's as its counterpart. Think of him as a sufferer, treat him kindly, and wait for the madness to pass. Nine times out of ten it *will* pass if only the wife can be patient, and the grateful husband, realising his folly, settles down to happiness more complete than before—shamefaced, he may recall the time when exactly the reverse happened and, as a youngster, he was thrilled because he could charm a woman old enough to be his mother. Men, at these times, are like pathetic little boys, anxious for the world to see their achievements. " There's life in the old dog yet," as the saying goes—and they want to prove it.

It is not a good idea to force the issue. If this happens to you, refrain, if you can, from saying : " Choose between us ! " Think it out calmly, and you will realise that he could not possibly be happy for long with such a slip of a girl, nor she with him. There can be no choice. You are his wife, and, in his heart, he knows it is you he loves, but, while this infatuation has him in its grip, the only thing you can do is wait, gently teasing him as if you could not take the matter seriously after all you have been to each other, and giving him the chance of saving his face and ending the matter himself.

Warding Off a Crisis

NEVER let the " other woman " have the satisfaction of seeing that the affair has upset you. Keep your chin up, and be too proud to let a slip of a girl think she can steal your husband under your nose. Let her know that you are just as confident of keeping him as she is of winning him, and treat her smilingly like the little girl she probably is. A crisis can so often be avoided—a dramatic incident passed off with a laughing remark— if only we can keep our heads. Bring out your sense of humour and let it take the sharp edge off your bitterness. Put yourself in the loved one's place and imagine your feelings in similar circumstances. Summon a little pride to help you hold your head up in front of the world—and a lot of love to help you forgive and forget and start again.

Husbands seem to suffer in the

late forties what many wives go through earlier—a longing for romance ; and it is not always only the husbands who take the first opportunity that comes along to get a little.

The ideal way, of course, is for each to keep the other so busy being happy with him or her that there is no time to look round for outside romance—nor any inclination.

But, after this last longing for a final fling, on both sides, there comes a happy peacefulness in the knowledge that they are together, growing old gracefully.

Growing Old Gracefully

A ND do not let the thought of growing old frighten you. If you have lived your life lovingly you will have around you crowds of youngsters who are thrilled by your stories, " young marrieds " who will appreciate the tips you can

give from your wealth of experience, and many friends who shared with you the good old days and will love to chat with you about them.

While you can help and encourage anyone you need never fear that you will become useless ; so long as you can love, there will always be somebody who needs that love. Avoid too much criticism, and remember that methods change, usually for the better. Keep that valuable sense of humour going, and, since age has its privileges, make the most of them !

You have led a full, exciting life ; you need the quietness of later years in which to think it over, to savour the full happiness of it. You and hubby together, free from the cares of struggle and bringing up a family, can wander away through fields of Memory, and smilingly watch your own youngsters set out on that journey which you have travelled so happily together—and which you know to be the most exciting adventure of all.

Married life, like a beautiful garden, must be watered and cared for, not only when it is new in the springtime of the twenties, but also through the summer of the thirties, and the crisp dawning autumn of the forties.

CHAPTER XVIII

The Fully Fledged Family

IN a previous chapter we have talked about the children's careers, and now we come to the point where, having left school, they start out in the world to pursue those careers—young men and women with the future before them, needing your sympathetic help and encouragement now perhaps more than ever before.

You, their parents, may find it difficult to believe that they will ever really reach the stage when they can think and act for themselves without consulting you—but though, in the happiest families, everything always is talked over together, the wise parents will have ensured that this is because the young people like to include them in their plans, and not because they are incapable of managing their own affairs.

You cannot be with them at their work; they must make their own decisions there unaided—but during their childhood you did your best to make them self-reliant by creating the right atmosphere at home. Keep this atmosphere still. For instance, when they bring their problems to you, do not give way to the temptation just to tell them what to do. You are older, of course, and, with your experience of life, it would not be surprising if the solution was perfectly clear to you. But the ideal way is to help the young people to think for themselves. Talk the problem over from every point of view, pointing out the advantages and disadvantages of any course of action—and then let the young folk themselves make the actual decision.

It is unlikely that young people

treated in this way would go blundering into serious trouble, for they would have learnt to think things out, and though they will naturally make mistakes, they will profit by them, with your sympathetic help—instead of feeling that you are to blame because things did not turn out as they expected ! They will be self-reliant, clear-thinking and level-headed, which is a grand start in life.

Following the same principle, there is only one way to dispel the fear that dwells in every mother's heart at the prospect of letting her child go out into the world. She knows that outside influences are bound to come along, that her " baby " must stand on his own feet now, probably rubbing up against undesirable people, or hearing the kind of conversation that has carefully been kept from him before ; and she is terrified that, even if this does not lead him astray, it will start him asking awkward questions she would far rather not have to answer.

Be Frank about Sex

BUT it is useless to try and keep young people in ignorance— and mistaken, for adolescent curiosity is one of those terrific forces that must be appeased at all costs. And rightly so. Are the young people not embarking on an adventure that contains a vast number of curious things ? Naturally they want to know about them, good and bad alike. It is not enough to keep them out of mischief by avoiding all knowledge of it. Ignorance does not lead to goodness ; and wickedness is not the natural outcome of knowledge—far from it. The best way is to answer all questions frankly, and the less

secrecy there is about the whole business, the less importance will the young people attach to it. In the early days, Sex is of no particular interest to the healthy-minded. It is the *secrecy* which so often surrounds it that drives them to feel they will be missing something if they do not inquire further. Once their questions have been answered sympathetically, they are likely to turn their attention to something more absorbing— like getting on well at work—safe in the knowledge that mother or father is there to help should any further difficulties arise.

So now, not only have you trained the young people to be self-reliant and level-headed, but perfect confidence exists between them and you—a very shield against those harmful outside influences— and you may rest assured that you can trust the young people out of your sight.

The third thing to consider is how you can help them to do well at their work. Their main necessities are plenty of rest and fresh air, with good food and regular meals. That sounds simple enough, but it is not always so easy to bring about without friction, for, once the kiddies leave school, they are apt to feel very grown-up and important, and they do not take kindly to being told what to do !

No doubt some parents would try to force the children to obey them for the simple reason that " mother knows best " as was the way when they were tinies—but it is a much happier idea to treat the boys and girls as intelligent people, and have a little discussion about the whole thing. Consult them as if you considered that they had now reached the age when you could cease treating them as children— and the compliment is sure to bring about good results. Reach a mutual agreement about bedtime, and see that daily fresh air is assured. The good food will naturally rest with you, except, perhaps, at midday, and then you would do well to keep an eye on what the young people eat, for there is a great tendency to save money by going short on the mid-day meal—and that is dreadfully bad for the system.

The Wages Question

WHEN young people start earning money, it is best to encourage them to be self-supporting—to contribute something towards household expenses, to pay for their own amusements, clothes and holidays, etc., according to their ability. Help them to look upon this as a privilege rather than a duty—for, as you yourself may know from experience, there is no fun in paying out money one has worked hard to gain if it is expected as a right ; whereas there certainly is a lot of fun to be had in the knowledge that one is now old enough to pay one's way—independent, and no longer a drag on dad's resources.

It is a mistake to let young people keep the whole of their earnings to spend on themselves and it is equally a mistake to make them give up the whole lot. Little by little, as each rise comes, they should be encouraged to take on more of their own responsibilities.

But if they are to contribute to the family budget, like dad, they should also receive some of the consideration he gets. Make a point of that, and let them feel their importance as wage-earners. Let them know how proud you

are of their achievements. Ask how they are getting on, and encourage them to talk, helping them to respect the authority of their " boss," and to learn to take orders with a good grace—for if they cannot understand why they should take orders, it is a sure thing that they will never be fit to give them.

If they have been working hard all day, they should not be given a lot of jobs on their return, or they will get over-tired. Do not ask for help, but, when it is offered, let them know how much you appreciate it—and, though you would do well to refuse it occasionally, sometimes you should say " Yes."

Young People's Friendships

ONCE the young people start out in the world, they will meet people you have never seen, and form various friendships in which you have no say. So far we have seen how to make them self-reliant, so that they can choose their own friends wisely—and how to give them confidence in you so that they will have no hesitation in telling you about them. The main thing now is to keep that confidence—and you will not do that by continually criticising their friends.

If they ask your opinion, by all means give it frankly, but do not offer it at first ; rather wait and see if the person concerned improves on acquaintance. Remember they are your children's friends, not yours—and, so long as there is nothing radically wrong with them, you are not really called upon either to like or dislike them.

If your son—or daughter—has two friends, one that you like and one that you do not, you would do better to encourage the nice one rather than openly discourage association with the other—for human nature is such that we always want what we are not allowed.

Soon the question will arise as to when you should allow the young people to go out with the opposite sex, and it seems that the ideal way of managing this problem is to let it take a natural course. Encourage your children to mix with both sexes at first—rambling clubs, cycling clubs, sports clubs, dramatic societies, and local church functions being the best way of meeting nice friends with the same interests. By degrees the large parties that often go about together dwindle down to foursomes. Four people is a better number than two, at this stage, for the conversation is not so apt to get personal, and the young people concerned are less likely to think they are serious.

Encourage your children's friends to drop in at your home, and, when the question does arise : " Mummy, may I go out with So-and-So to-morrow ? " you will know what the particular friend is like. Whether you give your consent or not depends on many things, but to withold it for no better reason than that the son or daughter is " too young " is a bad mistake. Such a reason might well make an obstinate child openly rebellious, and even an understanding young person might feel resentful.

There are many much more tactful ways of dealing with the question than that—and one is, supposing the young people should not be given permission, in your opinion, why not say something like : " Well, I had hoped you would come to the Pictures with dad and me, then. Couldn't we all go together ? " Nine times out of

ten that will do the trick, for all the young people care about is that they should enjoy themselves together—and if you tactfully walk home with dad, letting them go on ahead, they will still have a little time for a conversation-for-two, and no feelings will have been hurt.

That is a point to consider, for all young people are filled with a growing sense of their own importance, and it is much better to share that feeling with them, and help them to put it to good use, than to try and alter it.

Young Love

SO we have guided the young people through early friendships to the time when they are of an age to choose their life-partners. Strange as it may seem, Nature, almost as if she feared that human nature might become too dull, takes a delight in attracting completely opposite types together— perhaps in the hope that their children may have some of the instincts of both parents and keep up a certain amount of variety ! So it is that rarely do people choose the mates we would expect them to—and sometimes parents are bitterly disappointed with the children's choice.

There is nothing much that one can do in the matter. If you have brought up your bairns to be level-headed young people with a good knowledge of the facts of life, you have done your part splendidly, and, though you may seek to advise them in the matter of choosing a life-partner, you should not attempt to make up their minds for them. Love cannot be commanded or repelled at will, and when it knocks at the door of our children's hearts, the best we can do is to give them sympathy and understanding, and help them to see both sides of the question.

When the path of true love is running smoothly, parents usually find that tempers are calm and smiles are many, and nothing is too much trouble—but when things are difficult, then it is that tempers are frayed and nerves on edge, and, if things are not to become unbearable in the home circle, great tact will be needed.

The main thing is to treat the sufferer quite normally, for nothing is more irritating to a girl than to suppose that her family is pitying her; she is on guard the whole time. This is equally true of a boy in love. Naturally, it is best not to mention the love affair, but whichever parent is more pally with the child should make time every day for them to be alone together —casually, of course, as if it was not planned—when the boy or girl can talk as much as he or she wishes. Do not attempt to force confidences of this sort; they will come, in time, in answer to the right treatment, and, when they do, talk as man to man, and thrash things out together, so that the youngster knows there is help to be had at home instead of the criticism and harsh laying down of the law which used to be the case.

It is necessary to provide some occupation to keep the aching heart from doing too much thinking about the same subject. Ask for help in the house or find some little job which needs concentration—try and manage early hours, good food and plenty of fresh air, for the nerve-strain is very great at these anxious times, and attention should be paid to the health particularly.

Let things take their natural course, and, in time, you will find the youngster has "shaken out of it" as the saying goes, and will soon have full command of himself. Take it for granted that he or she will act in the common-sense way, and be too proud to let friends see how badly he or she has been hit. Help them to keep their heads up—to join a club, and take up some other interest—help them to face the world bravely and keep their heartbreak to themselves. Teasing, and constant reminders of the affair rarely heal the wound —they only rub salt into it and make it extraordinarily difficult to cope with, so younger brothers and sisters should be taught to be kind, as they would if the elder one was physically ill. The knowledge that the family is standing by, expecting the best of one, is a very sure way of bringing out that best.

Difficult Questions

BUT not only are parents called upon to help their children in this way—often they are expected to answer questions that need a vast amount of thought. Your daughter may say: "Mummy, how soon can I let a boy kiss me?" Your son may want to know why, if it is natural for men to love women, it is wrong for him to ask for more than kisses when he takes a girl out. "Why?" and "When?" They are little words that crop up a lot when there are growing sons and daughters about —and you must be ready to explain.

If you have brought her up to be frank, and to think for herself, your daughter will realise that, if she genuinely likes a boy, there is no harm in allowing him to kiss her—but she needs a warning word that all men are not alike, for this she cannot think out for herself —she needs a reminder that, if she makes herself cheap with any man, he will not respect her. And your son will realise that caresses more intimate than a kiss become valueless if they are not reserved for one's life-partner. They will try to model their behaviour on what they see of yours—so it is as well to remember that every day, whether you know it or not, your growing children are subconsciously watching you, and taking their cue from you.

Deal frankly with their problems and do not merely dismiss them with "Of course you mustn't—that's wicked." Humans never grow out of longing to know the whys and wherefores of every subject, and, no matter how delicate the subject may be, absolute honesty is always the best policy in the end, and is really the quickest way of taking their minds off it. When once we know something, there is no longer any need to go on thinking about it, and trying to find out all there is to be discovered.

And so we may safely leave the young people to take their place in the world with other young men and women.

When They Bring "Them" Home

DO you remember the day you said "Yes," and the day you were taken home to "his" people? Do you remember with what mixture of feelings you entered their home, and longed for their approval? And you, husbands, do you remember how you knew only too well that you could not possibly be good enough for her, but how you did hope her father would not be too hard on you—that he would give you a chance to prove your worth?

Of course you remember every minute of those days! But, if by any chance, you do not, then you would do well to spend a few minutes recollecting them. For one day your son—or your daughter—is going to bring his sweetheart home, and you will be to them in the same position as those parents you braved long ago.

Perhaps you have a good idea of exactly which man your daughter intends to marry—in which case you have plenty of time to think things out beforehand, and bring yourself into a cheerful frame of mind about it. Perhaps she is going to spring it on you as a glorious surprise—and that will demand much more self-control on your part. Whatever happens, you must not spoil her surprise. Do not "jump on her" straight away. Go carefully. Admit your surprise, and pretend it has quite overcome you, if you must—but do not crush the young couple's hopes without due consideration.

Once they have made up their minds to marry, very little you can say will stop them—and, if there is nothing really wrong with the match except that, from your point of view, it is not ideal, take a deep breath and determine that you are not going to spoil things for them. At first they will only be engaged, and there are such things as broken engagements, you know. Give the youngsters a chance. Welcome the addition to the family, and let him —or her—know that it will certainly not be your fault if things do not work out according to schedule.

If, during the engagement, the future "in-law" turns out badly, then you can openly object and do all you can do to stop the marriage. It will not be surmising on your part. It will be a fact,

If you haven't got a granny or grandpa you are very unfortunate, for no one can take the place of grandparents, those lovely cuddly people who grow more lovely and loving as they grow older.

and it is more than likely that your child will actually welcome your interference then, and your help in ending something that has become a little too much for her to cope with alone. If you are merely cold and unpleasant beforehand, and do not give the youngsters that necessary chance, then there is every likelihood that you will drive them into a much earlier marriage than they had planned —simply because they feel they would be happier alone. And then you can do nothing.

Youngsters in love are headstrong. All the world knows that. But they will usually pay attention to a reasonable parent—and, at any rate, you might be successful in prolonging an engagement that would, in time, prove its own worth —if you go tactfully about the whole thing.

Leaving the Nest

NOW let us suppose that the youngsters have come happily through the engagement days, and the marriage draws near.

Of course it will be a wrench for you, at first, but if you bring yourselves to realise that you can, if you wish, gain a son—or daughter —instead of losing the one you already have, by this marriage, you will store up unlimited happiness for yourselves as well as for the child for whose happiness you have slaved all your lives.

The details are rather a worrying part of the whole business—as no doubt you remember from your own experience—and it would be a great kindness to the youngsters if you undertook to help them as much as possible.

Offer to go with them to the clergyman or minister who is going to marry them, and he can explain just what they must do, and how much the ceremony will cost. Try and let all your friends and relations know about the wedding, for not only would they feel dreadfully hurt to be left out on such a great occasion, but no doubt the youngsters would appreciate a good send-off on this, the greatest of all their adventures, and the presents that may come flocking in will help them to set up house together, happy in the knowledge that so many people are confident of their success.

The bride's mother must help her to provide all the necessary linen for her new home, and she, too, is responsible for the reception after the wedding—where everyone meets to congratulate the happy pair personally, and to make it a day they can never forget. Of course there is no need for a " splashy " affair, but a simple ceremony with sincerity as the keynote is something the children can look back on with gratitude and happiness.

The best man must be the bridegroom's shadow. He should arrange to convey the guests from the ceremony to the reception—to get the happy couple themselves there, and to see that they go happily off for the honeymoon with the luggage perfectly safe, and the tickets in their pockets. His job it is, too, to hand the bridegroom the ring at the right moment during the service.

Your job, as parents, is to see that for your son—or daughter— this is really the day of days ; that happiness overflows, and that no thought of leaving you and dad alone to misery should ever enter his head. When you want to dwell on the loneliness ahead, busy yourself with attending to the guests instead. You will find your work cut out answering questions and spreading happiness. There will not be much time for sadness at the wedding—and afterwards, well, you are going to be much too busy getting back to " honeymoon " days yourselves to feel lonely for long !

Second Honeymoon

YES, with all your family married, and the last one off your hands, why should you not slip back to those dear days when you and dad were sweethearts and life was young and lovely ?

Now you will have time to go about together. Perhaps dad has already retired ? If not, perhaps he will soon be retiring, and together you can find new happiness in life and a thrill in each other's company that you did not know still existed !

Go visiting friends and relations together—and ask them all back to your home. Get about and see life. Do not sit at home and mope. Soon, very soon, you will be grandma and grandpa, maybe, and then you will have fresh duties to undertake. This is your little holiday from the responsibilities of life. Make the most of it. Spring-clean the house together and fix up new gadgets so that it is a fitting home for two such honeymooners as yourselves. Attend to the garden, and plant the flowers you have always longed to see there, but have somehow never found time to look after. You will have time for everything, for a little while—time to read your favourite books, and take up the hobby you thought you had forgotten—time to catch up with the world and learn all that is going on which you may have missed in these busy years of being devoted

parents—time to make yourselves up-to-date parents who may even surprise the real honeymoon couple on their return.

You will have time to look over your wardrobe and perhaps buy a new hat or two—time to discard that old suit, hubby, and order yourself another. You have more time and possibly less expenses. What are you going to do about it ? How are you going to make the most of such a state of affairs ?

Don't take it as a matter of course that life will be dull now that the youngsters have flown away, and left you alone in the nest. Life is *always* full of fresh wonders for us to discover if only we have the time and the will. And you can have both now.

When you think of something you all used to do together, and instantly the mournful thought flashes into your mind : " Ah, those good days are over ! " force yourself to think of something else that you could never do before, that you are going to do now—and look on the bright side.

Here is a splendid opportunity opening out before your very eyes. Don't miss it. Don't put off this other " honeymoon " either, for any reason whatever. It is yours by right now, and the chance may not come again. Seize it !

Grandparenthood

SO soon after your brief " honeymoon," the youngsters will be wanting your help. They are settling down in their new home, which means they will need your advice in a hundred and one different ways—there will be tea-parties to exchange, the other parents to get friendly with, new presents to admire, shopping expeditions together; intimate little talks between father and bridegroom, and mother and bride. Where, you will ask yourselves, is the time we thought we were going to have for feeling lonely and unwanted?

And then, swift upon that exciting time will probably come the half-expected, longed-for news that soon you are to be grandparents. Mother may catch dad looking in the glass, remembering the time when he first heard he was going to be a father, and wondering if he will look much like a grandpa with such crisp, only lightly-silvered hair! But what you look like will not matter in the least—the younger the better, the older the wiser. It is how you *love* that will matter now.

Think of your own waiting days, and remember your difficulties. Times may have changed since then, but human nature remains the same, and the little mother-to-be will need reassurance and help, encouragement and enthusiasm. Father-to-be, too, wants to be told all that he can do to help her. Do not dampen their joy with solemn doubts like: "Oh, my dears, but do you think you will ever be able to manage on your money?" The baby has announced his arrival now; you can't cancel him even if you would—so prepare to welcome him with as much ardour as if there was a fortune in the bank. Where there is enough love, money can usually be made to do.

The Great Day

OF course you will do all you can on the Great Day. Safe in the knowledge that "mother" is there to take over, and "father" will be with her husband, the little mother-to-be can place herself in the nurse's hands with confidence and joy.

Then, when the baby has safely come to town, you will see opening up before you a new world in which you are most important people—no longer are you just parents bereft of your child; in the eyes of your friends you have risen to the realm of grandparents, and can command respect as never before!

In the first flush of having a chubby little new possession, grandparents are apt to spoil him—to pick him up just when he cries, and rock him to sleep when he's fretful. But remember the fact that the new mother has probably prepared herself for this motherhood by earnestly studying the subject; don't sweep away her gentle protests with an insistent "My dear child, when *you* were a baby, I managed to bring you up quite well, and I never did this, that and the other"—for either you get the name for being interfering, or else the young mother feels that, after all, you did manage perfectly well, and she might do worse than give up trying to learn on her own while you are there to advise.

That, of course, would be fatal—for, while it is nice to know that grandparents are there, willing and able to help, it is every woman's privilege to bring up her own child, and unless she does she cannot make a good mother. Grandparents should pass on all they know, but let the new parents bring up their child in their own way, learning more every day about the happiness their task brings—just as you did yourselves.

There is one great way in which you can help, and that is in giving the new parents a night "off" occasionally. Take charge of the baby, and let them go out and enjoy themselves. They will be eternally grateful, for no matter how much they may love the wee mite, they love each other, too, remember, and it is particularly necessary that, at a time when nerves are perhaps in rather a weak state, after the recent strain, they should have a little while to devote to each other alone without the baby requiring attention every now and again.

If the new mother knows that you will not only mind her child, but you will also respect her wishes in the matter of looking after him, such as never giving him a dummy, or picking him up at the wrong time, etc.—her mind will be quite at rest.

And how grateful the young couple will be if you and the other grandparents get on well ! It is worth making a supreme effort to keep friendly with them, and to remember that they are just as excited as you are about being grandparents.

Grandparents' Privileges

AND so you and hubby go on learning together, sharing the joys of being grandparents, happy in each other's presence, sweethearts still—a splendid example to the young couple. Keep their admiring trust and faith in you and in your marriage ; you are giving them an ideal to live up to.

If you need to find fault with the kiddies or their upbringing, do it by all means—for it is a grandparent's privilege to assist the new couple in making the baby as perfect as possible—but do it gently, so that, when you go to the house, they feel an extra shower of love is coming, not, as so often happens with relations, that they must take cover and put on their party manners in order not to offend you !

So it continues, all through life —love and tact are what you need most. Do not worry too much if you are not blessed with this world's goods. Grandchildren do not need spoiling, and, anyhow, grandparents are particularly noted for the little packets of sweets they carry about with them, the unexpected penny they produce just at the right moment—not the big things of life. It is their ability to know just when a sweet would be appreciated, just when a penny would make all the difference—that makes them so popular.

They win the little childrens' affections, not by the gifts they bring—though they certainly are a joy—but by their loving hugs and grand stories of " When I was your age " ; their joy in the children's achievements. If you haven't a granny or a grandpa, then you are a very unfortunate little person indeed, in the eyes of the kiddies —for no one can take the place of grandparents, those lovely cuddly, exciting people, who seem to become more lovely and loving as they grow older, and who need the little ones' attention and care more and more.

Encourage the bairns to " look after you." Do not let them feel you are too independent, and do not want their help—or they will cease to offer it.

Being grandparents has a thrill all its own. It is up to you to enjoy it and make the most of it— and so complete the joy of a perfect Love and Marriage.

THE END